# Anthropology for Architects

# Anthropology for Architects

Social Relations and the Built Environment

**RAY LUCAS**

BLOOMSBURY VISUAL ARTS
LONDON • NEW YORK • OXFORD • NEW DELHI • SYDNEY

BLOOMSBURY VISUAL ARTS
Bloomsbury Publishing Plc
50 Bedford Square, London, WC1B 3DP, UK
1385 Broadway, New York, NY 10018, USA
29 Earlsfort Terrace, Dublin 2, Ireland

BLOOMSBURY, BLOOMSBURY VISUAL ARTS and the Diana logo are trademarks of Bloomsbury Publishing Plc

First published in Great Britain 2020
Reprinted 2021 (twice), 2022, 2023

Copyright © Ray Lucas, 2020

Ray Lucas has asserted his right under the Copyright, Designs and Patents Act, 1988, to be identified as Author of this work.

For legal purposes the Acknowledgements on p.xvii constitute an extension of this copyright page.

Cover design: Eleanor Rose
Cover image © Ray Lucas

All rights reserved. No part of this publication may be reproduced or transmitted in any form or by any means, electronic or mechanical, including photocopying, recording, or any information storage or retrieval system, without prior permission in writing from the publishers.

Bloomsbury Publishing Plc does not have any control over, or responsibility for, any third-party websites referred to or in this book. All internet addresses given in this book were correct at the time of going to press. The author and publisher regret any inconvenience caused if addresses have changed or sites have ceased to exist, but can accept no responsibility for any such changes.

A catalogue record for this book is available from the British Library.

A catalog record for this book is available from the Library of Congress.

ISBN: PB: 978-1-4742-4149-6
ePDF: 978-1-4742-4152-6
eBook: 978-1-4742-4151-9

Typeset by Integra Software Services Pvt Ltd.

To find out more about our authors and books visit www.bloomsbury.com and sign up for our newsletters.

*For Sandra and Andrew Lucas
for their support every step of the way.*

# Contents

List of Illustrations  viii
Preface: Rationale and Context  xiv
Acknowledgements  xvii

1  Introduction: Typologies of Social Relation  1
2  Inscriptive Practices and Anthropology  25
3  Home and What It Means to Dwell  45
4  Museums and Architectures of Collection  71
5  Marketplaces and Sites of Exchange  101
6  Routes, Walking and Wayfinding  137
7  Theatre and Festival: Performance and Liminal Space  157
8  Restaurants, Food Events and Sensory Architectures  185
9  Conclusion: Towards an Anthropological Architecture  217

References  232
Index  242

# List of Illustrations

| | | |
|---|---|---|
| 2.1 | Brush and ink drawing of Himeji Castle | 32 |
| 2.2 | Brush and ink drawing of Sumo wrestlers | 33 |
| 2.3 | Sketches of Harajuku cos-players | 41 |
| 2.4 | Watercolour painting of Gonpachi | 41 |
| 2.5 | Watercolour painting of Kappabashi crockery store | 42 |
| 3.1 | Movements of clothing for cleaning through author's homes in Manchester and Den Haag | 54 |
| 3.2 | Tatami dimensions and room layouts | 60 |
| 3.3 | Photographs from the *100m House* | 67 |
| 4.1 | Author's photograph of the Jewish Museum, Berlin by Daniel Libeskind | 81 |
| 4.2 | Author's photograph of the exterior of the Edo-Tokyo Open Air Architectural Museum | 84 |
| 4.3 | Author's photograph of the interior of the Edo-Tokyo Open Air Architectural Museum | 85 |
| 4.4 | Author's Photographs showing details of the Edo-Tokyo Open Air Architectural Museum | 86 |
| 4.5 | Author's photograph of hanok adapted to contemporary use showing ventilation and utility meters | 88 |
| 4.6 | Author's photograph of Namsangol Hanok Village: an example of the open-air museum approach | 89 |

# LIST OF ILLUSTRATIONS

4.7 Author's photograph of newly constructed house designed to look like a traditional hanok: detail of wall under construction. What is notable here is the manner in which the wall is decorated to resemble hanok construction rather than built using those techniques  90

4.8 Author's photograph of view of the Cheonggyecheon restoration  91

4.9 Author's photograph of teams of gardeners at work on the Cheonggye stream  93

4.10 Author's photograph of the East section of the stream, with expressway piers retained  94

4.11 Author's photograph of Seoul City Hall, with the old Japanese colonial administration building (now the central library) in the foreground  95

4.12 Author's photograph of roof lines of hanok house district  97

4.13 Author's photograph of modern hanok  98

5.1 Author's redrawing of Patrick Geddes's drawing 'The Association of the Valley Plan with the Valley Section'  105

5.2 Diagram of cyclical gift giving and of reflective obligation  109

5.3 Author's Photographs showing the architecture of various forms of economic exchange: Namdaemun Market, Wako Department Store, Prada boutique  113

5.4 Drawings showing front (a) and rear (b) of Tsukiji market stall and turret truck (c) used for transportation of goods within the market  114

5.5 Author's photographs of Tsukiji market  115

# LIST OF ILLUSTRATIONS

5.6 Contrasting layout of Tsukiji market (Tokyo) and Noryangjin market (Seoul) 117

5.7 Author's photograph of Namdaemun market field site 121

5.8 Section drawings of Namdaemun market 123

5.9 Author's photograph of pallets being dragged about to respond immediately to market conditions 124

5.10 Author's photograph of external spaces monitored by neighbouring stall holders 125

5.11 Axonometric drawings of Namdaemun carts packed away 126

5.12 Axonometric drawings of Namdaemun carts in open state 127

5.13 Axonometric drawing of Namdaemun cart showing the definition of front and back through simple means such as facing direction, position of ingredients and cutlery implying the territory of the vendor 128

5.14 Author's photographs of portering equipment and of portering company organizer 130

5.15 Elevation drawings of modular Namdaemun carts showing variations 131

5.16 Axonometric drawings of informal Namdaemun stalls and lunch table 132

6.1 Getting lost in Tokyo labyrinths 142

6.2 Author's photographs of HDB housing blocks in Singapore including hawker centres and flexible social space 144

6.3 Diagrammatic renderings of Augoyard's qualities and forms for everyday walking 147

6.4 Author's photograph of Kadomatsu decoration 151

# LIST OF ILLUSTRATIONS

6.5 Author's photograph of Kyoto street during New Year celebrations 152

6.6 Author's photograph of Yasaka Shrine, Kyoto with braziers, street food sellers and amazake 153

6.7 Author's photograph of Bell at Kodai-ji 154

6.8 Author's photographs of Hatsumōde at Fushimi Inari Shrine 155

7.1 Sketched plan-oblique drawing of the Kabuki-za stage 164

7.2 Pictorial notation of the interaction between stagehand and actor 165

7.3 Schematic section of the Kabuki-za theatre auditorium 166

7.4 Oblique drawings of NHA outside of (a) and during (b) festival 169

7.5 Sample route map for Sanja Matsuri on Sunday; these are modified slightly each year 171

7.6 Author's photograph of procession showing (a) neighbourhood association members; (b) musicians and dancers; (c) geisha; (d) heron hooded dancers 172

7.7 Axonometric drawing of an example of a neighbourhood *Mikoshi* 173

7.8 Author's photographs of street-side maintenance and preparation of the *Mikoshi* 174

7.9 Drawing of the various parts of the *Mikoshi* 175

7.10 Drawings of the material culture, street decoration and appropriations found during Sanja Matsuri, including (a) Mikoshi trestles; (b) ad hoc picnic table; (c) temporary tarpaulin and scaffolding pole enclosure 175

7.11 Drawings of temporary stages 177

LIST OF ILLUSTRATIONS

**7.12**  Watercolour studies of Sanja Matsuri participants showing *happi* coats and other uses of costume to identify affiliation   178

**7.13**  Author's photographs of Sanja Matsuri   179

**7.14**  Structural diagrams of *Mikoshi* parade   180

**7.15**  Axonometric drawing of *Mikoshi* bearers   181

**8.1**  Key to sensory notation   193

**8.2**  Oblique drawing of izakaya   195

**8.3**  Author's photograph of Golden Gai in Shinjuku   196

**8.4**  Sensory notation of izakaya in Shinjuku's Omoide yokochō   197

**8.5**  Sketch plan of *kaiseki restaurant* and typical arrangement of small dishes   199

**8.6**  Sensory notation of kaiseki-style restaurant   201

**8.7**  Drawing of tempura counter   202

**8.8**  Sensory notation of tempura restaurant   203

**8.9**  Drawing of gyoza restaurant showing similar counter arrangement to the tempura restaurant   204

**8.10**  Drawing of ceramic burner from katsu restaurant   205

**8.11**  Sensory notation of gyukatsu restaurant   206

**8.12**  Drawing of metro station ramen restaurant   207

**8.13**  Drawing of vending machine. Diners select their meal from the options on the buttons and pay outside the restaurant, handing over a ticket when seated   207

**8.14**  Drawing of shabu shabu table   209

**8.15**  Sensory notation of shabu shabu restaurant   210

| | | |
|---|---|---|
| 8.16 | Drawing of condiments provided to allow diners to adapt a dish to their tastes 211 | |
| 8.17 | Author's photograph down Nakamise Dori towards Senso-ji 212 | |
| 8.18 | Photograph of street food stalls at Senso-ji and Asakusa-jinja during the Sanja Matsuri festivities 213 | |
| 8.19 | Watercolours of yatai stalls from Sanja Matsuri 213 | |
| 8.20 | Sensory notation of yatai stalls on the Senso-ji precinct 214 | |
| 9.1 | Examples of sensory notation 226 | |
| 9.2 | Sequential photographs of junior Maezumo Sumo bout 228 | |
| 9.3 | Laban notation of Sumo bout 229 | |

# Preface: Rationale and Context

*A*nthropology for Architects aims to bridge the gap between two disciplines concerned in part with what it means to build and dwell. The book presents a series of building types and discusses these through appropriate anthropological theories. This is not intended to be an exhaustive catalogue, but instead presents a series of exemplar studies. Theories of economic exchange might, for example, be used to discuss domestic or sacred spaces just as marketplaces are used to elaborate that theory here. Many theoretical frameworks can map across to aid out understanding a range of architectural spaces, allowing for a more nuanced reading of the socially constructed aspects of architecture.

For some time now, cross-disciplinarity has been encouraged and enabled in academic research, particularly in Britain. It is in this context that the foundations for this work were laid. This book's earliest origins are in my 2002 PhD studentship in social anthropology as part of the Arts & Humanities Research Board's *Creativity and Practice Research Group* at the University of Aberdeen and Duncan of Jordanstone School of Art in Dundee. The group's aim was to reassess existing approaches to architecture and anthropology. Rather than producing an anthropology *of* architecture or an ethnographic account of architecture, our aim was to look deeper into the nature of creative practices as fundamentally *human* activities. As such, this study focused on how and why drawing and notation are used, encompassing the full scope of 'inscriptive practices' as ways of producing knowledge.

Over time, this approach developed into a discussion of how knowledge is produced in different disciplines and by which means. The resulting *Knowing from the Inside* project brought a wide range of disciplinary perspectives together (including anthropologists and architects of various sub-disciplines as well as fine artists, craftspeople, film-makers, product and industrial designers, mathematicians, philosophers, educationalists, archaeologists and many more), with both academic and practical knowledge production traditions under discussion as equal partners. In parallel, the work forming this volume has been under development through teaching at Manchester School of Architecture since 2010, informing undergraduate courses in *Architecture* and *Observation*, *Graphic Anthropology*, *World Urbanism*, and postgraduate studios in *Knowledge Production in Architecture* and *Intimate Cities*. The text that follows is the outcome of a long and ongoing engagement exploring what architecture and anthropology have to say to one another: not only in terms of anthropologists informing architects, but also for anthropologists to gain greater knowledge of architectural thinking.

One result of working across disciplines is an appreciation for clear communication. Every academic tradition has its own literature and an associated language, allowing experts in each field to communicate complex ideas efficiently either through the use of extensive referencing (safe in the knowledge that your reader shares that knowledge) or through the use of jargon and technical terminology. Whilst this provides a valuable shortcut, reliance on assumed disciplinary knowledge becomes problematic in cross-disciplinary work. Errors of misrepresenting the other discipline can be introduced by misunderstanding terms, misreading the literature, or using our home terminology uncritically and defensively. Of course, the potential is for creative re-use of ideas from another discipline, of montage-like juxtaposition of concepts can produce some of the most innovative works. This volume will use straightforward language wherever possible in order to make the text as accessible across academic and design disciplines as possible. Additionally as a book written with architecture in mind, the aim is for the text and images to be read together with the same attention, exploiting the generosity and space for multiple simultaneous and complementary interpretations.

This means that this book is not a series of ethnographic encounters based on the long-term participant-observation common to anthropological research. One aim is to explore the potential of existing research practices in architecture – primarily drawing and associated inscriptive practices to develop an understanding of the social aspects of architecture. Drawing grants the researcher access to different aspects of a phenomenon: more than illustrations, these drawings and notations are to be read as analysis: explicitly geometric understandings of the world organized according to conventions and shared understandings about how they can be occupied and used. The architectural drawing is an open-ended understanding full of suggestions and possibilities whilst simultaneously giving precise dimensions and locations.

The broad structure of the book is to associate architectural typologies with theoretical frameworks from anthropology. Homes are paired with theories of maintenance and cleanliness, reflecting the idea that dwelling is a perpetual work in progress. Museums are presented alongside literature on collections and decontextualization whilst marketplaces are explored through theories of reciprocity, exchange and gift giving. Sacred space is considered as part of the literature on movement and routes, further explored in terms of neighbourhood festivals and the ways in which performance can create temporary architectures. The nuances around food culture and agency are presented in the chapter on restaurants, and each chapter seeks to open up an everyday and ordinary topic, offering it as a site of potential and alterity. The aim is to equip the reader with theoretical frameworks which help to break down assumptions with the ultimate aim of encouraging design that responds to people's actual needs rather than presumptions or the repetition of established forms.

Most of the examples in the book are drawn from the author's field work in Japan and South Korea. The geographical focus could just easily have been any other part of the world, particularly given the wide-ranging nature of the typologies addressed: dwellings, collections, markets, routes, theatres, celebrations and restaurants. There is a logic in placing oneself elsewhere, away from home, in order to conduct field research. The value of being an outsider is that it allows the researcher to ask fundamental and often naive questions: such that every aspect of life, no matter how mundane, is available as a research topic. This has pitfalls at the same time and opens the work to accusations of fetishization, cultural appropriation, misunderstanding or exoticization. This last flaw is particularly sharp with reference to the literature on Japanese architecture, which often tends towards perpetuating cliches and heightening of differences, the idea of a culture-shock experienced when visiting a culture so different from the West. Events described are intended to be ordinary rather than spectacular such as highlighting the design implications of small differences in food cultures. Counter-seating introduces a relationship between diners and cooks; the provision of condiments allows a fast-food culture to adapt to the tastes of individual customers.

The range of graphic methods used in this volume builds towards a 'graphic anthropology'. This is intended as a parallel to visual anthropology, which has a focus on lens-based media and how anthropology can be built around film and photography practices. By sketching, drawing, notating and mapping, the skillset of architecture can be brought into contact with anthropological theory more directly. The aim is to make use of the process of making meaning by transferring our understanding of a scene or phenomenon, be that visible or non-visible, into a series of traces into a surface. These are organized according to conventions that allow another to read the drawings: the codes of architectural drawing are an obvious example here, but less mimetic and more gestural traditions still have conventions, even if these are more open to interpretation. Graphic anthropology is a way of slowing one's engagement down and spending some time with an observed scene, unpicking materiality, relationships in context, gesture and posture, overlapping meshworks and knots of dense social interaction.

The ideas from this book are intended to be integrated into the practice of architectural design, most directly informing the process of site and context analysis and the understanding of precedents.

# Acknowledgements

This book is the result of a long period of development, with some of its origins to be found indirectly in my PhD research. Much of the material was developed early in my career as a lecturer at Manchester School of Architecture through the lecture series and electives in *Observation and Architecture*, *Graphic Anthropology*, *World Urbanism*, *Rewriting the City*, and a research-led studio workshop on *Knowledge Production in Architecture* as well as a wonderfully varied range of MArch dissertations on related topics. As such, the book owes a debt of gratitude to the many students who have engaged with this version of architectural and graphic anthropologies since 2010. The acknowledgements that follow are each a kind of home for this work, appropriate given the theme of dwelling that unites architecture and anthropology. Whilst all errors and flaws in the argument are the fully owned by the author, the work is the result of figurative and literal homes in Cumbernauld, Aberdeen, Manchester, Seoul, Tokyo and Den Haag.

My view of anthropology is shaped by a long conversation with a cross-disciplinary group of scholars centred, but not always based at the University of Aberdeen. The leader of this group is Tim Ingold, whose academic generosity has shaped so much of our approach, driven by genuine enquiry and an openness to the ways in which we might know our world better. Tim's faith in me as a young architectural academic navigating his way into anthropology has been invaluable. This has meant taking practices seriously, making and doing as ways of analysing and demonstrating an understanding of the world by immersing ourselves fully in it. Creativity, according to our earliest research group, is *understanding in practice*: a formulation that has remained with me. The group is so broad as to defy completeness in listing here, but my key colleagues during this time have been Mike Anusas, Stephanie Bunn, Jen Clarke, Anne Douglas, Emilia Ferraro, Caroline Gatt, Wendy Gunn, Liz Hallam, Rachel Harkness, Marc Higgin, Elizabeth Hodson, Murdo Macdonald, Trevor Marchand, Sandra McNeil, Alyson Miller, Ricardo Nemirovsky, Amanda Ravetz, Griet Scheldeman and Jo Vergunst.

Many of the above group came together most recently under the banner of the ERC Advanced Grant project 'Knowing from the Inside' which provided funds to some of the projects detailed in this volume, particularly the investigations into Sanja Matsuri in Tokyo. Further funding was provided by Manchester Metropolitan University for research in Seoul, and the University of Manchester which supported further field research and conference presentations essential to developing my arguments. I would like to thank Alfred Hwangbo for his hospitality in Seoul, and Darko Radović, Davisi Boontharm, Kyota Yamada and Ryuzo Ohno for their welcome and assistance in Tokyo.

Academic leave granted by the University of Manchester in 2018 was important for the development of the manuscript. Earlier research projects are also represented, such as the AHRC & EPSRC 'Designing for the 21st Century' funded project *Multimodal Representation of Urban Space*, where I developed the *Sensory Notation* method used in Chapter 8 alongside Ombretta Romice, Gordon Mair and Wolfgang Sonne.

Of my colleagues at the Manchester School of Architecture, I would like to give particular thanks to Stephen Walker who gave valuable feedback on an early draft of this book. I would also like to thank the team at Bloomsbury – James Thompson, Alexander Highfield and Sophie Tann – for their patient advice throughout the publication process.

As with any project with a long development process, my family have had an essential role in steadying me during the highs and lows of producing the manuscript. As ever, the continued support of my wife Morag has been absolutely essential throughout the course of writing this book through our moves from Edinburgh to Manchester and now split with Den Haag; I have leant heavily on her confidence in my work when my self-confidence was at its lowest ebb. Thanks for the latter edits of the work are also due to my 'co-authors' – our cats Omar and Odessa, who have an academic following in their own right due to their Instagram appearances.

My parents Sandra and Andrew Lucas, to whom the book is dedicated, supported me through the foundations of this work during my PhD research, and continue to be a source of stability. My sisters Katrina and Rhonda also contribute to that importantly familiar and restorative home environment whenever I manage to make it back home to Cumbernauld.

# 1

# Introduction: Typologies of Social Relation

## Introduction

In framing this book around *typologies of social relation*, the intention is to discuss building types and the theories derived from social anthropology best suited to understanding them. Some of these relationships are tightly intertwined, as in the case of dwelling or performance, whilst others are broader theories such as exchange or practice. The book's intention is to present anthropology as directly relevant to architectural design and theory. In some instances, this gives further elaboration to tacit knowledge within architecture, the embedded knowledges passed down through studio cultures but rarely made explicit, whilst in other cases the theories will offer new perspectives on the ways we interpret architecture.

The broader intention of the book is to propose a productive relationship between architecture and anthropology, with the ideas developed through anthropology taken seriously as prompts for architectural design and theory. In short, architects and others can benefit greatly from reading ethnographic works and the theories derived from them. Most architects will not have the opportunity to engage directly in ethnographic research, so closely tied to anthropology as a discipline, but other opportunities present themselves: as Ingold reminds us, anthropology is not ethnography and vice versa. Architects can engage in alternative anthropological enquiries more suited to their skillset and resources. The discipline of anthropology is opening up beyond its well-established textual and lens-based practices of ethnography, and other ways of knowing are being developed. The key lesson is that one must not take the social world for granted: that the most everyday occurrences have complexity and variation, open to analysis and heavy with further implications for the worldview of participants.

Anthropology offers us the potential for an architecture of broader ecologies, where skills and practices provide insights into the ways people understand the world in a broad range of mutually inclusive ways. Anthropology offers architects ways of understanding materials and their life stories; economies and their networks of trust and obligation; how conservation strategies can be understood through museum studies and the critique of the collection; how practices of maintenance define ideas of cleanliness and the concept of dwelling as a perpetually unfinished project; and the co-production of people with their environments, how roles are performed in both dramatic and religious contexts as well as everyday encounters. The architectural implications of this are broad, suggesting the architectural humanities might turn their eye away from both the canon of Western antiquity and the othering practices of vernacular architecture, and towards understanding the full range of our deliberate environmental adaptations that might be considered as architectural.

## Architecture and the lifeworld

Anthropology is a well-established and defined discipline in which a concern for the social and cultural lifeworlds of people is described. This concern with *being human* is central to the discipline and lies at the root of the possible collaboration between the disciplines of architecture and anthropology.

The *lifeworld* is a fundamental concept when considering how architecture and anthropology inform one another. This concept allows anthropologists to consider the intermingled nature of people with their environment: context in this case is inextricable from *being*. Conventionally, this is presented by the anthropologist as a series of encounters with people who live their lives in a way which is different to the anthropologist themselves: this space of otherness is problematic, but introduces a useful critical distance to the discussion. As such, anthropologists often work away from their homes.[1]

Architecture deals with people and their *lifeworlds* in a different way, seeing the facts of our everyday lives as the raw material from which new possibilities can be wrought. A more detailed and fine-grained understanding of the facts of these lifeworlds, in all of their diversity, offers the potential for accommodating (in both senses of the word) the lives of people in a more nuanced and intelligent fashion. The potential is for a more socially informed and engaged architecture to emerge from a deeper understanding of what it means to dwell in space. Anthropologist Michael Jackson (2013) considers his preference for the term lifeworld:

> If I prefer the term 'lifeworld' to 'culture' or 'society', it is because I want to capture this sense of a social field as a force field (*kraftfeld*), a constellation of both ideas and passions, moral norms and ethical dilemmas, the tried and true as well as the unprecedented, a field charged with vitality and animated by struggle. (Jackson, 2013:7)

By eschewing categories such as 'culture', the lifeworld avoids some of the assumptions of a bounded social group sedimented within the term. Whist not perfect in itself, it does assist us in thinking of how concepts of the world are bound up in individuals and how they live their lives within it. One of the things anthropology excels at as a discipline is the discussion of knowledge and its production. Anthropology challenges structures of knowledge based on conventional power relations, such as patriarchal, imperialist, academic or capitalist constructs, and gives equal weight to knowledge possessed by other groups and won through other ways of knowing and understanding the world. These challenges to the conventional structures allow for a more holistic understanding of the many ways in which it is possible to be human, to dwell within the world and to construct a coherent lifeworld. In order to do this, anthropological approaches ask us to understand where we ourselves come from and to make fewer assumptions about the world around us. Living is, therefore, to produce working knowledge of the world.

It is this principle of observing, asking, participating and questioning the world rather than walking into a context, situation or place knowing everything about it that is most valuable to the process of architectural design: how can we mobilize the methodologies and practices of anthropology in order to situate our design practices more carefully, responding more fully to the needs of people and the wider environment.

The importance of the lifeworld concept is that it suggests we cannot understand elements of social life in isolation, but must have a holistic approach which considers the following at a range of scales from micro- to macro-scale: environmental conditions, historical legacy, politics, ecology, economics and many more aspects. Even if the eventual account focuses on a small set of examples, these are chosen as representative of the entire context, highlighting its most significant features which demonstrate an alternative way of living.

This introductory chapter discusses some key methodologies in anthropology, suggesting where these cross over with architectural concerns and practices. This allows the body of the book to focus on specific examples and theories developed by way of anthropology. By engaging with participant participant-observation, auto-ethnography, and methodological atheism/philistinism visual anthropology and design anthropology amongst other methods, one can begin to draw parallels with not only architectural theory, but also aspects of the design process itself from specification of a programme, context analysis, spatial and formal design, materiality, construction process and post-occupancy analysis.

A range of practices already exist in architecture in order to integrate elements of the social more fully into architectural design processes. The results of these as practices have specific aims, often aimed at particular types of community, such as vulnerable or disenfranchized groups. User-centred design, co-design, people–environment studies, environmental psychology, space syntax, and other systems and processes have sought to reduce the distance between architects and the people they are working for, but are designed to address particular aspects of socially responsible design. My intention is not to be dismissive of these important and evolving practices, but rather to add further nuance to conventional design practice rather than suggest additional work packages of activity and enquiry.

*Anthropology for Architects* offers a substantially different approach, one which places the architect as someone who *draws, models, designs* and hopefully *builds* culture; intervenes upon and provides *context*, where anthropologists classically *write* it.[2]

The introduction concludes by summarizing the approach taken by subsequent chapters, which are arranged according to site typologies and their associated anthropological interpretations.

## The anthropology of architecture

In situating the intentions of this book, it is helpful to consider some of the possibilities in sketching a relationship between architecture and anthropology. This is often discussed in terms of the distinction between anthropologies 'of' architecture and *anthropological architecture* or *architectural anthropology*. The anthropology *of* architecture often takes architecture and its practices as the unit of analysis, studying the agency of designers, clients or users and their buildings through participant-observation with the aim of understanding the complex network of social interactions which contributes towards the construction of our built environment. Similar approaches exist within the study of vernacular architecture, where building conventions alternative to the dominant paradigm are charted.[3] The potential of an anthropology *with* architecture suggests that the disciplines work closely with one another in order to produce a new manner of understanding, exploring a wider range of methodologies and approaches in order to produce a new social and spatial context.

This book presents a survey of the theory that underpins the strong correspondence between contemporary social anthropology and architecture with the aim of moving towards an *anthropological architecture* or *architectural anthropology*. As the study of people and their lifeworlds, anthropology has a great deal to contribute to architecture, with implications for long-held assumptions, reinforcing and elaborating as much as it contradicts and complicates. The central contention is that this is good for both disciplines and lies at the root of any cross-disciplinarity. Anthropologists often seek to engage with architects and academics in architecture, a shared interest in dwelling and how we make places in the world makes for fruitful discussion.

Above all, the book is to be read from the point of view of what assists us with the practice of architectural design. This idea of practice is broadly sketched to include more than the professional and commercial office familiar to bodies such as the Royal Institute of British Architects (RIBA) or American Institute of Architects (AIA), but rather to consider the practices which constitute the built environment at the scale of the building. The more explicitly urban scale presents another set of problems of course and lies outside the scope of this study.

The initial research question is: what can architects learn from anthropologists?[4] This swiftly developed to ask how architects can integrate anthropological thinking and processes into their work.

As architects, reading ethnographic accounts written by anthropologists gives us a window into other peoples' worlds: precisely the aim of anthropology. This is, of course, highly specific and problematic when we attempt to mobilize this directly into designing. Where anthropology can contribute, however, is at the level of theoretical structures: the scaffolding for thinking about complex, messy, real-world situations – more appropriate than the fashion for philosophy with its essentially reductive approach and abstraction of problems. Anthropology can also offer methodological approaches: not only the fully engaged ethnography, which takes a great deal of time, but other ways of knowing are certainly possible.

The book seeks to demonstrate the applicability of anthropological thought and ethnographic practices to both the understanding and the design of the built environment. This is fraught with as many difficulties as correspondences, of course, and the fundamental nature of architecture and design as broadly interventionist is the most problematic of all. Anthropology is conventionally understood as an observational practice – one which stresses engagement and participation, but methodologically atheist, apolitical and philistine: taking a position apart from our own desire to interpret through our existing belief and value systems. The notion of taking these observations and making fundamental changes to the environment in question is often anathema to anthropologists, where it is second nature to designers such as architects and other designers.

Our definitions of architecture must change to encapsulate the social sphere in a more holistic manner. In order to do this, the lessons of disciplines such as anthropology must be attended to, their practices understood and adopted as appropriate, allowing architecture to enter into informed collaboration with its practitioners. Exploiting existing disciplinary intersections relies upon collaboration with contemporary practitioners rather than solely upon our reflections on the writings of anthropologists. Our alternative reading of these theories as designers informs this collaboration significantly: we approach the material differently as architects. One way to discuss this is to consider what a parallel discipline of *Architectural Anthropology* might look like, borrowing from the recent and continuing development of *Design Anthropology* with its focus on industrial and product design but with the aims and needs of architecture kept in mind. Design anthropology's methods use provocation and prototypes in a way that architecture cannot: different concepts of scale are a significant issue in this, where the size of a building often precludes building a prototype leading to adaptation and conversion after construction to resolve issues, whereas the scale of industrialized production requires product design to have a high degree of refinement before committing to a run of thousands of units. Despite a clear kinship between architecture and the other design disciplines, the terms of engagement between architecture and anthropology are distinct from those found in design anthropology, so it is mainly the process of forming this sub-discipline and how it established its methodologies that is of interest to us here.

The potential is a more socially informed, engaged and sensitive architecture which responds more directly to people's needs. It is crucial for architecture to move away from the technocratic models developed during Modernism, but which remain persistent today – and perhaps more efficiently enacted with automation in the design and construction processes. The profession can adopt alternative models of practice which surpass the demands and economics of professional and commercial practices in order to produce a more holistic built environment.

The enormous potential for anthropologically informed architecture lies in a reassertion of what architecture is as a discipline. It is more than merely economic activity, building what is determined by market forces in a manner determined by vested interests. Instead, we must build resilient and sustainable architecture fit for people to truly dwell in. This indicates that an approach towards anthropology needs to be embedded within architecture rather than as an add-on or sub-discipline. Care needs to be taken in the manner of architecture's adoption of anthropological thinking, particularly around the idea of making use of traditional or vernacular knowledge. Whilst such recoveries of historical precedent can be appropriate, they are only ever one option for architectural design: it is not the role of a recast architecture to police what is acceptable and what is not, whether that is as a form of cultural appropriation by learning from other cultures or the denial of modernity and its technologies. These options must remain on the table, articulated in new ways by an architectural anthropology.

There are opportunities for close collaboration between architecture and anthropology, and, it can be argued, a need for it. Buildings fail or succeed based on social conditions as often as material failures: yet the questions are rarely framed around the social status of the building, such a massive investment of time, materials and other resources. More than a curiosity or study in the collaboration possible between two cognate disciplines, this book suggests that the social aspect of architecture is crucial rather than luxurious, pragmatic rather than philosophical.

## A brief history of anthropology

It's helpful to have a little context to the discipline of anthropology, noting important developments such as structuralism as well as its origins in colonialist practices. This progression of dominant ideas is sometimes rendered by historians as a sequence of discrete schools of thought, but the actual developments are more fraught and overlapping than this might suggest. The identification of a dominant school of thought often occurs after the fact (with some notable exceptions), noting a trend, a series of common concerns and a shared approach. This is why we can never say with any certitude what school is dominant at this moment, but it is clear that a set of concerns are apparent across architecture, including an increased concern for environmental technology and sustainability as well as the formalism afforded by developments in computer-aided design and manufacture. In architectural history, there has been a recent phase of postcolonial theory looking at the mechanisms of transnational movement of ideas and practitioners, and a recent move to the examination of second-order manifestations of architectural practice such as journals, exhibitions and competitions as ways of constructing architectural taste. Each such development looks not only to examine something under-represented in the existing literature, but to build upon what we have learned from prior movements. More than mere fashions, such collections of scholarship allow us to learn collectively, discussing common challenges and issues with the aim of making substantial progress in understanding.

In anthropology, the discipline was founded by missionaries, explorers and adventurers. This origin has marked the study of cultures deeply and creates a problematic deep at the heart of the study, where power relations between the studied people and the anthropologist are potentially unethical. This early anthropology conceptualized people as Other, often with a capitalized 'O'. The problem with this approach was that it was based in and supported by Colonialism. This means that the people examined by such early anthropology were seen as exotic, often expressed in the terminology of the 'Noble Savage'.

one simultaneously interesting and anachronistic example of this is James Frazer's *The Golden Bough*. He was trained as a philosopher and engaged on a project to describe the history of humanity and also of the contemporary non-Western world. It is easy to criticize his work from the point of views we have nowadays, as some of his work misunderstands the cultures he encounters in fairly fundamental ways. Indeed, his work can be understood as potentially racist in many ways, and whilst we are properly critical of this racism nowadays, it does not entirely invalidate his work, which must be read in the context of the times. Despite these failings, his writing until his death in 1941 sets him as one of the precursors of the modern movement.

Frazer is, as a product of Britain in the nineteenth century, an imperialist. The United Kingdom had an empire and held dominion over vast swathes of the globe at this time. This lack of self-determination is, of course, politically problematic, and as an imperial power, Britain subjugated and exploited these countries as a self-professed benevolent dominion. The belief of such imperialists was founded in an idea that such countries were not as advanced, and as such, we could help them at the same time as integrating their people and raw natural resources into a globalized economy. There was no choice involved in this; this was rule imposed from the West; which establishes an unethical power imbalance in the relationship between any researcher and the people he (for it was at this point invariably a male domain) came across. Romanticism was a great part of this era, where the so-called savage state of people was granted a kind of cache and fashionability in the place of true understanding of the sophisticated lives being lived on a different set of terms, and with completely different reference points.

There is a reason we still read his work, based on his own observations as well as a vast literature:

> Because Frazer was a product of the nineteenth century we think of him, confusedly, as an imperialist and a romantic. He was at bottom neither, believing fixedly in a kinship of the intellect that transcended cultures, and above all in the primacy of thought. Magic was this: schematized though; and ritual was thought-in-practice. His aborigines, like his Romans, come with a completely worked out, if fallible, system of epistemology and ontology, even of technology. They had views, so do we; they got things wrong; but which of us, in the last resort, is wiser? Robert Fraser, Introduction to *The Golden Bough* (Frazer, 1994[1890]:xxxix)

The book is comparative in its approach, taking thematic approaches to diverse themes such as *The King of the Wood*; *Killing the God*; *Scapegoats*; and the *Golden Bough* of the title (which refers to the Roman myth in which a golden-leafed bough enables Aeneas to travel safely in the Underworld). In what was a particularly daring observation for the time, Frazer drew parallels between the Christian story of the Crucifixion with other religions and traditions in which the king or god is sacrificed and consumed, mirroring ancient traditions in which a ruler is slain ritually before becoming old and infirm.

Such notions that any human being could be understood as 'savage' have, over the course of the twentieth century, been entirely eradicated from anthropological discourse. This is deeply embedded in the politics of anthropology as a movement, which began as a way of understanding people with radically different lives, as an extension of natural history in a way. This science aspect of the social sciences has been supplanted by a stronger association with the humanities.

This association sets anthropology apart from these European missionaries, setting an agenda of so-called methodological atheism. This approach was required in a time when the majority of practising anthropologists were themselves Christian: that such beliefs are actually difficult to reconcile when in the field with the various belief systems held by people across the world. The criticism inherent in holding a religious belief system was impossible to reconcile with an accurate and sensitive study of the life of people with even slightly different views of the world, be they alternative Christian traditions, small regional religious traditions or the other great world religions. This remains a difficulty for researchers of faith today, but has developed further into a generalized approach for the discipline, making the anthropologist methodologically apolitical, philistine and even to an extent amoral: not making judgements on the people they have chosen to study.

We are now at a stage where anthropology is fractured into sub-disciplines based on either a thematic differentiation or a regional one. As such, there are groups of medical anthropologists, anthropologists of art and anthropologists who look into skill. Others might focus on the anthropology of Africa, East Asia, Australia or 'The North'. Each of these groupings allows anthropologists to consider a similar set of issues, cross-comparing and offering up generalizable theories about humanity, and the multitude of ways in which it is possible to be human. There are some notable exceptions: some anthropologists directly engage with development work, actually attempting to make a difference when visiting troubled areas of the world. Others, such as feminist anthropologists, engage directly with the gender politics of their chosen field. This is another important exception from the trend of uncritical anthropologists: where the lives of women are examined in terms of their freedom, opportunity, equality and power.

One of the founding figures of the contemporary discipline of anthropology is Claude Lévi-Strauss. As an anthropologist, Lévi-Strauss is famously associated with the structuralist tendency in anthropological theory. Whilst such schools of thought and the development of ideas might seem completely academic in interest, it is worth considering in detail the development of intellectual discovery. Any field, such as architecture, anthropology or philosophy, has certain dominant characteristics at any given point.

Structuralism is a key development in this history of anthropology, and it is understood to be a watershed moment in the discipline. Anthropologists continue to use the term to define a work as being either structuralist or post-structuralist. For these reasons, it is worth considering precisely what is meant by a structuralist theory. Lévi-Strauss abstracts human life into common structures held to be universal. These categories include *kinship*, *religion*, *mythology*, *language*, *art*, *magic* and *medicine*. We shall see later that there is not only an influence and continuing utility for this notion, but also a rejection of it – particularly on the basis that it promotes an idea of universality. Anthropology is founded on the specific rather than the general, so how is it possible to reconcile this idea of universality at all?

Lévi-Strauss's approach to this, which draws a distinction between ethnography and ethnology in that ethnology, is the comparative study (1963:2) enabled by the process of conducting an ethnography. In this understanding, ethnography is source material and anthropology the analysis and understanding that is made of this. Ethnology has been superseded by social anthropology in the UK and cultural anthropology in North America, with ethnology remaining the prevailing terminology in the European discipline.

Lévi-Strauss examined the history of anthropology and developed four fields of investigation:

sociocultural anthropology (primarily social anthropology)

linguistic anthropology

biological anthropology (also known as physical anthropology)

archaic anthropology (strongly related to archaeology).

This model is strongly associated with American anthropology, where British schools of thought would consider social anthropology to be their primary area of concern. This sketches a broad discipline of human development which can accommodate the study of ancient humans, differences in physical biology and also in approaches to language and how this affects cognition. Archaeological anthropology, for example, deals with similar issues to social anthropology as it seeks to understand the lives of ancient people. The evidence available drives a methodology resulting in an anthropology based on the material traces people leave behind rather than having direct access to them for ethnographic, fully embedded research.

Such categorizations of the discipline are not universally accepted, even considering the British focus on social anthropology, there are a great many sub-disciplines each with a different regional or topical focus.

Boas achieved a great deal for anthropology, in particular moving on from Frazer's era where there was assumed to be a singular thread of human development and evolution; Boas established the idea that there are multiple forms and variations of this human development, opening the door for there to be parity between such evolutions.

After Boas, Malanowski moves the discipline closer to what we now understand as anthropology by formulating methodologies which reduce the distance of the observer to the observed. Malanowski helped to establish the idea of participant-observation as the primary technique of social anthropology. This research practice embeds the researcher in the field and involving extended periods of months or years living with a community and participating fully in their world. This overturned the presumptions of earlier ethnographic research which stressed the distance of the observer; that in order to remain objective, the researcher cannot get involved in the lives of the people he is studying.

Lévi-Strauss accepts this new model of anthropological methodology, but is more interested in the theorized results than the reportage. Rather than merely describing, Lévi-Strauss is concerned with drawing out the meaning of what is happening in the field site. For this, he argues that there are common and universal structures to human life and activity. This structuralist approach is sure of itself, consisting of the analysis of field notes and abstracting their content from the specific towards irreducible elements. Lévi-Strauss notes the similarity in approach between the anthropologist and the historian in this regard, with reference to his rejection of an earlier and commonly held idea that anthropology is an equivalent discipline focused only on non-literate cultures (1963:23).

In this model of anthropology there is an objective of reaching deeper into a phenomenon, of a lifestyle, of a culture in order not only to understand the surface of what is happening, but also to discern the true motivations and meanings at the heart of what is being observed. Such reasons might be conscious, but are more often unconscious and the result of a long tradition of knowledge and understanding. We can begin to understand the difference between anthropology and history not to lie in the form of the evidence available so much as the qualities of the temporality. History attempts to find patterns in decision making and the wider cause and effect, where anthropology has a concern for the way lives are lived, the relationships between people and how we can find similarities or differences therein.

## Ethnography and anthropology

Anthropology is closely associated with the methodology of ethnography, specifically of participant-observation. Early ethnographic enquiries would position the researcher as an observer, scientifically maintaining a distance to ensure they do not influence the subject of the study. The impossibility of this, together with developments in methodologies which place the researcher firmly within the context, resulted in the development of a mode of participant-observation, where the ethnographer recognizes and allows for their own presence.[5] Ethnography generally consists of a long-term study, often presented as a *rite of passage* for the anthropologists themselves, where they would typically travel to another place, living there for a period of months or years and learn how people live in the process. Like most disciplines, there is a continual crisis within the discipline concerning the practices of conducting research, with classic ethnographies adopting a version of the scientific method. This involves attempting to remain apart from the object of study, so as not to influence it. This could never really be the case, however, and a more nuanced approach of participant-observation became the norm.

The ethnographer is implicated in their research, present at all times, and objectivity is recognized as an impossible aim to achieve. This makes for a very subjective social science, verging on biography and autobiography at times. Ethnographic studies consist of pertinent stories which allow the anthropologist to begin to develop theories about the underlying meaning of what they have observed and participated in.

There is a growing body of literature around the ethnography of architectural practice. Often framed as a form of science and technology studies (STS) and informed by the work of Bruno Latour and Isabelle Stengers, these texts seek to unpack the processes by which designers work, how decisions are made and the nature of architectural design as a technical practice. These studies are fascinating insights into the workings of practice which allow us to avoid the myth of the individual genius architect and to see the process in the round. Examples include Sophie Houdart's work *Kengo Kuma: An Unconventional Monograph* (2009), the result of an extended ethnographic engagement with the office of Kuma Kengo; this text describes the day-to-day activity of the practice, including the social nature of architectural drawings, and the place of such materials in the design process. For further discussion of the full extent of a building process, Rachel Harkness's (2011) study of *Earthship* builders in Scotland follows the materials used and the transfers of knowledge among a group of self-builders looking for more environmentally sustainable ways to live.

Other significant writers in the field include Albena Yaneva and Victor Buchli. Yaneva's ethnographic account (2009) of the work of OMA focuses on the use and re-use of models from one proposal to the next, seeing the design process of an architectural firm outside the bounds of individual projects, and is one example of the confluence of architecture with anthropology, specifically of the ethnographic method – partly on account of the difficulties presented by attempting a more informed and contemporary form of participant-observation (problematized by the necessity for specific expertise). Buchli's *Anthropology and Architecture* (2013) is written more explicitly from the disciplinary perspective of anthropology and written from the perspective of material culture studies with a regional focus on the ex-Soviet Union. Such an approach explores the life stories of materials and objects as well as people, noting that inanimate objects have narratives of making, use, and disuse which intertwine with the people who own them. Buchli's approach is to see architecture as an agent, one which acts in a variety of ways on the people who encounter it, and which can be used as an instrument of state control over peoples' lives. The historical context of the relationship between the two disciplines is important and useful, discussing art historical, archaeological and anthropological discussions of vernacular architecture.

Architecture and anthropology share a common root of observation. Whilst anthropology goes to great lengths to problematize its observational practices through the discussion of ethnographic field work and participant-observation modes of working, it is clear that observation remains a part of that story. The drawings I discuss later are in this observational mode, developing the idea of the sketchbook as comparable to ethnographic field notes, highlighting its role in forming theories, contexts and a basis for future action. It is this future orientation present in architecture which anthropology has had an issue with historically, but various forms of activist anthropologies and design anthropology have begun to find routes out of this: anthropology can be as interventionist as architecture. Thomas Binder, writing in *Design Anthropological Futures*, notes that recent developments in the field indicate that *collaborative encounters* (in Smith et al (Eds.), 2016: loc.6114) allow for new lifeworlds to come into being.

Further discussion in design anthropology reveals that design can be understood as a provocation, that design is a *mode of knowledge production* (Donahue in Yelavich & Adams, 2014:38). New methods might be required in this case, rather than simply adopting existing processes which carry a great deal of theoretical baggage with them. The model proposed by Donahue (2014) is an alternative to the positivist model of design as problem solving. Both Donahue and Binder, as well as other contributors to these collections, are part of a movement in contemporary anthropology around emergent conditions rather than operating with presumptions of stability and continually re-enacted social rituals. Design is recast as relating to *futures* as plural possibilities of change, framing the intervention of the design professional within ideas of emergence (Smith & Otto in Smith et al., 2016: loc. 692).

This conundrum of intervention with regard to anthropology has long been an issue – it is raised by Smith and Otto but not fully resolved: how can anthropology, as conventionally defined, reconcile the idea of intervention given its fundamental opposition to action? The co-production argument and socially engaged practice only take us so far once we recognize expertise and specialism in design disciplines and designers themselves. Anthropological approaches are uncomfortable with conventional practices of design, where individuals or teams work from a client's brief, gather information and produce variations on the design before presenting them to the client again. Often, anthropology tries to avoid such conventional instances in preference to fully engaged practices where designers collaborate with clients and users. The fact remains, however, that design, much of it good, exists within the dominant paradigm.

Smith and Otto draw upon Rabinow's *contemporary anthropology* (2016: loc.718), referring to the notion of the *emergent* that is used to oppose conventional anthropology of societal reproduction, where the new, the altered and the changed are all smoothed out. What we have in emergent models of social life is an anthropology which has an eye on continual reinvention, of creativity and cultural improvisation as we might have understood it elsewhere. The idea of what the contemporary means in itself is also challenged:

> Tradition and modernity are not opposed but paired...the contemporary is a moving image of modernity, moving through the recent past and near future in a space that gauges modernity as an ethos already becoming historical. (Rabinow, P., Marcus, G., et al., 2008: loc. 645)

Rabinow complicates the accounts of emergence coming from Deleuze and his source, Bergson. Virtuality and potentiality are then added to the terminology of futures and emergence. There are some distinctions in the inflection each of these give, but there is perhaps a lack of precision, but it is important to report on not only what facts can be observed on the ground, but also the possibilities people understand to exist:

> Anthropology has paid more attention to what is than to what might be, and has had a greater interest in how societies are reproduced than how they are transformed. (Smith, R.C. & Otto, T., in Smith et al (Eds.), 2016: loc. 747)

There are other approaches to anthropology beyond participant-observation including ethnographic film[6] and the photographic practices of visual ethnography.[7] The presence of the lens and recording media is theorized carefully as a sub-discipline related to documentary filmmaking, not only accounting for the influence of the lens on what happens in front of it, but also accentuating the multisensory nature of what can be captured and conveyed through non-textual means.

Further methodological innovations are present within design anthropology, and these are perhaps most relevant to architecture. Still relatively young as a sub-discipline, design anthropology[8] still has an issue in applying across all of the design disciplines: architecture is a particular case in point. The use of prototypes within design anthropology is particularly interesting, with the anthropologist working alongside designers and end users of products, observing and collaborating throughout the process in order to understand how a designed object might be used, what it is actually needed for and how best to achieve this.

Controversially, some anthropologists are beginning to question the near-exclusive focus on ethnography as anthropology's method. Tim Ingold (2014, 2017) has written about the habit of conflating anthropology with ethnography:

> Anthropology, I maintain, is a generous, open-ended, comparative, and yet critical inquiry into the conditions and possibilities of human life in the one world we all inhabit. (Ingold, 2017:22)

In defining anthropology, Ingold describes its concern with considering all of the ways in which it is possible to live life as a human being in a social context. The question asked by anthropology is, given that no way of life is simply 'natural' or the way things must be, *why* is social life arranged in this way? As such, he defines it as a *comparative* discipline.

I've long avoided positioning my work as *ethnographic*, preferring to call it anthropological. This is perhaps strategic, as I am most often presenting work to anthropologists. This discussion stems from my early work in anthropology, where I spent my time at my own drawing board interrogating a research question about creative practice through my own work. The result of these conversations was to underline that this upstart architect was resolutely *not* doing ethnography.

Despite projects which relied on my observations of another context, Japan, this has made me a little uncomfortable about describing my work explicitly as ethnographic, but instead arguing for it as an alternative form of anthropology.

The distinction might lie in the nature of ethnography as a non-judgemental form of reportage, accurately and unflinchingly accounting for what happens within a social context. By drawing and using other inscriptive practices, I feel that I have already made a step towards interpretation, making sense of things and theorizing through drawing.

It occurs to me that this might be different if my drawings were conducted in situ and over a longer period, rather than from brief visits and drawn up afterwards in the studio. The immediacy of the data of ethnographic field notes is akin to the hurried sketch made whilst in a place; this is typically followed by a longer consideration of the recorded events afterwards in order to bring some order to them, and this sense-making process could be considered as characteristic of anthropology. Ingold has argued several times for a disentangling of ethnography and anthropology. This is not to be protective of either term, but to be more precise in what we mean by them: and importantly, opening the door for anthropology to be conducted by a range of alternative methods – not only ethnography, but also by creative practice such as drawing, dancing, pottery, pedagogy and more.

I was trained to understand anthropology as an alternative to the philosophical tradition whereby theory was grounded in the lifeworlds of people, and the aim was not to find a single universal truth, but to celebrate the multiplicity of ways to be human in the world.

The research that follows maintains a tension between what I will call an ethnographic aspect and the anthropological interpretation of that condition.[9] The argument made by Ingold is perhaps internal to anthropology, but it underlines some of the ways in which ethnography is being made to stand in for anthropology: as a kind of reportage without the reflective element of anthropology. Ingold positions anthropology as follows:

> Anthropology, as I have presented it, is fundamentally a speculative discipline. It is akin to philosophy in that sense, but differs from philosophy (at least as practiced by the majority of professional philosophers) in that it does its philosophizing in the world, in conversation with its diverse inhabitants rather than in arcane reflections on an already established literary canon. (Ingold, 2017:24)

The key phrase here is that anthropology does its philosophizing *in the world*. There is more to it than this, however: anthropology, unlike philosophy, is not looking to establish a singular truth applicable to every context: anthropology respects the various possible truths which people construct for themselves in order to live their lives, seeing them as having validity and not imposing a normative view which can never be neutral or universal.

## Structure of the book

The book is arranged broadly around the familiar concept of building types, describing these with the aid of appropriate and relevant anthropological theories. The types are broadly sketched, including some unconventional entries such as temporary festival events and iteratively designed marketplaces. Each of these types of building can be argued as a different social context, meaning that the established canon of anthropological theory has something to contribute.

The range of case studies is largely drawn from my field work in Japan and South Korea. This engagement with East Asian cities such as Tokyo, Kyoto, Seoul and Daegu is not accidental and not only allows for critical distance to be established, but also offers opportunities for examinations of other architectural cultures, socially constructed buildings and understandings of the built environment which can challenge and elaborate the more familiar paradigms. The field sites are not presented with the intention of being exotic or strange, instead representing alternative types of ordinariness. Being an outsider has its benefits, however, as a researcher can sometimes identify things which residents take for granted and highlight precisely why these are valuable and interesting. These case studies demonstrate how methods can reveal other ways of building and dwelling, with other observations possible in other places and through other methods. The selection is not intended to be definitive so much as demonstrative of the potential of anthropology for architects. A second selection of cases is drawn from my engagement with anthropology over the last two decades, most importantly the group *Knowing from the Inside* and its precursors, including the *Creativity and Practice Research Group*. These groups have centred around the department of social anthropology at the University of Aberdeen and the leadership of Tim Ingold: a hub for the investigation of the intersections between art, architecture, design, craft, and anthropology and alternative pedagogy. The working process of these groups has been to engage directly in practices of making and then to reflect on how each member of the group contextualizes this within their own practice. This engagement is more than the usual acknowledgement section for a monograph, but fundamental to shaping the approach of the work included in this book.

The book is based on a broad ranging literature which combines established texts in both disciplines in addition to recent scholarship. Each chapter includes a discussion of the context, the relevant literature and appropriate methodologies to that instance. Theoretical frameworks are used alongside graphic conventions, both informed by anthropological theory and practice. The aim is to combine these approaches to form a truly *architectural anthropology* rather than an anthropology *of* architecture.

One aim of this book is to solve the conundrum of how to integrate anthropological thinking into architecture as a design practice as well as a field of academic study. Anthropology helps us to think about the social life of buildings at an appropriate scale: that of the personal and individual lifeworlds which make up our everyday lives.

We begin with a discussion of the intersections between architecture and anthropology in Chapter 2. This is not with the conventional point of contact, of vernacular architecture, but a discussion of contemporary anthropology and its methodological experimentations. As such, the discussion of *Anthropology in the Studio* takes in the revival of drawing practices as this overlap between architecture and anthropology. The discussion is one of knowledge traditions. As a discipline, anthropology considers knowledge to be plural and produced by engaging in practices, using skills and various ways of being in the world. The key theoretical framework for this chapter is the seminal collection *Writing Culture* edited by James Clifford and George Marcus. Anthropology famously turned inwards at this point, problematizing the production of ethnographic texts and questioning the evidential and scientific intentions of some writers against the poetic and narrative explored by others writing in a biographical mode. Whilst no clear resolution was found to the debate, it provides a useful framework for discussing the role of drawing in both architectural research and anthropological research. Despite recent moves back towards the graphic, drawing has found itself devalued by the academy and profession. Beyond merely restoring its status, however, it is important to understand how we produce knowledge when we draw.

Chapter 3 discusses the most familiar of spaces: the home, and concepts of dwelling. This is informed by a rich literature on domesticity and dwelling across both disciplines. The first point is to make as few assumptions as possible when discussing the home, as it is all too easy to fall in to framing engagements with homes on familiar terms, through our own experience of what it means to be at home, to have a home.

Understanding the home through this lens of material culture allows a different understanding of the home as a storehouse of the things that share our lives and intersect with our own biographies. Other readings of the home are also possible. Recent work on sensory ethnographies considers the ways in which, as an extension of phenomenology, there are social and cultural differences in how we engage with our environments through a rich and overlapping set of senses. We hear our homes, smell them and have a tactile engagement with them. This intersects with one of the key operations of *making* a home: the continual maintenance of it. To think of the dwelling as a place continually under construction by its inhabitants might seem to be overstating the case, but the processes of occupation are essential for architects to understand: the ways we keep our homes clean, in good order, with everything 'in its place' suggests that it is constantly *in the making* rather than finished once the construction is complete. Classic literature on cleanliness helps with this: Mary Douglas's work on the nature of cleanliness and dirtiness suggests that these are far from being universal categories. If we think of dirt as a 'matter out of place' (2002:44–50), we can immediately see that the presumed 'place' of that matter is important to consider. What is neat and tidy for one person, one family, is impossibly cluttered for another, be they in the next house down the street or in another continent.

Dwelling is itself an important concept, and its elaboration by Tim Ingold into a broader understanding of our own co-production by/with our environment. Ingold argues that we cannot be understood in the abstract, but must always be discussed – as humans – in the environment, be that a rural setting where people interact more directly with wilderness or the most densely occupied city. These environments make us as much as we make them: and the home is central to this as one of the places we have the most power to alter in our everyday lives.

Anthropology intersects with other disciplines which are useful to architectural issues. Chapter 4 considers another of these in discussing collection and its associated spaces such as museums. The discussion of material culture studies continues here with the further complication of Suzanne Küchler's discussion of Malanggan funerary sculptures, a classic trope within anthropology. The sculptures collect elements of a person's life through symbolic motifs and are then left to gradually decompose in the forest. There appears to be no clash with the collection of these by Western art collectors and curators, however, as the sculptures have served their purpose. Eventually, these objects are reproduced in order to be collected, asking questions of the influence collection has as a process.

This is connected to appropriation and display: museums are designed to place objects within the reach of people who would not normally be able to experience them in their context. This gives the museum a fraught relationship with the object, argued to divest it of function and reduce it to a representative of a larger series, a kind of 'pet' as Baudrillard (1994:7–24) describes it. In the example given, the idea of the museum is pushed towards its limit with an open air architectural museum similar to those described by Joy Hendry (2000). Here, buildings are disassembled in their existing context and rebuilt within the museum, placed alongside other exemplars of building types and periods.

Conservation in architecture has a common root with this kind of collection, where discernment is applied to examples of buildings and curatorial decisions are made over which ones to retain and which ones can be demolished. This can be observed in the preservation of Hanok courtyard houses in Seoul, where some examples are moved and placed into clusters of Hanoks for tourist appreciation; others are moved into 'Hanok Villages' but retain their residential use, and new Hanoks are also built, often near to the preservation villages, but sometimes with concessions made to contemporary life such as incorporating car garages in the stone base of the structure.

Economic exchange is another fundamental human activity which has been explored by anthropologists. This intersects with literature on gift exchanges which implicate the recipient of a gift in a return of the favour. As such, Mauss's theory of gift exchange, which has been subject to commentary by a great many anthropologists, forms the foundations of economic exchange – of which, capitalist exchange is but one model. Chapter 5 discusses these ideas of cooperation, competition and obligation with reference to urban marketplaces in Seoul and Tokyo's recently vacated seafood market.

The informal architecture which forms this market can be considered as a prototype for a different kind of architecture, playing against the presumptions of what is, and is not, architecture according to the Western canon of architectural history; the suggestion here is that reconsidering the ways in which space is defined, altered, maintained and managed can provide an alternative manifesto for architecture. Indeed, once it is explored as architecture, if architecture is to encompass all human space-making activities, then a substantially different architecture of co-existence, minimum material means, cooperation, portability becomes possible – an architecture that can be packed away at night when it is no longer needed, or adapted to the needs of different stock on the part of the vendor, a different position within the market.[10]

Chapter 5 discusses material culture studies: this time the work of Arjun Appadurai and his definition of the commodity phases and candidacy of things. When a thing is considered to be a commodity is something of a moving target, and architecture has a complicated relationship with this. Contemporary practices of land banking and the use of homes as a convenient place to store wealth[11] are part of a broader continuum of the financialization of housing and property, rendering it increasingly difficult for younger generations to own their home without significant amounts of capital coming from family.

Movement is an important feature in our experience of space, from the small movements which allow us to interact with door handles and other openings to the promenades designed deliberately into Victorian cities and Corbusian villas. Chapter 6 discusses this most quotidian of practices in detail, considering the manner in which we might become lost or find our way. Walking is such an everyday activity for able-bodied people that it might seem strange to cast a critical and theoretical eye over it. A multitude of different practices of walking exist, with each social implication. These *techniques of the body*, as Mauss describes them, would include the endurance of hill walkers in collecting peaks and the choreography of a large subway system (Lucas, 2008b).

## INTRODUCTION: TYPOLOGIES OF SOCIAL RELATION

The activation of spaces by altered practices of walking is a feature of religious and secular festivals, and this is addressed with reference to Kyoto's new year celebrations, which bring the city into use as the stage for a celebration. Various routes, movements, stoppages and returns are described in the *peripatetic social science* of Jean-François Augoyard. Here, assumptions are broken down and a broad range of variations in the practices of everyday navigation are exposed, showing the complexities behind a simple walk to the shops, with all of the decisions made in the process of determining a path.

Whilst much anthropology deals with the everyday, there is a case to be made for discussing deliberate performance and its associated spaces as I do in Chapter 7. There is of course a great deal of writing on the anthropology of performance, the best known of which would be Victor Turner, whose exploration of the threshold conditions and liminality of theatrical performances are expressed in language which has a close kinship with architecture. Once again in Chapter 9, examples are drawn from Japanese architecture, beginning with Kuma Kengo's account of designing a Nō theatre.

Other Japanese theatrical traditions include a similar bridge element for subsidiary performances, and the chapter describes the various elements on and off stage of a kabuki performance. This uses ideas from narrative theory such as diegetic space to supplement the liminal spaces detailed by Turner. What emerges is a complex arrangement of participants in the performance, some of whom exist within the story world and some of whom are understood to be adjacent or entirely outwith. This provides a framework for understanding how performance can activate an entire city district as in the case of Sanja Matsuri, an annual festival in the 'low town' Asakusa ward of Tokyo. The city is embodied and performed, with activities including formal processions, bearing divine palanquins and street parties. This constellation of temporary architecture, mobile buildings and alternative presence in familiar space illustrates many of the ways in which display and performance can form and inform the built environment.

Chapter 8 considers the place of food in everyday life by examining a range of restaurant spaces designed to accommodate particular aspects of Japanese cuisine. This is framed through a literature which extends from the very earliest ethnographies to contemporary anthropology; such is the fundamental nature of our eating habits. The spaces described show how a variety of dishes co-produce quite specific forms of restaurant, suggesting again that we need to break down assumptions about how people prepare food and eat, even within the commercial context of a restaurant. Claude Levi-Strauss famously discussed the distinctions between raw and cooked food, abstracting practices of food preparation as *gustemes*. Aside from the abstractions of cultural and natural processes detailed by Levi-Strauss, various societal pressures generate forms of food consumption, such as demonstrations of fresh ingredients and cooking to the infrastructure of dormitory towns and long hours of work.

Our food is more than a reflection of cultural codes and attitudes, but *is* an important element of that culture in itself. Understanding more about the underlying politics, economies and social class of what Mary Douglas calls *food events* allows us to better understand this important element of everyday life and how it is framed architecturally. Japanese cuisine provides a set of examples ranging from elaborate multi-course kaiseki meals to informal street dining at festivals. Each example shows a clear multisensory relationship between architectural form and the sociality of how we eat.

The conclusion in Chapter 9 suggests how we might begin to assemble anthropological architectures: plural in nature, these assemblages might find different approaches in each context.

The book is arranged around various building types: studio, home, museum, market, sacred space, theatre, restaurant and festival. The intention is not to tie specific anthropological theories to each example: Ingold's dwelling perspective can be just as useful in understanding a theatre, Douglas's notion of purity and cleanliness has clear application to religious spaces, Pink's sensory ethnographies can apply as easily to museums, and agency theories such as Gell's apply very well to marketplaces and performance spaces. The aim is also not to provide an exhaustive list of anthropological theories. Kinship and ritual are not discussed explicitly, for example, but might well find relevance in a number of chapters.

There is a general applicability of anthropological theories to architectural contexts, which shall be explored in greater depth in the concluding chapter, which presents the question of what architects can make with this, what can you do or make with an *anthropological* architecture and *architectural* anthropology?

# Notes

1 As with many things, this is not *always* the case, and there are many good reasons for anthropologists to discuss their 'at home' condition. This is most common where the anthropologist wishes to represent their own lifeworld, either as a member of a marginalized or under-represented group, or as a form of auto-ethnography: a development drawing on autobiography, critically engaging with one's own life, practice, interactions and context.

2 See Clifford & Marcus (2010) for more on this notion of 'writing' a culture and the controversy around it within anthropological discourse.

3 See, for example: Brunskill (2000), Glassie (2000), Oliver (2003) and Rudofsky (1981).

4   I have also, in my discussions with anthropologists, addressed the question of what anthropologists can learn from architects. The focus here is on what architecture can learn from anthropology, but this is not to suggest that architecture as a discipline is in a junior position: anthropology can benefit greatly from the sophistication in discussing spatial conditions, materiality and construction understood by architects. Our knowledge base is both well established and greatly in demand by anthropologists.

5   See Lucas (2016:10–11) for a discussion of the etic and the emic with regard to architectural history.

6   See Grimshaw (2001) and Grimshaw & Ravetz (2005) as well as MacDougall (2006) for more on visual anthropology, particularly its relationship to ethnographic filmmaking.

7   See Pink (2007) for visual ethnography methods focusing on lens-based media.

8   For further exploration of methodological issues in design anthropology, see Gunn (2008) and Gunn & Løgstrup (2014).

9   I have an event organized by Laurent Stalder and Momoyo Kaijima on *Architectural Ethnography* in Einsiedeln, November 2018 to thank for triggering some of these observations on the ethnographic qualities of my work. This remains a tension within my own work, but hopefully a productive one. See Kaijima, Stalder & Iseki (2018).

10  Other aspects of this market, such as its nuanced provision of surface, and the limits placed on it by infrastructure are discussed elsewhere. See Lucas (2017a and 2020).

11  Wade Shepard (2015) gives a convincing account of this in relation to the construction of empty cities in China, where the apartments are built and purchased as investments ahead of the settlement's completion. Indeed, the infrastructure required to make these places liveable may be many years away in these cases.

# 2

# Inscriptive Practices and Anthropology

## Introduction

As so much of this volume relies on drawings, diagrams, notations and other forms of trace, it is important to explore what this can mean. This makes for an unusual anthropology in itself, but it is intended to bridge the practices of architectural research and anthropological research. The starting point is to situate this work within the theories of practice. The primary importance of drawing is not the 'finished' article, but the processes of making it. This process can include the form of attention and perception employed, the hand–eye coordination required to make the gestures and the materials which allow for a trace to be left upon a surface. The practice continues through the reception of the work: it is never truly finished so long as another audience can produce new meanings from it.

Drawing is gaining traction within anthropological practice, most often in the form of sketched perspectives and graphic novel style sequential art. The argument of this chapter is that this can be expanded substantially to include the conventions of architectural drawing. Architects use a mixture of idiosyncratic personal notations and stable, codified conventions when drawing. These have alternative roles in the process of architectural design and can also serve different purposes in anthropological research. The term 'inscriptive practices' is used to sidestep debates around what 'drawing' might include or leave out, and to redirect the debate to the practice of making meaningful marks on or into surfaces.

This chapter gives a brief survey of the status of drawing in anthropology followed by a personal, perhaps auto-ethnographic account of what knowledge can be produced through drawing. It is not sufficient to state that inscriptive practices allow for the production of alternative knowledge, equivalent and supplementary to the ethnographically driven text of anthropology. The character of this knowledge is quite furtive, a dense knot of potential meanings and understandings made possible through the codification of an object in to plan, section, axonometric or other forms of drawing.

## Anthropology in the studio

Design anthropology and anthropologies of architectural practice have, to date, concentrated on the design studio itself as a subject for anthropological gaze. Whilst the focus of this book lies elsewhere, there is much to be learnt from this, particularly in understanding the studio as one of the sites in question.

The studio can stand in for the design process, representing architectural thinking and knowledge production. Whilst there is more to the practice of architecture, many of the key decisions are made in the studio, in the office: at the drawing board or in the CAD interface. Understanding this as a skilled practice is then essential to opening the discipline up to the influence of other disciplines. Studies such as Gunn (2009), Yaneva (2009) and Houdart & Minato (2009) all explore this notion in different ways, either in the pedagogical studio or in the international professional practice.

Architecture is a set of activities which can be bound together as a praxis: a coherent set of practices which have embedded skills and opportunities to produce knowledge. The principle of *ecological thinking* established by Gregory Bateson (1972) is helpful in this regard, as it is a framework by which our own presumptions and operating biases are challenged and placed into a wider context. This deepening and broadening of context is essential to the development of a more anthropologically sensitive architecture, and Bateson is in agreement with others such as James Gibson (1983, 1986), in seeing the production of knowledge as linked to the context where and when it is produced: the historical context, the institutional and professional contexts, the physical and social contexts, the political and economic contexts. Each of these contributes to the production of knowledge, whether this manifests itself as a piece of writing or as a building. Bateson (1972:xxviii) insists that each domain has its own *authority*, suggesting that in order to conduct research, the established abstract fundamentals need to come into contact with direct observation in order to fully exploit each way of knowing.

This chapter looks to understand both studio practice and, more specifically, inscriptive practice, as capable of anthropological insights. The knowledge produced in this way differs from the conventional forms of text-based argumentation, operating within a quite different framework. I use the term 'inscriptive practices' to group together mark-making activities such as drawing (in its many guises), cartography, notation, diagramming, sketching, painting and even handwriting or calligraphy. Each of these has its own benefits and drawbacks based on the rules used to narrow the focus of the inscriber. Every convention edits the world down, limits the scope of the graphic representation through conventions of outline, shading, symbolism, scale and position. A sketch can capture a moment, but without the great accuracy of other forms of representation; a map can describe a terrain, but only suggest what actually happens there. Every drawing then is an edit, a selection of the pertinent issues.

Whilst studio practice suggests a location, a site, it enters into architecture via the profession's educational model and some ideas of practice. Teaching in studio allows the teaching of architecture to operate projects with complexity and context appropriate to the level of the students, gradually increasing in both complexity and the autonomy of the student. Contemporary architectural education mixes emulations of architectural practice with an environment where experimentation and risk taking are encouraged as part of the learning process. The complexity of architectural design is such that it necessitates several strands of education in technology; theory, history and humanities; professional and legal practice. Skills such as draughting and model-making are also part of the process alongside learning how to conduct site surveys and analyse precedents. It is studio where each of these elements comes together and, despite differences in office environment in architectural practices, the metaphor of studio looms large.

## Drawing culture

This book carries a title that suggests there is a great deal for architecture to learn from anthropology on a disciplinary level. This is undoubtedly the case, as in any cross-disciplinary transfer. This transfer of knowledge is important in terms of both content and methodology. The same can be said in the other direction: anthropology should not emerge unchanged from its encounter with architecture. As outlined in the introduction, the overlapping spheres of interest between architecture and anthropology are one basis for collaboration, but a more fundamental question remains over precisely how knowledge is produced.

One of the ways in which architecture produces knowledge is through drawing,[1] and this is a practice of increasing interest within anthropological circles. Drawing opens up a range of options regarding the ways in which we think. The pursuit of drawing is often spoken of in terms of creative, craft-based practice, but this is not the whole truth. Indeed, drawing has a similar status in architectural discourse to the discussion of writing in anthropology: recent titles include *The Death of Drawing* (Scheer, 2014) and *Why Architects Still Draw* (Belardi, 2014), both illuminating a crisis in the concept of drawing – particularly with the advent of ubiquitous digital practices such as Computer Aided Design (CAD), Building Information Modelling (BIM) and three-dimensional (3D) model-making and printing. The conclusions of such apocalyptic proclamations are often to restore drawing to its position, now encompassing a wider range of practices as constituting a form 'drawing'. The element pulling these different ideas of drawing together is spoken of loosely as a common logic of drawing. How can it be that practices as different as freehand sketching, measured perspectives, sets of orthographic projection drawings, parallel projections and CAD drawings rendered models composited through several pieces of software, and a range of individualistic diagramming and notational practices are all considered to be drawings? There is a professional suspicion that 'beautiful' drawings are hiding something, with arguments similar to those raised below by the influential anthropology text 'Writing Culture' edited by James Clifford and George Marcus.

Recognizing the utility of drawing and other inscriptive practices as knowledge-producing activities, there is increasing interest in graphic or drawn anthropology and social science, with Michael Taussig's *I Swear I Saw This* (2011), Andrew Causey's *Drawn to See: Drawing as an Ethnographic Method* (2017), and books such as Anja Schwanhäusser's collection *Sensing the City* (2016) and Ingold's *Redrawing Anthropology* (2016). Nick Sousanis's *Unflattening* (2015) is a particularly notable instance, as the work is presented in its entirety as a graphic novel, having been submitted as a PhD thesis on this basis. Annual field schools are held on the use of graphic novel and sketching techniques in ethnography, and the work of research groups such as *Knowing from the Inside*[2] has pioneered the validation of graphic works *as* anthropology. Marc Higgin gives an account of what we do when we draw from an anthropological perspective (2016), concluding that we make things present by drawing them. Recent work has moved towards the consideration of imagination and its role in anthropological discourse. Elliot and Culhaine's edited volume *A Different Kind of Ethnography* explores a number of options, situating alternative practices as other forms of ethnographic engagement rather than as something different. A model of three branches of ethnography is put forward, which is more inclusive (2017:9). Here, the familiar model of participant-observation is joined by interview and the analysis of documentary evidence, archival research and scholarly study. This allows extension to the postcolonial 'insider' ethnography as a move away from the presumption of outsiders travelling to do their fieldwork, reaching a conclusion of sorts with the ethnographer-performer which investigates the creative practice wholly from the inside of that practice.

One of the aims of this book is to develop the notion of an architectural anthropology. This has been suggested in the context of design anthropology, an established field of enquiry where anthropologists and industrial or product designers work with end users in order to enhance the design process. Whilst this approach is of great interest and is a potential model for the engagement of designer with the user, my intention is to develop *Architectural* or indeed *Graphic Anthropology* in a slightly different direction.

Forms of drawing, graphic representation or *inscriptive practices* are important to the development of the practice of an architectural anthropology. *Graphic Anthropology* then is to *Architectural Anthropology* what *Ethnography* is to conventional *Social Anthropology.* The intention is to develop this approach with both architects and anthropologists, to encourage architects to consider the social life of their spaces in more detail and to open the anthropologists to the alternative logics available to drawings as opposed to writing. The drawing is capable of carrying every bit as much content as a written essay. Indeed, a drawing (broadly speaking) offers a wide range of communicative opportunities not open to the text.

An influential work in anthropology provides a useful analogy for drawing, *Writing Culture* was compiled in 1986 by James Clifford and George Marcus, and concerns the project of anthropology to *write* culture. The focus on such a fundamental practice exposes some of the complexities of the discipline as a whole. Given anthropology is conventionally disseminated as a thesis, monograph or article (notwithstanding the more recent developments in the documentary films made in visual anthropology), what is the nature of this practice? There is a danger that such a query can result in some disciplinary navel gazing, and the prospect of returning to this debate often fills anthropologists with a degree of dread. My intention here is to discuss the possibility of *drawing culture* in the same manner as Clifford & Marcus argue it is written.

The aim of the collection is not simply to raise the question of ethnographic writing, but to move the discipline in the direction of more engaging texts, and away from the 'science' ambitions of the social sciences. There are a number of drivers behind this, drawn from the nature of the discipline at the time. The aims of a dispassionate account would all too often erase the elements of greatest interest, and the authors argued that there was no way of truly erasing the anthropologist from their account. The authority claimed by such accounts was unwarranted and unsupportable, making contested circumstances appear to be fully resolved. The collection is part of a general trend within anthropology towards the co-production of knowledge with respondents in the field rather than writing accounts *of* their lives; anthropology was becoming committed to writing *with* the lives of others. The researcher was always present and implicated, such that a neutralized and dispassionate language became increasingly disingenuous.

Marcus and Clifford and their authors found that there were, when care was taken over the ethics of the account, benefits to writing in a biographical mode, even drifting towards the poetic. The increasingly phenomenological positions of anthropology necessitated a greater focus on sensory perception and, as we shall see later in this chapter and in Chapter 8 on food cultures, the senses are a part of cognition and knowledge, not merely a precursor to it. The contextualization of ethnographic accounts and anthropological theory had to include the researcher's presence, particularly where their presence might have altered or challenged social dynamics substantially as in the case of female researchers in male-dominated circumstances.

The manner in which we represent things is important, and *Writing Culture* consolidated a broader movement towards considering the means of anthropological production more carefully and opening the possibilities for creative practices such as drawing to be used to express the experience of ethnographic fieldwork as contingent and personal. A suspicion of the beautiful is rather unexpected in architecture, understood to be a creative and artistic discipline, particularly from the outside, but this discomfort has its roots in the use of spectacle to disguise shortcomings in the functionality of the design.

## Why I draw

In this section, I borrow my title from a well-known short essay by George Orwell, who meditated on the theme of *Why I Write* (2004 [1946]). It is a deceptively complex question, one which I feel bears a great deal of scrutiny as, like Orwell's writing, I have drawn and painted throughout my childhood and adult life.

Orwell structures his argument across four motives:

a sheer egoism;
b aesthetic enthusiasm;
c historical impulse; and
d political purpose.

This first category of *Sheer Egoism* is less flippant than it might at first appear and speaks to the simple urge to make things for the appreciation of others. This is not seen as a bad thing, of course, simply a fact in the creative impulse; very rarely are things made solely for one's own appreciation or benefit. Indeed, Orwell celebrates this egoism to the extent that it allows the creative individual to continue to live their own life, rather than to subsume it to the will of another, be that through a job or other lifestyle which precludes non-utilitarian, original, free thinking.

*Aesthetic enthusiasm* is also not to be dismissed too easily. Despite aesthetics being rather unfashionable, it remains a powerful consideration and driver for activity. This is a 'desire to share an experience which one feels is valuable and ought not to be missed' (Orwell, 2004:5). This motive is sometimes seen as being 'auratic' as in the case of Adorno's aesthetic theory (2004 [1970]), which was suspicious of the beautiful, often with quite valid reasoning. The category of the aesthetic does include not simply the beautiful, but also the sublime, the uncanny and the absurd. Getting lost in a detail, a colour in a composition or a scene which encapsulates an experience are all examples of this aesthetic impulse: the desire simply to depict is a strong motive.

The *historical impulse* has at its heart a desire to understand, to find some truth and to bear witness to events. This can be in the manner of documenting scenes and events as much as experimenting with abstracted models or lenses through which the world can be seen and understood. As such, every mark made can be understood as being 'of its time' whether that mark is an attempt to break away from convention or a revival of traditional forms of representation. Such avant-garde movements aren't immune from being considered a part of the historical record any more than the quotation or pastiche of older forms.[3]

Finally, and showing the intertwined nature of these motives, is the *political purpose*. This is intended in its broadest possible meaning and might be interpreted as some form of theoretical or moral intention or reflection. The key to this is the 'purpose' rather than the invocation of politics, which is given the simple definition of the 'desire to push the world in a certain direction', and continuing to say that 'the opinion that art should have nothing to do with politics is itself a political attitude'.

This final category is interesting also, as it is identified by Orwell as the one which he, as a writer, finds to be of greatest importance. This should come as no surprise given the explicitly political nature of his writing, but the reasoning behind this preference is instructive and feeds into one of my own concerns with drawing: that it is purposive and potentially rich with theoretical meaning on a level and manner complementary to, but entirely different from, the written word.[4]

The first drawings I would like to discuss are a series of brush and ink drawings on paper (Figure 2.1). The ink is Chinese, ground into ink from a solid stick with an inkstone and water. The paper is Japanese calligraphy paper, translucent and porous. The drawings are from photographs taken during visits to Japan. This introduction of photography complicates matters

**FIGURE 2.1** *Brush and ink drawing of Himeji Castle.*

a little, as we are already one remove away from the immediate experience. We shall see later on that this is a difference of degree, rather than in kind. The materials of the drawings are important to note. The qualities of the support in particular, with the absorbent nature of the surface, have a fundamental impact on the lines made by the brush. The ink, which can be varied in its consistency by virtue of being mixed with water as required, works in conjunction with the whole technology of this drawing to force my hand into a certain set of strokes.

Most notably, watery ink blots immediately, resulting in feathery outlines at best, large grey blobs at worst. More concentrated ink still blots unless the strokes are forceful and deliberate, difficult at this small scale as the paper is a little larger than A4. The blotted marks also have their function, and as I learn to work with the medium and support, my range of strokes increases.

Contained within each drawing is the trace of the gestures that made it. The speed, direction and hesitancy of these marks are evident, allowing the drawing to be deconstructed and the intention of each mark read. The viewer can, in drawings such as this, connect with their own practice or tacit knowledge of making marks on paper. This is not the main focus here, however, as I am discussing why *I* draw. This is a more interesting question in many ways and responds well to Orwell's motives for writing.

This question might usefully be phrased: what kind of observations does drawing lead to? These drawings constitute a meditation on the form and movement of the subject. The movement can be suggested, as in the case of the tree; explicit as shown by the series of Sumo scenes (Figure 2.2); or even absent in the solid permanence of Himeji Castle. The process of such representational drawing is a form of attending to the scene in great detail, focusing and, perhaps more crucially, of editing carefully in order to find an essence of the scene at hand.

Such work on paper can often serve a purpose different to other forms of representation. This can be seen clearly in the drawings produced by the director and film theorist Sergei Eisenstein. Eisenstein drew constantly through his life these drawings more than mere doodles and for a completely different purpose to his films. One might assume a preliminary quality for the drawing, similar to the sketch made by a painter in order to organize the composition or form of elements in a larger work. The directness of the drawn line is one of the first aspects to consider; these are drawings made very

**FIGURE 2.2** *Brush and ink drawing of Sumo wrestlers.*

much for their own sake. Catherine de Zegher of the Drawing Center New York notes that the drawings were an outlet for 'drives and emotions that he could not articulate with words' (de Zegher, 2000:5).

In a fascinating meditation on his own drawing practice, Eisenstein reflects upon the kinship between drawing and dancing, holding that: 'drawing and dancing are branches of the same tree' (Eisenstein in de Zegher, 2000:26). His account of *How I Learned to Draw* documents his fascination with the line, from early attempts at a pure, critical, 'mathematical' line towards his rediscovery of 'the free run of a line' when thinking about his enthusiasm for the foxtrot, considered as a 'peg from which to hang any free, improvised movement' (2000:29) when contrasted with the tap-dancing lessons of his youth with prescribed, discrete steps.

More than the suggested freedom of subject matter – political satire, and erotic and religious imagery – noted by de Zegher in her introduction to the catalogue, Eisenstein's different purpose (and we can see Orwell's *political* purpose motive at work directly here) can be expressed with modest reference towards Eisenstein's method of rapid, juxtapositioning, highly didactic montage in film.

> There is deep within me a long-standing conflict between the free course of the *all'improviso*, flowing line of drawing or the free run of dance, subject only to the laws of the inner pulse of the organic rhythm of purpose (on one hand), and the restrictions and blind-spots of the canon and rigid formula (on the other). (Eisenstein in de Zegher, 2000:31)

My brush and ink drawings are an attempt to understand what I have seen and recorded. The drawing moves beyond the record of the photographic representation and towards an extended meditation on a moment, the forces at work, the massing and forms, the play of light and dark. The objective quality and value of the works isn't so much an issue here, so I make no claims as to the quality of the drawings, but rather focus on the process and purpose of making them. This dispenses a little with Orwell's first motive of egoism, but an element of this remains. More important here is the second category of motive: of aesthetic enthusiasm. By this definition, aesthetic appreciation is a form of understanding that focuses on the moment and the experience. The act of drawing from such experiences is an attempt to extend that moment, to see the image not just as a single frame in an un-filmed continuity, but as an exemplar or encapsulation of that whole movement. The movements suggested by these drawings depict the totality of the dance-like nature of Sumo wrestling, the points at which contact is anticipated and made, with the contested nature of the outcome relying on viscerality as well as balance and poise.

I am also aware of the materiality of the drawing itself. As a technology, the ink and paper lend a quality to the representations, best viewed from the distance of an arm's length rather than digitally projected, enlarged many times their original size. The handling of drawings in a studio learning context is simultaneously respectful and pragmatic, with a preciousness afforded to the paper, but once permission is given, an opportunity for addition, amendment or erasure.

The drawing of Himeji Castle is particularly interesting in this regard. When drawing in this way, I work with several layers of blank paper underneath the drawing I am working on, and these sheets often absorb a trace of ink from above. In this case, the drawing didn't work – part of the risky nature of the medium, where one must make marks quickly and commit to a course of action with no option to repair a mistake. Whilst the intended drawing was rejected as a failure, the under-sheet, for all its flaws, carried the intended composition. Once these wet marks had dried, I used the undersheet to produce a new drawing closer to my intention. Some unintended marks remain, such as the blob of grey in the sky, which I could have disguised as a cloud, but chose to leave in as a trace of the origin of the drawing. This drawing was, then, a direct result of the technology used to make it.

# On bearing witness

Charles Baudelaire is best known as a poet, writing on the early modern phase of Paris in the nineteenth century. Baudelaire was influential on the later work of essayist Walter Benjamin, who celebrated the life of the modern city on Baudelaire's instigation. Until Baudelaire, the default approach was to criticize and decry the modern city as an appalling, hellish place to live: crowded, alienating, impersonal, chaotic and inhuman.

Baudelaire found wonder and beauty in the city. In particular, Baudelaire categorized and wrote about the characters found in the city, ways of being that were unique to the city and which could not be found elsewhere.

As well as his poetry, Baudelaire is recognized as an early example of writing in art history and critique. Of particular interest to us here is his essay *The Painter of Modern Life* (2006 [1863]) in which he discusses the work of an artist not widely regarded as important to the canon of art history, Constantin Guys. What is of interest to Baudelaire is the way in which Guys is recording everyday life: bearing witness.

Writing on a series of fashion plates depicting the styles of clothing from the Revolution to the time of writing in 1863, Baudelaire finds it to be a historical document of great interest and reflective of the everyday philosophy of the time. Rather than establish an 'academic theory' of absolute beauty (2006:3), Baudelaire sought to promote a theory of beauty that was based in both rationalism and historical context: the second factor being almost anthropological in intention. His aim was to move away from the singularity of classical understandings of beauty and to have a layer of circumstance over the top of this. Baudelaire is writing at a time when concepts of beauty and aesthetics are fiercely debated, and the prevailing opinion is that there is a fundamental, classical concept of absolute beauty: a perfection that would be universal to all people in all places and times. Baudelaire is challenging this a little, but not entirely, by suggesting that there are two parts to beauty that interact in a balance that is difficult to discern without the historical document of which he writes.

The challenge is an important step away from the classical model, if not an outright rejection of it, which would come later. What is important to note here is Baudelaire's focus upon the contextual element of beauty represented both by the fashion plates and by the work of Guys.

This is important in structuring the essay and offers the opportunity for discussing the themes of drawing and observing, making a record and seeing the value in the everyday:

> And so, as a first step towards an understanding of Monsieur G., I would ask you to note at once that the mainspring of genius is *curiosity*. (Baudelaire, 2006:7)

This concept of curiosity is crucial to Baudelaire's understanding of the artist. That one must be truly curious is an interesting focus, but it is important to underline the context of art was changing at this time, with a realization that the everyday lives of people, wherever they might be found, were just as interesting as the rich patrons of the Church or nobility. In the nineteenth century, art is moving towards increasing democratization, where the gaze of the artist is directed at his peers as well as towards the rich patron.

Driving this must be a genuine interest in human nature, the condition of the city and the ways in which we arrange ourselves socially. Baudelaire is enthusiastic and oversells the work of the artist a little, but a number of important points remain. Most notably, he writes of the duty of the artist to record the 'gait, glance and gesture' (2006:13) specific to their age. This suggests an importance for sketching in capturing these finer points of poise and costume which are pertinent to the times. Take, for example, the idea of comportment, that is to say, the posture and way of moving people have. This is affected by the clothing that people wear to a great extent. Recording the fashions of people, how they sit in cafes, and how they go about their business is an important role for the artist to take. We will discuss walking in a later chapter, but it is worth noting at this juncture that something as simple and everyday as just walking is culturally and socially specific.

> The spectator becomes the translator, so to speak, of a translation which is always clear and thrilling. (Baudelaire, 2006:15)

This short passage speaks to the theme of this chapter broadly: that the act of spectatorship is important and cognitive. To speak of an act of spectatorship is important: indicating that it is deliberate, directed, attentive. This is not some passive reception, but a gaze and perception that is turned towards a scene in a particular way. Baudelaire goes further to describe a little of the actual process of this perception, as focused through the act of drawing and painting: of sketching proper (2006:17). His process moves from lightly indicated pencil sketches designed to note the composition. This is followed by tints and washes to give some substance to the territory marked out. Once these are done, the ink lines are selected from the under-drawing, finishing what was started. The process reportedly allowed Guys to complete multiple drawings in short succession, working swiftly on a series and selecting all the while which lines to follow through and which studies to complete.

There are several elements which are worth discussing from Baudelaire's account. The movement from light pencil lines to more permanent ink lines is important and interesting given the selection process inherent to any sketching practice, as is the application of colour in between the line-making steps. Inscribing in pencil and then pen exposes a process which also occurs in single-media sketches, but in a more involved and obvious manner. Sketching is a selection process in which a scene is observed and inscribed on the surface of the paper (also known as support – allowing for alternative drawing surfaces to be discussed). Sketching does not allow everything to be represented, particularly when a scene is in motion, people and vehicles moving, flags fluttering, or clouds drifting.

> He has everywhere sought after the fugitive, fleeting beauty of present-day life, the distinguishing character of quality which, with the reader's kind permission, we have called 'modernity'. Often weird, violent and excessive, he has contrived to concentrate in his drawings the acrid or heady bouquet of the wine of life. (Baudelaire, 2006:41)

This leads us to the concept of a drawing as a 'study'. Indicating that a drawing is in preparation for another work, it suggests a plural nature for drawing: that we might not always refer to a single work as one item or instance, but an entire stack of sketches which contributed to a work.[5] This is an almost academic turn of phrase for a creative practice, in that a concentrated form of attention is turned towards a subject. Formal aspects are examined in detail and rendered in outline, given contours and detailed. A sketch can be considered as a form of research, an academic pursuit.

## Arnheim's visual thinking and its applications

Psychologist and art theorist Rudolf Arnheim has a great deal to contribute on the role of representation as a form of cognition. By cognition, we are talking about thinking: so, stated simply, sketching and other forms of inscriptive practice from notation to diagrams and measured drawings are a form of thinking, almost a form of research or kind of investigation. He substantiates this claim in a detailed manner, examining the role of perception in understanding and all the while reinforcing the idea of vision and perception *as intelligence*.

This runs counter to the prevailing opinion at the time of writing in the 1960s. Despite widespread respect and acceptance of Arnheim's work, it remains controversial and deeply ingrained that cognition is a process of reflection that is inherently divorced from first perceptions, a position that describes thinking as something conducted by verbal language. Several terms are fundamental to Arnheim's research. Cognition refers here to the broad range of mental activity that deals with sensory perception, its sedimenting in memory, and our ability to recall it and deploy it (1969:13). He notes that at the time, psychologists worked with a definition which excluded sensory perception from cognition, a situation that Arnheim and others such as James Gibson (1983, 1986) sought to overturn, particularly by placing people within their broader ecology rather than as abstract laboratory subjects.

This perceptual basis for thinking is not exclusive, and not to the detriment of other forms of thinking: but is instead additional to them. Perceptions, particularly (but not exclusively) visual perception, form the basis of inscriptive practices. Arnheim discusses the development of *perceptual skills* as an acquisition process that takes time and effort to develop. Rather than being a given condition, skill acquisition is something which we are all able to do equally well. These perceptual skills are distinct from raw perception, which have a basis in our biological capacities which vary from one individual to another. In short, we can be trained to pay attention more closely, to observe more acutely and to listen more keenly (Arnheim, 1969:31).

In developing his response to visual perception, Arnheim discusses the role of context in measuring our understanding. He does so in an interesting way, one which underlines one of the main themes of this book: the fundamental importance of context. Context can be understood as a variable, one which we are charged, as architects, with understanding comprehensively and holistically, before we act to modify, modulate, mutate or otherwise alter that condition. The fundamental role of architecture is to change the context, to work within the bounds of what already exists, but also to understand that it is possible to change that context in some way and to be mindful of what each of those changes might result in.

This approach to context is fascinating on its own terms: that we see things firmly in a context, as part of a flow, a continuum of space. Things belong to a place, appear in that place, but we must be able to go through an operation of extracting objects from that context in order to understand them as discrete, individual objects.

> To see an object in space means to see it in context. The preceding chapter pointed to the complexity of the task accomplished every time the sense of vision establishes the size, shape, location, color, brightness, and movement of an object. To see the object means to tell its own properties from those imposed upon it by its settings and the observer. (Arnheim, 1969:54)

Arnheim details visual perception through a variety of qualities such as scale, colour, texture and so on: breaking down the visual field into a variety of component parts. This is counter-intuitive when compared to the experience of reality, but this difference is hugely instructive. The practice of observing for sketching and drawing is a substantially different operation to the kind of visual perception required for recognizing people, navigating or any other purpose. In order to reconstruct the world by sketching, one must begin to understand it in terms of these individuated categories. These terms may be borne of the logic inherent to our graphic practices. It is worth considering whether the root of our understanding of outline, texture, contour, shading and even colour lies in the technology of graphic representation.[6]

This aside, it remains that such distinctions can be understood as being artificial but operationally necessary in representation. Take, for example, a landscape with rolling hills and cloudy sky. When drawing such a scene, we are trained to draw the outlines of these elements as discrete, but what is the nature of this line? What does an outline of a cloud as drawn in pencil on paper actually represent? Obviously, there is no graphic, defined edge on such a phenomenon: the world doesn't work like that, but when presented with such a graphic description, we read it as the edge of the cloud: a threshold between cloud and not cloud. This outline suggests a stronger, more defined threshold than exists in reality: our visual thinking of the phenomenon demands that an outline is defined. It is worth an aside to John Ruskin's thoughts on the matter with relation to a sketching exercise he proposes in his book, *The Elements of Drawing*:

> And observe, in this exercise, the object is more to get firmness of hand than accuracy of eye for outline; for there are no outlines in Nature, and the ordinary student is sure to draw them falsely if he draws them at all. (Ruskin, 1969[1856]:33)

Arnheim's influence is significant, as his work underlines the role of inscriptive practices in our thinking processes, opening up a field of research which recognized the production and making of drawings as a unit of analysis rather than the image, the result of that process as pursued by art history.

## Harajuku's cos-play Zoku

I present a series of my works here: watercolours of scenes and characters found around Tokyo. These paintings share a common theme, reminding us of Baudelaire's *Painter of Modern Life* in which an artist who is now unfashionable and considered to be fairly minor is celebrated for the documentary nature of his works. This celebration of city life is unusual for the time. The novelist and essayist Georges Perec gives useful advice on how and why one ought to concentrate on the quotidian (1997:50); he develops an interest in life as observed that reveals a great deal simply through attendance – by being present and bearing witness.

The first series of paintings here are character sketches of a weekly promenade in Harajuku, Tokyo. Youngsters gathered at the bridge to the Meiji shrine to celebrate the latest fashions in youth culture. In this case, it is the so-called *Cosplay Zoku* (Figure 2.3), who gathered to display their costumes and meet with friends. This site has been a source of fascination for some time, with the film director Chris Marker[7] documenting this zone of permissiveness and individuality in the 1980s, where rock n' roll hand jives were particularly popular. In the early 2000s, popular manga, anime and video game characters were faithfully recreated by the cos-players in a combination of hand-crafted and off-the-peg costumes before the promenading trend died out around 2010. Other parts of nearby Yoyogi Park continue the subcultural display, with rockabilly dancing, and synchronized pop idol inspired dance troupes sharing the space with strollers and joggers.

The watercolours move beyond the photographs as an attempt to get to know the scene in a deeper fashion. By tracing the outlines, examining the patterns and textures, recreating the postures, I meditate on the scene in a more concerted fashion. I aim also to communicate my understanding of the scene through the studies. One cannot, after all, replicate every detail, so a process of editing and rationalizing is necessary. This editing is part of a cognitive process and determines *what I want to show* to my presumed audience. These paintings select characters or groups from a dense throng of people, often erasing the background as relatively unimportant.[8]

The second series of these paintings is more ambitious and looks to scenes such as Gonpachi Restaurant (Figure 2.4), an overscaled izakaya establishment

**FIGURE 2.3** *Sketches of Harajuku cos-players.*

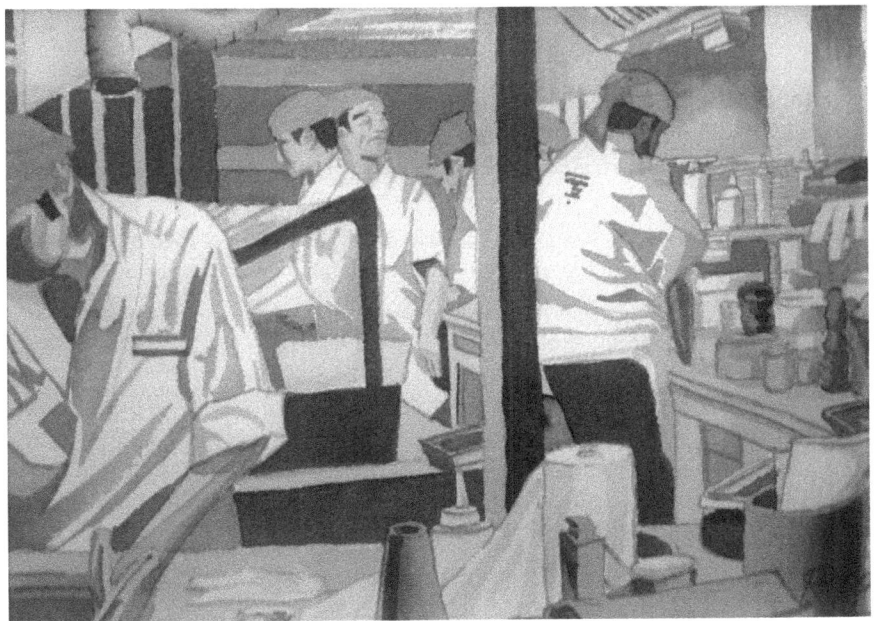

**FIGURE 2.4** *Watercolour painting of Gonpachi.*

**FIGURE 2.5** *Watercolour painting of Kappabashi crockery store.*

with an open kitchen and hollering staff; or the downtown wholesale district of Kappabashi (Figure 2.5) with its piles of kitchenware in bright colours and contrasting patterns. The desire here is to simply understand and to show. The banal detail of a stainless steel working kitchen with worn plastic containers and expert staff putting on a theatrical show for the customers arranged around the counter; or the concentration on the faces of restaurant owners browsing the wares in Kappabashi as they make decisions about the rice bowls they want for their establishment.

Bearing witness to an event is a manifestation of Orwell's *historical impulse* behind the drawings, not only to record the event: after all, my photography does that well enough, and books of photographs by professional practitioners are readily available. The drawing is a form of practised understanding, however, and a way of extending that moment. A close study of the photograph might yield some further understanding, but to replicate the visual effect exercises a visual knowledge and understanding, suggesting that – as Gibson[9] and Arnheim would support – perception is not a passive reception, but an active engagement. This engagement is heightened and channelled by the practice of drawing.

The question of why I draw is by necessity a reflexive activity and hopefully not tiresomely the case. My intention is to consider the nature of inscriptive practices more broadly as fundamental creative practices, finding them to be more than simply a record and also a process by which understanding can be both sought and shown. My knowledge of these scenes and characters is displayed by the drawings, and this motive is something, which, in Orwell's categorization of the writer's craft, might be seen as a *political intention* – perhaps more broadly understood as a theoretical or critical enquiry into the world around us. This is an intention wholly in line with the investigation into the many possible ways of being, dwelling and living conducted by the discipline of anthropology.

# Notes

1. It is not of course the only practice; architecture is a famously diverse profession involving a broad range of skills from model making, client negotiations, finance, construction, community engagement, contract law, landscape and interior design, historical and theoretical research and much more.
2. See https://knowingfromtheinside.org for more details and outputs from the project.
3. See Tafuri (1976) for a problematization of Utopia in architecture, and a discussion of its status as a *system*.
4. Interestingly, Orwell contends that:

    it is also true that one can write nothing readable unless one constantly struggles to efface one's own personality. Good prose is like a window pane. (2004:10)

    This concept of effacement is counter to the concept of the autographic mark in drawing, and it is true that art history is littered with attempts to occlude and complicate this relationship, from Sol le Witt's instruction-based wall drawings to drawing with the less dominant hand. This is related to the advice given by Georges Perec regarding the writing of a scene, where he recommends the writer attend to the banal and ordinary:

    'Observe the street, from time to time, with some concern for system perhaps.

    Apply Yourself. Take your time.

    Note down the place: the terrace of a café near the junction of the Rue de Bac and the Boulevard Saint-Germain

    the time: seven o'clock in the evening

    the date: 15 May 1973

    the weather: set fair

    Note down what you can see. Anything worthy of note going on. Do you know how to see what's worthy of note? Is there anything that strikes you?

    *Nothing strikes you. You don't know how to see.*

You must write about out it more slowly, almost stupidly. Force yourself to write down what is of no interest, what is most obvious, most common, most colourless.' (Perec, 1997:50 my emphasis)

'force yourself to see more flatly' (Perec, 1997:51 my emphasis)

5   For more on the multiple nature of drawing and stacks of tracing paper as a single work, see Lucas (2017b).

6   See Ingold on the lines that act as outliers (2007:50–51), *lines that do not fit* for more on this – outlines are an artificial form of perception; it is a necessary component of many inscriptive practices.

7   Marker, C. (Dir.). 1983. *Sans Soleil*. France: Argos Films.

8   It's something of an aside at this juncture, but I am also interested in colour, with the readymade aspect of watercolours contrasted with the mixing of colour in an acrylic painting. In this respect, my acrylic paintings often engage more with the motive of pure aesthetic enthusiasm, as a source photograph mingles with strong memories of a colour I can often find myself in a fugue over replicating this remembered and recorded colour; finding the right opacity and saturation becomes an all-encompassing activity. This is, perhaps, an issue for another essay.

9   See Gibson (1983:33) and Merleau-Ponty (2002:7) for more on the active nature of perception as opposed to passive reception.

# 3

# Home and What It Means to Dwell

## Introduction

This chapter discusses a space of familiarity, the home. Domestic space is where we tend to have greatest agency, we have control over our surroundings, are able to select objects that are useful and meaningful, and often able to decorate or remodel space in order to meet our individual tastes and needs. The very ordinariness of the home is what makes it of greatest interest and importance. As such, homes have a well-developed literature in both architecture and anthropology.

Several theories are used to draw out the nuance of home. These are often applicable to other building types, but heightened in the case of residential architecture. The first is to consider the home not as a physical structure so much as the outcome of a set of complex social relations. This overturns the notion that the home might be a container for social interaction and expresses it instead as the outcome of ongoing relationships. One aspect of the ongoing nature of domestic space lies in practices of maintenance and repair; the home is a perpetually unfinished project and is constituted of what we do there. Whilst acts of cleaning might not seem *architectural* at first glance, the theoretical implication of discussing maintenance offers a position towards architecture as a continuum rather than a finished article.

This continuum perspective is in tune with broader theories of material culture, placing the home within a broader set of intertwining biographies. The home is one way in which we both express and establish our identities. The choices we make regarding how we wish to live can be informed by cultural norms or iconoclasm, and this narrative of co-construction is one which can be carried through into other typologies and areas of interaction between architecture and anthropology. Material culture studies are a major cornerstone of anthropological theory, crossing over with a number of other disciplines, including archaeology and museum studies. Material culture is long overdue critical attention in architecture and offers perspectives towards buildings that might enable the full life cycle of components and structures to be reassessed. Again, it is relevant to many of the building typologies presented in this volume, but discussed most thoroughly in terms of the home.

Cleaning offers greater nuance than one might expect, and the discussion of dirt opens up the contested nature of the most basic categories. We might express cleanliness in terms of common sense or tacit knowledge, but our attitudes and definitions of dirt are subject to social construction and agreement.

## Home as a set of social relations

The home, that most quotidian of spaces, allows us to consider issues of gender, domestic objects, and everyday life. This is clearly an issue of some concern for architects, whether working on private residences or public social housing.

The home is at the same time as being resolutely ordinary a special category of space, carrying with it an aspect of our identity, related as it is to the most intimate details of our everyday life. This idea of everyday life, of the banal is particularly important to interrogate, as there is a temptation to make assumptions about how people live based upon our own experiences. Breaking down operating assumptions is one aim for this book as a whole, and it is appropriate that the home is central to this argument. The reality of the home and dwelling is open to a great deal of variation: perhaps as many ways of making home as there are households. Fundamental categories such as home, dwelling and household are all contestable terms which can have an impact on our understanding if articulated bluntly. There are so many approaches towards domestic space that it resists simplistic categorization, meaning that it must be discussed with a great deal of nuance. Home spaces are important to architecture, as they are often what we are called upon to design. How can lessons be learned from anthropological understandings of dwelling without arguing ourselves into complete inaction?

The literature on dwelling in anthropology establishes that these most familiar spaces can carry variations on a set of themes: how we understand our lives, organize our self in relation to the world and how we continually construct, maintain and reconstruct an idea of individual or collective selfhood.

It is therefore important to investigate the most ordinary things in order to understand the complexities which we might not question on a day-to-day basis. Each home represents, in Claude Lévi-Strauss's terminology, a set of *social relations*. In order to act upon these observations, Lévi-Strauss argues that we must establish what the *social structures* are governing this state of domesticity. The discussion of home and dwelling introduces us to several phases of anthropological debate. We start with structuralism, most closely associated with one of the discipline's most important figures, Claude Lévi-Strauss. We then develop our argument beyond structuralism's mission to discover underlying commonalities and into the acceptance of diversity and variety found by post-structuralism. This opens anthropology up to a wide range of approaches and sub-disciplines, allowing us to explore gendered space, sensory perception and some of the politics of space. Structuralism offers some useful insights of course, but it is important to move into the contemporary concerns of anthropology as well, rather than have architectural theory repeating debates already settled elsewhere.

Whilst Lévi-Strauss considers a number of other phenomena, it is his account of 'social structure' which is most instructive in the following discussion of the home. One interpretation of the home is that its status as a social structure might be more important than its material, physical form.

> Passing now to the task of defining 'social structure', there is a point which should be cleared up immediately. The term 'social structure' has nothing to do with empirical reality but with models which are built up after it. (Lévi-Strauss, 1963:279)

This is to argue that the concept of social structure is already an abstraction, a second-order phenomenon removed the immediate experience of living with a society, analysis is integral to any attempt to understand or define a social structure. Lévi-Strauss encourages anthropologists to move from immersion in a social situation to a model of how its underlying structure works. Thus, description itself can be understood as a theorization, if often a surface level of understanding which deepens with Lévi-Strauss's notion of structural analysis.

Lévi-Strauss continues with his definition by stating that social relations are the 'raw materials' for social structures (1963:279). Expressing this causal correspondence between *social relations* and *social structures* establishes *relationships* as the immediate experience of sociality, and the *structures* as analysis which follows. This model requires further exploration, and Lévi-Strauss finds this to have its origins in scientific discourse. His structures need to be systematic and rule based, predictable and assist in interpreting the observed world (1963:280). In searching for that which is systematic, structural analysis chooses to deal with quantifiable and knowable facts rather than tendencies or impulses. An example might be the conventional understanding of art in anthropology, which concerns itself with the outward signs of creative practices: the items created, the roles they fill in ritual and economic exchange, patterns of patronage and commissioning, and a great many interesting and useful aspects. What is forgotten in all of this, however, is the creative impulse itself. Where does this desire simply *to make things* come from. Creativity can be argued to be impulse and desire common to many, if not all, cultures across the world; yet, this very aspect of the act is erased from anthropological accounts by structuralism.

In this way, we can see that there is both utility to this approach and also a danger, for there are a number of aspects to our lives which cannot be so easily quantified and systematized, but which remain an incredibly important part of our lives. Lévi-Strauss does acknowledge this in his account, but is relatively untroubled by the loss (1963:285). We shall see below that the home can be understood as a set of social relations, leading to an understanding that constitutes a social structure.

This intersects with more contemporary theories such as theories of practice and of material culture. Sarah Pink (2004),[1] Daniel Miller (2001),[2] Victor Buchli (2000)[3] and Inge Daniels (2010)[4] all develop the position established by Pierre Bourdieu which describe human agency and practices to be at the heart of our engagement with the world, much of which is co-produced between people and their homes. The home is a special category of space – deeply embedded socially and culturally – and demonstrates a great deal about the position an individual or family (however such is described) relates to the broader world.

Home is a physical structure of a house and the material culture of its contents, and also a set of practices from cleaning and maintenance through to cooking, ablution, recreation, and framing social encounters with family, friends or colleagues.

## Domesticity and practices of maintenance

Anthropologist Sarah Pink, in her ethnography of the home, concentrates on how we engage with domestic practices of maintenance, with a particular focus on how these can be understood as gendered activities. This is clearly an issue of some interest for architecture, whether addressing privately owned residences or public social housing; detached structures or terraces; houses or apartments. As with other chapters in this volume, the material is intended for discussion both by the designers of homes and with researchers in architecture.

Pink conducts fieldwork in a collection of residences in England and Spain. There is a potential for a comparative study in this selection, but Pink resists attempting to describe a typical or normative home in each of these countries, noting the impossibility of this pursuit (2004:16). An important starting point for Pink is found in the language used by her respondents to describe their homes. Establishing that there is a great deal of sensory description in these accounts, Pink interprets the material to suggest that there is a visual bias in conventional design discourse. This is to the detriment of multisensory discussions, where the scents, sounds, textures and temperatures are either included in a reductive manner or not considered at all. Interviewees would describe their homes using rich sensory metaphors as well as through the activities or practices they engage in there. There is a richness in the simplest of tasks such as cleaning communal stairs, undertaking repairs or washing and drying clothes. These activities engage the body of the householder, engage their senses, and often instigate social interactions. As such, it is important to understand the home not as a site or fixed point in space: rather, it is constituted of a continually unfurling, knotting and tangling set of *social relations*.

Small changes in the conditions under which we dwell can make a more fundamental shift in how we understand the home. Pink notes that the Spanish practices of engaging with the *communidad* of an apartment block involve not only a financial contribution, but also responsibilities towards the cleaning and maintenance of communal areas and facilities (2004:17). This is not seen as a full social interaction, as such activities are often conducted by individuals in isolation, but the common effort is recognized and offers an opportunity for more direct social engagement to take place, in the case of either a smooth-running apartment block or one where the attendant neighbour to neighbour relationships are fraught with tensions or dysfunctional in some way. The provision of exterior spaces in housing is a feature of the Spanish context and includes elements appropriate to the climate such as communal pools. The shared responsibility can help to engender a community spirit and even result in close friendships between residents who, in another culture, might rarely come into contact with one another at all. Small changes in the conditions of our living can make a disproportionately large impact socially.

Most importantly, Pink suggests that the home is an important site for the *production of the self*. In this, there is a great deal to understand. Firstly, that selfhood is a construction, a process and an activity rather than something predetermined, fixed and final. Secondly, that our material possessions, the arrangements of these and our practices of home-making either reinforce or assist us in defining these aspects of selfhood, rather than merely being secondary representations or reflections of who we are.

> Much knowledge is produced and used through embodied experience that involves sensory engagements with the environment. Such knowledge is experienced by sexed bodies and is gendered itself as it is associated with different identity types. To understand how the multiple femininities and masculinities that make up the contemporary gender pattern are lived, I suggest it is instructive to account for how sensory experiences, knowledge, metaphors, meanings and actions are bound up in this. (Pink, 2004:147)

This notion of the production of self is, for Pink, a gendered process. Gender can be understood as distinct from sex in a number of ways, but primarily as an expression of the difference between the biological aspects of one's sexuality as opposed to the social and cultural factors which determine our roles within society. This offers a great deal of variety in human experience, with gender understood differently from one family or household to the next never mind between one culture and another.

Pink discusses the possibilities in both *multiple* femininities and *multiple* masculinities: different ways of being considered masculine or feminine. These overlapping categories are bound up in a knot of self-definition and social constraints. Given these differences, it becomes possible to map out the social relations represented by the various activities and spaces of the home (Pink, 2004:147). These multiplicities allow for alternative experiences of the same physical space, as those experiences are given shape by what each person practices there. If people adhere to a given society's traditional roles for men and women, then they experience spaces differently according to what they are expected to do, how they behave and what is not permitted. This extends beyond gender categories and into other areas such as social class.

The implication of constructing our idea of home around practices, the things that we do there, is that we can begin to understand that different people have radically different experiences of a space based on the activities they take part in there. Even within a single household, the experiences of the members of that unit each have their own idea of home; their own understanding of space; their own set of practices by which they live their lives. Taking the example of a notional nuclear family, children's practices will be different from their parents: their associations with selfhood constructed differently from the adults, their responsibilities towards the space expressed in quite different ways. Home is complicated by social relations, resulting in a much more nuanced concept with the potential to be a site for radical rethinking of identity and selfhood.

This is not intended to paralyse architects into inaction with all of the possible permutations, particularly as each understanding of the home can coexist without physical adaptations. Home is more than a physical structure, but those material aspects can have an impact on how we dwell there. The accounts given by Pink are very ordinary, with simple answers to simple questions revealing a great deal about how differently our neighbours might live. As such, it heightens our awareness that we might make assumptions or accept stereotypes without asking how people actually live.

Conceptualizing the construction of selfhood as an ongoing process is mirrored by one of the other ideas explored by Pink: that the home is incomplete and in transition through continuous home improvement and maintenance strategies, whether decorative, complete remodelling of the space, or simply storing or rearranging items and accumulated possessions. This is framed as an everyday creativity expressed through our dwelling in a place, finding pleasing or functional arrangements for our possessions (2004:56).

The manner in which we make alterations to this incomplete home is made with reference to a framework of social constraints and personal creativity. Even where a given constraint or trend has been rejected, that decision might be made with reference to a normative projection. This is where the generalizable opinions of home occupation and living are useful and interesting, as people use patterns projected by television programmes or magazines as reference points from which to hang their personal opinions and responses.

Adaptations are a key way in which people make a place their own, making their mark on the place. Despite this, a significant amount of design resists adaptation in any substantial way: change is rarely accommodated by the design, and improvements or alterations have to be made in spite of the original, against the express wishes of the architect, or in a manner deemed unsympathetic to the original. Enshrining some architecture as worthy of preservation is the furthest expression of this idea: where the agency of the 'original' design overpowers the needs of contemporary inhabitants and historical preservation seeks to freeze a building to a certain moment in time. This is of course a complex argument, and the wealth of literature on building re-use and conversion attests to a fruitful and valid form of architectural expression and intervention: it is notable, however, that this field is continually undervalued in the discussion of architecture as an art form with an established canon of individual geniuses each producing singular designs.

Pink's account of homeowners' adaptations and modifications to their homes helps to rewrite this narrative, describing the interior design cues for 'country house' aspirations and how these influence decisions about the home (Pink, 2004:55). The home is defined by these suburban respondents with reference to a normative idea of country living, one which is expressed through the loosely defined term 'countrified'. The home is associated with a coherent aesthetic which is a key driver behind the purchase of one property over another. This stylistic preference is further reinforced through subsequent changes. This is in part expressed by the householders as an expression of the agency of the house, restoring it to an ideal or original state. This idea of agency gives the house, despite being an inanimate assemblage of material objects, the power to influence the actions of the human inhabitants either directly or indirectly.

Pink expresses each of her analyses in terms of the sensory experiences of that place. Multiplicity of experience emerges as a theme, setting this anthropology of home in opposition to earlier readings of domestic space, which lay important groundwork in politicizing the domestic sphere, but which fail to fully grasp the practised nature of such spaces. Early gendered readings of the home see the practices of different householders as fixed and unchanging, where Pink explores a number of the ways in which activities fluctuate. Homes are defined by the practices or activities which take place there. Gender remains an important category in this particularly when the identity of 'housewife' is interrogated in a number of differing cultural contexts.

> Existing analyses of the housewife situate her in terms of a series of theoretically constructed binary oppositions. Although such analyses are useful for understanding some cultural representations of domestic gender, they fail to account for everyday sensory embodied experience and diversity and do not accommodate change. (Pink, 2004:81)

This possibility for change is suggested by the practice-based theory driving Pink's critique of earlier anthropologies of the home. These remain influential foundational texts, but gender roles are practised and as such can be subject to change, say when one moves from one country to another, from one home to another, or even as the household makeup develops and changes. This idea is developed in later research by Pink, where the home is 'ongoingly made' (Pink et al., 2017:31), encouraging us to see the home not as a fixed structure or space, but as a constellation or knot of interrelated practices which continually *produce* home through the activities of dwelling there.

Pink begins with the existing literature on homes, analysing the theories presented there and beginning to understand these within the paradigm of her own work. This is then developed towards understanding the self-definition of her respondents, the interviewees and collaborators in the research. This is crucial to understand people's perceptions of themselves before beginning to abstract and theorize into social structures as suggested by Lévi-Strauss (1963).

Self-identification is an interesting concept, as it reflects both the way people actually see themselves and the image they would like to project. On top of this are external influences such as social and economic constraints, larger cultural conditions and the home itself with its agency affecting the individual. A large house requiring a great deal of upkeep, for example, can actually determine the life of its inhabitant to a large degree. The twentieth century sees advances in this, with the modernist focus on the kitchen as a site of efficiency and postwar introduction of domestic technologies such as washing machines and vacuum cleaners which served both as class signifiers and as ways of reducing the extent of manual labour required to maintain the home.[5]

Self-identification also reveals some of the methodological issues with interview-based research, as it relies on the power of an individual to fully articulate their situation. The self-awareness necessary and the skill to convey such observations require a degree of honesty on the part of the respondent as well as a lack of judgemental behaviour from the researcher when interviewing or architect meeting a client. Practices of cleanliness are useful indicators of how people understand their homes. Pink uses this to get to the heart of how her informants conceptualize their everyday lives from sensory experience through to the morality of making sure the home itself, the items within it and all of ones clothing is clean in a verifiable manner. Multinational corporations aid in constructing this conception of cleanliness, to the extent that the soap commercial has agency over the home in a worrying manner. There is, for example, an associated scent signifying this concept of cleanliness, which is often the result of market research rather than in the reality of how clean a thing is, or a culture of cleaning practices.

The underlying suggestion that a dirty home is one where there is a moral lapse is an idea that is losing its foothold, but still employed as a reference point. Other moralities emerge, with the division of labour in the home as a process of a gradual societal shift, drifting away from the traditional or conventional model and towards an equity as gender equality becomes the norm in both research sites investigated.

The idea of the clean and its flip side of the unclean has resonance with a key text in anthropological theory: Mary Douglas's *Purity and Danger* in which the cultural construction of the idea is interrogated, writing in the preface to the 2002 edition:

> There is no such thing as absolute dirt: it exists in the eye of the beholder. If we shun dirt, it is not because of craven fear, still less dread of holy terror. Nor do our ideas about disease account for the range of our behaviour in cleaning or avoiding dirt. Dirt offends against order. Eliminating dirt is not a negative moment, but a positive effort to organise the environment. (2002:2)

This relates to the definition of dirt as 'matter out of place' (2002:44) and redefines the discourse as one between order and disorder rather than a

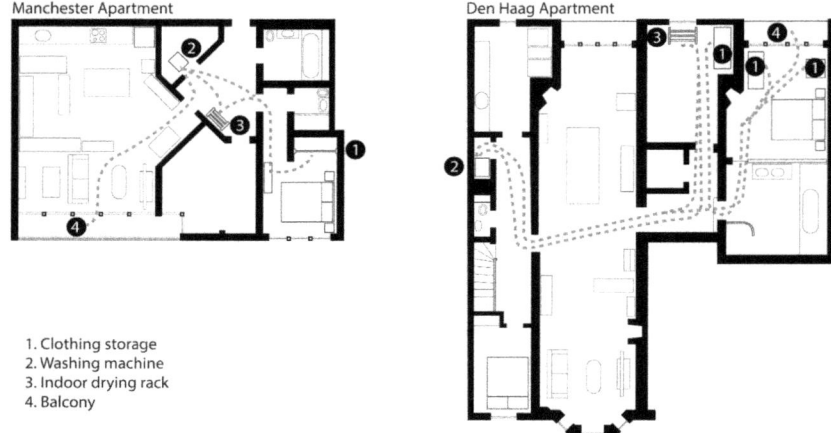

1. Clothing storage
2. Washing machine
3. Indoor drying rack
4. Balcony

**FIGURE 3.1** *Movements of clothing for cleaning through author's homes in Manchester and Den Haag.*

real fear of disease, judgement or of failure. The practice of cleaning is one of bringing order to a place: most importantly, in eradicating chaos from our homes. This order and disorder is a strong thematic, extended in a number of ways by Douglas into a discussion of the danger of liminal zones: of thresholds. The threshold, such as the door, is a well-understood architectural figure and one in which a great deal of energy is spent in the design process. Douglas indicates that it represents the passage between the ordered world of the interior and the exterior which, being out of our direct control, can be understood as chaotic. The point of transition between these states is fraught with potential danger (Figure 3.1).

As a unit of analysis, home offers the researcher a great many potential projects. Where Pink explores the gendered and sensory home, others have focused on the material culture of space, the power relations of a state imposing its will on the everyday life of citizens as an increased and enforceable agency of home, or even using a single aspect of the home such as storage, as a way of discussing the process of accumulating and organizing possessions.

## Material culture and the home

Material culture studies are a major field of enquiry in contemporary anthropology, crossing over with other disciplines such as archaeology. Daniel Miller gives a comprehensive overview of this field in his recent introduction

*Stuff* (Miller, 2010). In this text, Miller establishes the idea of material culture as fundamental to our understanding of contemporary society, to the extent that our lives are lived closely enmeshed with materials of *things* and of *stuff*. His use of this potentially flippant turn of phrase, of *stuff* is intended as a way of moving the debate away from reified categories of items with strong symbolism, the status of art objects or religious artefacts and towards all the everyday things we tend to take for granted. This reiterates anthropology's general focus on the aspects of life that are quotidian, that we take for granted, the supposedly banal details of life where some of its most important aspects are revealed.

Miller begins his work on material culture with a discussion of clothing as a demonstration of how such goods define aspects of our life, informed by, or formative of, our character. Miller notes that there is an interesting comparison with the home as another aspect of material culture, distinctive in terms of scale and costliness, but in the end developing our sense of selfhood through materials in a similar way (2010:80).

Discussing the home, Miller describes the possibility of Londoners having a common set of issues regarding their housing; that despite the variety of social and cultural groups within the city, a set of external forces are applied to their living conditions, including the economic and political situations as well as the physical morphology and density of the city. Miller's argument is that these external forces run counter to theories of mutual co-constitution between people and their environment: Miller's description is of housing shaped by the socio-economic forces of late capitalism and of individuals whose lives are in turn shaped by that architecture. The condition of the city, broadly understood to be made up of all those factors we must accept as a given, the urban condition, all have an influence on how we live there. Close quarters living often makes sound abatement an issue, for example, or the maintenance of common grounds: stairwells, doorways and gardens. In terms of agency, Miller takes much of the control of the environment out of individuals' hands, preferring to see larger global forces at work, with people largely at the mercy of these.

Whilst I would argue that this is overstated, Miller's distinction between clothing and the home is helpfully articulated in terms of relative investment. The relative ease with which we can wear alternative clothing, but not escape the mortgage or rental markets in London is determined by the relative levels of investment required: compared to property, clothing is affordable. Even where homeowners have a desire to remodel their house to suit their needs, the local authority can deny permission for substantial structural changes, and even modest decisions about decor can have an impact on resale potential. Relative investment is not an absolute measure, but an important one which includes the mechanisms by which:

property attracts a great many more interested parties: the state, landholders, local councils, building societies and the like. Against these forces, any desire by us, the mere people who dwell in houses, to engage in a certain relationship to them can find us way down any pecking order of power. (Miller, 2010:81)

In engaging with the home, we immediately insert ourselves in some relation to wider economic and political forces which are incredibly difficult to extricate ourselves from. Indeed, as with cultural norms noted above, the attempt to reject such forces is in itself a reaction to their power and presence. As such, there is a normative model for housing, residing and ownership in London and the UK as a whole. These forces mean that the home can be said to have a strong degree of *agency* over residents. Taking the concept of home to include all of these forces can seem at first to be a bit of a stretch, perhaps even a paranoid expression of theory, but it is consistent with exploring the Lévi-Straussian *social structures*[6] which are the result of observed wider *social relations*.

For Miller, the theory of agency is a way of combatting a reductionist approach to the power relations represented by the home. We do not, on a day-to-day basis, make explicit reference to these power structures, however much they might govern elements of our lives. They form a background against which we constitute our lives in a variety of different ways, foregrounded at particular points in the process of dwelling such as during the purchasing process. In order to increase the fidelity of our studies of the home, we must look to different theories as lenses or filters through which we understand the world. One such lens is agency.

Reductionism is dangerous, as it represents an essentialist impulse which resists the complexity of life as we live it. This messy complexity of the lifeworld is the unit of analysis for anthropology: firmly of the world, it is impossible to extract social theories entirely from the context where they are formed. Were we merely to seek to understand one element of our domestic, home lives, we leave a great deal unconsidered and omit many of the ways in which we manage and mediate these large external forces creatively. Whatever our circumstances, we are able to make our mark on where we live through the choices that we make.

Miller hangs his idea of agency on the concept of accommodating. Accommodation refers here to both the amount of space afforded by a house and the adaptability of that space for inhabitation. Establishing the importance of *accommodating* as a term encompassing not only a place to live, but also the process of adapting that spaces to suit our needs and including the social agreements and compromises for living, the term decouples from some of its more market-led connotations. Whilst anthropologists might see the home as a site of analysis, householders are rarely in the business of producing a deliberately constructed image which represents their life for the consumption of outsiders.[7]

The aim of studies of the home is twofold: to study the way we dwell as a fundamental human activity and to examine the intersections of these quotidian routines with grander narratives. Miller notes that 'the little details and the grand ideologies are usually linked' (2010:99). Living is experienced over time. This might seem like a self-evident observation, but many attempts to understand and theorize our lives abstract this fundamental foundation of experience in place and time. Living, simply stated, is a process which unfurls over a period of time. It also takes place somewhere. Our relationship to objects changes over time. Every event we undertake in the home, from cleaning to cooking, moving home or settling in, even failing or refusing to maintain a place – each of these acts is illustrative of our approach to life as an individual, member of a social group and in culture more broadly.

This approach to material culture suggests that the power relationship we have with external influences and the agency of the home itself are both important to our understanding of how we live today. It would be my contention, then, that as architects we need to understand our clients in order to be able to accommodate their needs better. This 'knowing' needs to have the same dispassionate and non-judgemental eye as the anthropologist and can be acquired through various forms of consultation, interview and observation informing the decision-making process of a design or through a sensitive response to the variety of inhabitations which might be both desirable and possible within a space.[8] Architecture also has the intention of proposing something new, a provocation to which people respond. This can also be informed by a greater understanding of the lifeworld.

Miller is, in the end, an anthropologist and sees the actions of the architect as simply one more level of agency or power relation between home and inhabitant. By beginning to approach an architecture more embedded in social anthropology, there is the potential for an architecture which is more attuned to the needs of a client. By understanding the day-to-day intersections between people and broad socio-economic forces, we can allow for greater flexibility, accommodate the specificity of a plural and multicultural life, offering both the possibility for change and the meeting of specified needs: handing some agency back to the householders.

Our task, then, is to take material culture studies and further analyse the outcomes: to operationalize the social relations revealed, the processes of living preferred, offering viable and useful alternatives, and embedding such understanding firmly into the design process.

## The home as a flow of materials

Inge Daniels is another anthropologist with a strong interest in the home, in domesticity and in how we live. Her focus in her ethnography of Japanese homes is the material culture of the home. Daniels worked with families around Osaka and examined the storage and display strategies of families of different sizes and types. This examination seeks to understand what we can learn about our lives through our attitudes towards material objects, the flow of such objects and what they represent.

Daniels identifies in the contemporary Japanese home that there is an acute issue regarding storage. This discussion becomes a focal point for the study, reflecting a number of things about Japanese home cultures within a clearly bounded case study. This might seem to be a curious element to focus on, and Daniels also considers the structure of the family, maintenance of family shrines and alcoves dedicated to deceased relatives. It is, however, the flow of possessions through the home, strategies of display and storage that are of greatest interest here. It is useful to see this as a model of how to theorize a set of social practices in the home. Storage is a case study through which one can explore a wider set of issues: it allows the research to be of both wider interest and more specific to the Japanese context.

Examining the idea of home in Japan presented Daniels with several methodological problems to resolve. In particular, the home is not generally understood as a space for visiting or receiving guests. This stands in contrast to some Eurocentric assumptions, where entertaining in the home has a longstanding culture, particularly in the middle classes.[9] Daniels observes that Japanese people generally prefer to socialize in public spaces and discusses the approaches she used in order to gain access to this most private of space by canvassing a particular area, placing adverts and posters for respondents to self-select. Daniels eventually abandons this idea in favour of exploiting the social relations she has built up during earlier research in Japan; utilizing the help of pre-existing contacts to extend the reach of the research is often known as a 'snowball sampling' approach. This raises important issues about how to safely gain access to peoples' lives, however, as a methodological issue, as well as the self-selecting nature of the research sample: reaching out to different social classes and groups becomes difficult if this method is adhered to exclusively.

The visibility of a domain to research is a pertinent issue, as many topics can remain unexplored largely due to practicalities of how to access the relevant people, places and information. Daniels outlines her approach as longitudinal, but in different terms to the conventional participant-observation study:

> Some anthropologists studying the home have successfully transcended the limitations of the interview by adapting 'traditional' *in situ* fieldwork techniques to modern, urban conditions. By paying multiple follow-up visits to the same homes, or by living for extended periods of time in the particular community studied, even if not inside the participants' homes, one may build up a relationship of trust with the people studied and gain a more profound insight into the aspects of life behind closed doors that are taken for granted. (Daniels, 2010:20)

Pink et al. also note their methodology in detail throughout their study (2017), focusing upon the ongoing nature of the making of the home: it is not a static assemblage, but a dynamic process continually producing a place. Daniels underlines trust as a major factor in the ethics of her research methodology. The subject of the research is, after all, intimate and personal: investigating the homes of people who are by and large uncomfortable with sharing this space. In this case, Daniels lived with several of the families for around a month each, supplemented by interviews with a larger group conducted over a long period. This time period is important, and it is important not to rush the process, as building and maintaining trust requires that this time is spent.

The development of the Japanese housing market in the twentieth century eventually came to settle on promoting the LDK concept, where the home is arranged around a central *Living–Dining–Kitchen* area. The combination of kitchen with dining area has a living room adjacent or adjoining it, creating a central hub for the home experience. This has associations, as we have discussed earlier, with economics, mainstream media and, specific to this example, the explicit desires of governments from the Meiji era onwards. Other external influences shifted the tastes of people from the traditional Japanese home towards a modern form quite distinct from those found in Europe or the United States.

This trajectory takes us from the model of the *tatami* (Figure 3.2) home which was designed around the reception of guests and towards a family-oriented, inward-looking home environment. The earlier organization was reserved for high status families, consisting of tatami matted rooms open to an ornamental garden at the front of the building, with darker, more private quarters to the rear, away from the garden. Arrangements of rooms without a separate circulation space mirrored early European models, meaning that one had to pass through spaces we would now presume to be private in passing from one space to another.

Daniels expresses the major move in this history as a deliberate shift from tatami-based to chair-based living. This is always associated with a new kind of family values ethic in the government posters of the time, as part of a deliberate move towards modernism as observed in the West. There was,

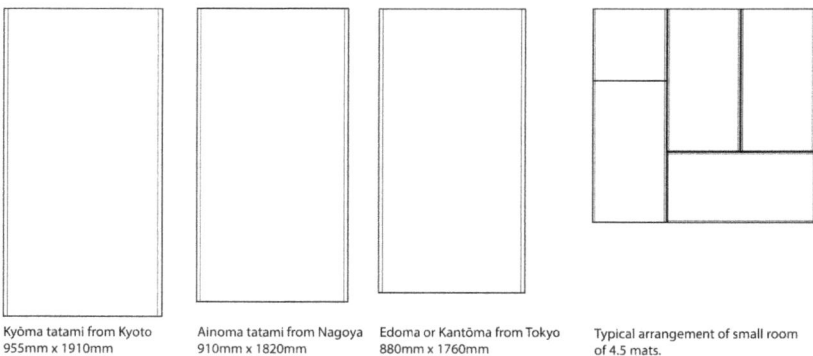

**FIGURE 3.2** *Tatami dimensions and room layouts.*

however, a long gestation period between this initial promotion in the late nineteenth century and direct government intervention in the 1920s, as only the very wealthy could afford these new modernist homes.[10]

Interestingly, the intercultural exchange of architects brought the influence of Japanese architecture to the West, with figures as diverse as Frank Lloyd Wright and Bruno Taut visiting Japan both to instigate a modernist revolution there, but also returning home unexpectedly influenced by the traditional forms of architecture they encountered. Such intertextuality is observed in a great many other points of contact, including literature and film. In cinema, the work of Kurosawa, as influenced by John Ford westerns initially, is instructive as his work then inspired works such as *The Magnificent Seven* and *A Fistful of Dollars* based on *Seven Samurai* and *Yojimbo,* respectively. A similar reflection and re-reflection also happens in architecture.[11] The LDK takes hold in the postwar period, when Japan's economy experienced a massive upswing, particularly from the mid-1960s. The intended Westernization, however, was only partly adopted and was adapted by the Japanese people in order to maintain many of the benefits of traditional living. With LDK, the guest reception rooms were removed, and the living room was used to accommodate this function. The tradition for families sharing a bedroom and sleeping on futons was largely maintained and is one of the practices most distinctive from the Western modern model of living.

Daniels (2010:37) elaborates that there is some variation in how sleeping is arranged, and it has now become a matter of preference for Western-style arrangements or Japanese-style rooms. In many ways, this is a more open approach than in the UK, for example, where a normative notion of sleeping arrangements prevails. Other elements of the home, for example, bathing, have a similar history and plurality of contemporary form. The move in this case is from local community bath houses which would serve an entire neighbourhood. The introduction of bathing in the home, whether Japanese style or Western style, has brought about the closure of many of these community facilities across Japan. This indicates a loss of community, as people would meet and socialize at the bath house in a manner that is impossible with the privatization of this space.

The most pertinent element of Daniels's study is the chapter on storage, with the intriguing subtitle: *the ideology of tidiness* (2010:131). The flow of material items through the home is examined in this chapter. The focus is on places to tidy things away and a never-ending need for more storage. This is elevated to an ideology: an almost religious fervour surrounding neatness and cleanliness, giving everything its appropriate place in the home. One of the challenges presented to householders is the culture of gift giving and souvenir gathering in Japan. Broadly speaking, gift giving is an important theory in itself within anthropology.[12] Gift giving and receiving has a strong social function in Japan, tied closely to social status and obligation.

As such, a flow of items enters a household; these are expected to be given some house-room, kept and stored carefully. This explains a preference for gifts which are edible or otherwise impermanent in certain circumstances, as they impose no obligation on the receiver to keep them. A survey of popular culture reveals television home makeover shows and interior design magazines with this very obsession: storage and an association with the efficiency of the home resulting from a good storage solution or strategy (2010:133).

One innovative example described by Daniels (2010:133) describes the *kura-house*, a new-build design by Misawa Homes, a volume house-builder which references the sixteenth-century typology of a masonry treasure house. The original kura-house is a separate structure designed to resist both fire and theft, whilst Misawa Homes' reinterpretation of the form resembles a regular modern house, but with additional storage built in to the ceiling to floor void, increasing storage space significantly in order to keep seasonal homewares and clothing tidied away. The *kura-house* illustrates the importance of historical referencing to marketing, and the manner of promoting modern homes to the purchaser. Methodologically, Daniels uses this specific, self-contained example to direct the reader's attention to a much larger, possibly hidden concern. By establishing that storage is important and apparent to the researcher, and finding such a clear example, Daniels affords herself the space as a writer to fully explore this relationship of gifts and homes. A tangible, material response is made to a social constraint: a structure arranged around the ceiling to floor voids for storing seasonal or unwanted items that cannot simply be disposed of. Other solutions to the same issue would include continually moving home, climbing up the housing ladder. The Japanese housing market encourages a different approach, whereby families build ever larger homes on the same plot: decreasing the lifespan of a building significantly but maintaining an attachment to place. Speed of construction is therefore a crucial factor. Families might also rent storage from businesses established to serve this need, compounded by the high urban density of Japan, creating an ecosystem of businesses around the issue.

The other side to this hiddenness is, of course, display. What items are chosen to be out in the open, on display or in everyday use. This is revealing a different set of choices and has some connections to the discussion of wrapping in Joy Hendry's anthropologies of Japan. Hendry takes the idea of the *furoshiki* wrapping cloth to stand as a metaphor for various aspects of Japanese culture (1993, 2000:11, 12; 210). This is extended to the ways in which other cultures are packaged neatly and presented in theme parks (see Chapter 4 for more on this) and further discussed by Jean-Pierre Warnier (2006) in his material culture of containers: inside and outside. The process by which practices of wrapping and containing might begin to inform wider activities is discussed in detail by both writers. The habituation to a particular tool eventually brings that tool, however broadly sketched, into the sphere of our own bodies: an extension of the hand which begins to form our engagement with the world: *furoshiki* wrapping becomes a sedimented practice extended into other aspects of life.

Daniels's study overturns conventional narratives of Japan as a throw-away consumer society, as she shows the great difficulty that her respondents go to in order to hang on to gifts and other things to give them their place and maintain an orderly existence at home. This is supported by other evidence, such as the industries of home building, external storage, television and magazine coverage. This is an example of why we must find out how people live rather than to simply make assumptions based on our own experiences of prejudices. The answers are always more complex, more interesting and more valuable to the design process than the easy assumptions we might make, whether this is eventually expressed as similarity or Otherness.

A combination of tradition and modernity co-exists in the Japanese homes described by Daniels, who makes no aesthetic or other judgements in the way that glossy magazines attempt to depict the Japanese home as either 'exotic' or 'minimalist'. Indeed, one can see that a parallel of British or American or European homes would be similarly rich, differing in many ways, but the point is to maintain a methodological philistinism and not to make value judgements. These can come later, in conversation with clients about the best way to move forward as, whilst anthropology is a fundamentally descriptive discipline, architecture has, as its end product, a change in condition; a change in space; the altering or creation of a new place.

The study of home can be seen as the study of a culture in miniature, a way of drawing cross-cultural comparisons to find similarities and differences, allowing the development of a theory of dwelling as a fundamental human activity. This notion of a theory of dwelling itself is crucial for architects to both contribute to and make use of.

## The dwelling perspective versus the machine for living in

Home and dwelling suggest the qualities of comfort, familiarity and accommodation. These words are warm, welcoming and suggest an approach at odds with the famous position taken by Le Corbusier, that: 'the house is a machine for living in.' (Le Corbusier, 1989 [1923]:107). This statement, often cited in isolation (as here), is part of Corbusier's influential manifesto, *Towards a New Architecture*. Here, Le Corbusier establishes the grounds for his brand of modernism, presented as a series of aspirations towards the prototypes of the ocean liner, the automobile and the aeroplane. A fuller citation discusses the aeroplane in further detail:

> The airplane is the product of close selection.
> The lesson of the airplane lies in the logic which governed the statement of the problem and its realization.
> The problem of the house has not yet been stated.
> Nevertheless there do exist standards for the dwelling-house.
> Machinery contains in itself the factor of economy, which makes for selection.
> The house is a machine for living in. (Le Corbusier, 1989 [1923]:107)

Corbusier's prototypes are drawn from engineering, where the form is determined absolutely by programmatic constraints. His exemplars are refined over iterations of design, giving formally interesting results, but these are not sculptural gestures. It leads him to ask the question of what, in an echo of Lévi Strauss's approach, are the underlying structures emerging from the relationships depicted. The structural logic he identifies is the machine, hence the machine *for living in*.

In interpreting the selection of prototypes, precision engineered for performance in their relevant context: an expression of the forces expressed by the road in the case of the automobile; the stresses of air travel on the plane's fuselage; and the pressure of the ocean on the liner. Corbusier is asking what are the forces, stresses and pressures which correspond to these for the home? His fascination continues with a consideration of the totality of each design; the appropriateness of every fixture and fitting to the vehicle encourages Corbusier to think of the home in a similar fashion. This was the model Corbusier expected architecture to follow.

Alternative implications of *dwelling* are explored in detail in the work of anthropologist Tim Ingold. Ingold takes two primary influences: Karl Marx and Martin Heidegger.

> Dwelling is not merely the occupation of structures already built: it does not stand to building as consumption to production. It rather signifies that immersion of being in the currents of the lifeworld without such activities as designing, building and occupation could not take place at all. (Ingold, 2011:10)

In further elaborating the concept,[13] Ingold asserts that dwelling is intertwined with concepts of *being*. This transcends simple occupation of space and is a meshwork between the individual and their environment, an ordered interaction between the two which is often described by Ingold as a kind of knot. The aim of this approach was to establish a distinction between the *building perspective* and the *dwelling perspective*.

This finds its fullest exploration in Ingold's *Perception of the Environment*, tracing a trajectory from Marx and Heidegger through James Gibson and towards Merleau-Ponty. The worlds inhabited by sentient beings are understood to also be sentient themselves. Here, the *dwelling perspective* is described as follows:

> By this I mean a perspective that treats the immersion of the organism-person in an environment or lifeworld as an inescapable condition of existence. From this perspective, the world continually comes into being around the inhabitant, and its manifold constituents take on significance through their incorporation into a regular pattern of life. (Ingold, 2000:153)

The implications of the dwelling perspective for architecture are profound. Were we to contrast what we might rename as Corbusier's *machine perspective* with that of Ingold's *dwelling perspective*, we can find the roots of modernism's greatest flaws[14]: the machine, whilst requiring maintenance and attention, is a predictable and knowable phenomenon. We know what happens when a machine is active; there should be no unanticipated functioning. Extending the metaphor further, Corbusier's aeroplane fails under exceptional circumstances, those situations where the wider environment misbehaves through extreme weather, collisions with birds or human error.

This suggests that the dwelling perspective remains appropriate as it accommodates that wider environment fully, as it is co-producing of human lifeworlds. A sketch for an architecture of *dwelling perspective* follows: building on longstanding discussion of threads and traces, the experimental anthropology of the *100m Dwelling* takes those metaphors and analogies literally, building on memories of homes and describing them directly in the landscape with a ball of twine.

## The *100m Dwelling*

By way of conclusion, I present an experimental piece of distinctly *architectural* anthropology. This workshop was presented as part of a residential workshop for the *Knowing from the Inside* research group, where the production of knowledge by creative practices from art, architecture, design and anthropology was examined. This example formed part of a wider investigation into the nature of lines, making them material in the form of coloured twine. The project challenges the ways in which anthropology is done, and this collaborative experiment co-produced some modest knowledge about the relationship between homes, dwelling and memories.

For this exercise, a group of participants (5 in number) were given a 100-m-long ball of twine[15] and, using the nearby forest, asked to design a house based on their memories.[16] Participants were asked what this idealized dwelling needed in terms of its accommodation and arrangements; how can the terrain and natural features be used or appropriated to represent this imagined house; and how might we collaborate with one another in this 1:1 scale design process?

After an introduction drawing on literature, including parables by Gaston Bachelard and Italo Calvino,[17] participants were asked to consider the following archetypal elements:

*Threshold*: most often thought of as doors, but including a wide range of possible ways of passing from one spatial condition to another. How are such transitions managed and marked?

*Garden*: in the house of our memory, is there a garden? What are our memories of gardens, from childhood play through to the careful long-term tending of plants and invitations to animals to share that space. Gardens can be modest balconies with plants in containers, or idyllic protected spaces. The temporality of the garden is an important feature.

*Windows*: the placement of windows features strongly in the imagination; the aperture captures a view: rendering a kind of image from reality.

*Hearth*: whether an actual fireplace or another focal point, the hearth as a concept is the centre of the home, a gathering point. This suggests that the home is a gathering of people as much as it is a physical structure, a shelter.

*Kitchen*: the preparation of food often features in our discussions of the home, and the kitchen is a centre of activity. The kitchen is often considered in temporal terms in line with the main meals of the day.

*Bathroom*: a closed and private space, often the only place in the home that is fully private. It remains a practical space, of course, and the processes of cleaning are compounded in some cases with the relaxation of bathing or the invigoration of a shower.

*Attic*: a hidden area devoted to storage, often filled with objects we only use seasonally – or simply cannot bear getting rid of. The attic is rarely visited, but figures in the imagined house strongly, featuring in Bachelard's archetype as well as a presence in fiction outweighing its importance to everyday life. The attic is quite different to a cupboard, so the role of storage is not its primary one in the subconscious.

*Cellar*: if the attic is rarely visited, then this is further compounded in the case of the cellar. The subterranean qualities of this space are important and, whilst much modern house building eliminates such spaces, increasing density in our urban centres has necessitated the use of such spaces for fully fledged dwellings.

Whilst we have earlier been suspicious of Le Corbusier's machine analogies for homes, Mary Douglas describes the home as a 'memory machine' in an evocative discussion of home:

> Each kind of building has a distinctive capacity for memory or anticipation... The home makes its time rhythms in response to outside pressures; it is in real time. Response to the memory of severe winters is translated into a capacity for storage, storm windows, and extra blankets; holding the memory of summer droughts, the home responds by shade-giving roofs and water tanks. (1991:294)

In this account, the home is also an economy of relative efforts between family members and draws an interesting comparison with the hotel in Douglas's account:

The idea of the hotel is a perfect opposite of the home, not only because it uses market principles for its transactions, but because it allows its clients to buy privacy as a right of exclusion. This offends doubly the principle of the home whose rules and separations provide some limited privacy for each member. (1991:303–304)

This experiment is a direct appeal to the houses and homes of our memories, enacting these through a simple drawing task in an environment rich with affordances (Figure 3.3): a forest with different ground conditions, inclines, trunks and branches, rocks and leaves. The home is romanticized and idealized to an extent, but the exchange of stories and memories enabled a practical engagement with the rooms of the house and, crucially, how these connect up: the circulation, the composition, the relationships between spaces.

The task clearly draws upon Gaston Bachelard's classic text *The Poetics of Space*[18] and Italo Calvino's *Invisible Cities* – both texts perennially popular with architects due to the spatial possibilities presented therein. The task was framed by a brief reading describing the city of *Ersilia* (Calvino, 1974:76), a city of traces represented by an accumulation of colour-coded threads which represent bonds of *blood*, *trade*, *authority* and *agency*. The process itself is both a negotiation and exchange of stories. Discussions of spaces from participants' remembered houses included unusual or unlikely uses of space. The duration of long-term and short-term occupation featured

**FIGURE 3.3** *Photographs from the* 100m House.

strongly in descriptions, narratives filling the space left by the sparse nature of the representation afforded by a 100-m-long ball of twine. The means of representation encouraged an abstraction and efficiency in representation. The transformative nature of the line in space as inscribing a boundary, denoting interior and exterior, thresholds, windows and promontories demonstrated a sophistication in the interaction between memory and context. Extant features such as an abandoned camp fire, fallen tree branches and the topography of the site were all used descriptively.

Our collaborative house of the imagination made use of the existing topography, a steep incline taking the place of stairs. One contribution suggested the landing as an important space where, in a cramped terraced house, a small private space had been carved out. Elsewhere, a break in the foliage stood in for a window framing a view of the sea (where in reality the view was of the Perthshire hills). This was accompanied by a feature representing a jetty into a body of water, a particularly happy memory for one participant. Spaces of agreement also existed, a tree stump became a kitchen table where families would assemble, and more intimate enclosed spaces were defined further up the hill, representing bedrooms.

The construction of the house at 1:1 scale was physical and embodied: rooms were paced out and related to the size of our bodies. Distances indicated by numbers of steps, arm spans, indications of height and space overhead: each of the bodily coordinates of left/right, ahead/behind, above, below, were all imagined through demonstration. Dwelling is an embodied activity after all, and reminding ourselves of this when it comes to design is crucial: we inhabit spaces, they become extensions of the human body to the extent that we often reach for things without looking: practiced movements in the kitchen are disturbed when a well-meaning guest has washed up and put things away in the 'wrong' place.

Another group who were taking part in a material collection exercise organized by another facilitator happened upon the resulting house with it's bay window, jetty out to the sea, hearth and threshold, stairs and landings: so they were taken on a tour, buying in to the fiction of a home that we had created collaboratively and imagined into being.[19]

## Notes

1. Focusing on gendered space as well as the sensorial and experiential aspects of home.
2. In this title, Miller addresses the concept of home with regard to material culture studies.

3   Buchli gives an account of the intervention of the State in the home in Soviet Russia, noting the extent to which the state would specify appropriate furnishing and decorations for the home. This was consistent with the promotion of the Soviet Union's opposition to bourgeoisie ways of living.
4   Describing the contemporary Japanese home in relation to its storage and display functions.
5   Most notably, Margarette Schütte-Linotzky's *Frankfurt Kitchen* design of 1926, charted as part of a wider cultural history of the kitchen by Kinchin (2011).
6   See Levi-Strauss (1963:279).
7   There are exceptions of course, and there is suspicion or derision of individuals who might live in this way as affected or poseurs, presenting an unachievable image of how to live to lifestyle magazines or other outlets to display an 'ideal' home.
8   A detailed exploration of this issue can be found in the work of Victor Buchli (2000, 2002) on Soviet-era housing.
9   As with all things, there are regional and other variations to this.
10  For more on this, see Japanese architect Arata Isozaki (1986) who discusses the floor orientation of Japanese traditional architecture.
11  See Goodwin (1993). For an architectural case, the literature surrounding the place of Katsura Rikyu (Gropius et al., 1960; Ponciroli, 2004; Ishimoto, 2010; Lucas, 2018a), an Imperial villa on the edges of Kyoto. The villa was famously visited by early modernists, including Bruno Taut, whose account of the planar geometry proved highly influential. Japanese architects have also noted the influence of Katsura alongside the Ise Shrine as foundational to Japanese architecture in a manner equivalent to the Parthenon's influence in Europe (see Isozaki, 2006).
12  See Chapter 5 of this volume as well as Mauss (2002[1954]), Hendry (1993) and Sansi (2015). *The Gift*. London: Routledge.
13  It's important not to misrepresent Ingold's work as explicitly Heideggerian here, however, as he has significant divergences from Heidegger's hard distinction between human and animal dwelling (2011:11). The greater influence on this aspect of Ingold's thought are the environmental psychologist James Gibson and phenomenologist Maurice Merleau-Ponty. Movement is implicated directly in the perception of the environment by Gibson's reckoning, and the entire organism is engaged in finding the useful affordances that environment has to offer.
14  For better or worse, of course, as modernism has a great many benefits over what came before it and represented an attempt at democratization of architecture.
15  This gave the experiment a fixed duration: we were to continue until the 100 metres of twine were used up, unfurled as a single strand without cutting or splitting.
16  The experiment was part of an event discussing pedagogical methods in a practical setting, posing alternative ways of knowing and mobilizing the idea of learning as understanding in practice. The residential event, at Comrie

Croft in Perthshire, Scotland, was part of the ERC Advanced Grant project *Knowing from the Inside* for which the author is an associate researcher. The so-called KFI Kitchen included a wide range of activities designed as alternative forms of attention: introverted attention, extravert attention and social attention. My aim here was to investigate how forms of drawing could inform anthropology, moving the discipline away from the idea that ethnography is the sole form of valid investigation.

**17** Bachelard (1992 [1958]) and Calvino (1974).

**18** Bachelard (1992).

**19** The artist Do Ho Suh, in his work *Home within Home within Home within Home within Home* of 2013, created 1:1 scale replicas of several homes he had lived in. These replicas are made from carefully detailed textiles, hung from the ceiling and nested within one another. The work is designed to be walked into and around, engaging the visitor to the gallery in a multisensory embodied experience of the spaces and their relationship with one another.

# 4

# Museums and Architectures of Collection

## Introduction

Continuing the discussion of building typologies through anthropological theory, this chapter addresses the museum. One of the most contested spaces in postcolonial literature, the museum represents a process of accumulation and display, often with its roots in historical plunder or domination. Whilst this is not always the case, examples of colonial artefacts' presentation in museums equip us with many transferable theories to less contentious materials.

Anthropologists often deal with the problematic nature of indigenous communities' relationships with Western collectors. These relationships can become embedded over time to produce a market for goods once produced for specific cultural reasons: as in the case of the Malanggan funerary sculptures described by Suzanne Küchler. The trajectory towards deliberately produced artworks providing a financial lifeline to marginalized communities complicates the narrative of Orientalism described by Edward Said. This trajectory or biography continues the thread of material culture studies from the chapter on the home, but with greater political implications.

Rather than document a museum building itself, I have chosen here to work with examples of buildings which have themselves entered collections. This sharpens the discussion of the status of the object, as one defence of the postcolonial critique of museums is that the building itself is mute, and it is the acquisition policies of curators that are in question. By discussing buildings which have themselves been decontextualized, made safe, interpreted and displayed, it becomes apparent that the status of a building can alter radically from its original functions. This argument can be extended towards other practices of building re-use and conservation and opens up a debate about the ruptures inherent in such re-categorizations. Rather than avoid such status shifts altogether, I would instead propose greater recognition and acknowledgement of the process being undertaken, deliberately designing it in to the display rather than studiously avoiding it.

## The problem of the museum

At its core, a museum is an architectural structure devoted to memory and the presentation of a collection. Anthropology and other disciplines have developed a critique of this, transforming what appears at first to be a public good and educational good institution into a deeply contentious site of colonialism. Issues related to collection have included the objectification of our material culture and relocation of artefacts from their context. Baudrillard[1] notes that the object becomes divested of its function as soon as it is placed into the collection: it is an act of decontextualization, robbing things of their use value, preventing them from continuing their original purposes enmeshed in everyday life.

This critique of the museum might appear to run the risk of abolishing this public good, but instead, by complicating our approach to the institution, we begin to understand the core value of museums as well as the problems they can cause. It is important to develop nuance and refine our relationship with items held by museums or deliberately exhibited elsewhere. Questions of who is saying what about whom should be at the forefront of our encounters with such displays.

Museums and collections have enormous power to educate and act positively in the world, so it is important to introduce a more positive note. One approach to this lies in the dual intentions of evoking *resonance* and *wonder*. Steven Greenblatt[2] examines these twin concepts in his essay of the same name, evoking the sympathy we can feel for other humans, whether separated by time or distance: to understand things made by human hands and to see ourselves in their lifeworlds.[3]

This moves us towards a discussion of the artefacts and the responses they are capable of evoking in the museum-going public. The aim is, after all, to share and educate – to deepen our understanding of one another. However much we might problematize the underlying mechanisms of that activity, there is something edifying and positive in this intent – to the extent that it must remain possible and be an aim worthy of achieving.

Honest stories related to the artefacts are the key to this. Rather than only showing a perfect, Platonic ideal of an object, it might be a more useful narrative to accompany a broken object ore one that shows clear traces of being well used, everyday rather than ceremonial. This might sound subtle, but represents a substantial shift in a collection's focus. By moving away from the finest examples in a series, the objects displayed might instead be the most informative about the lives of the people who used it. We can find traces of life and use in these artefacts, and it is this connection with others, this resonance and appeal to common humanity that ought to lie at the heart of our attempts at the display of a culture.

*Wonder* represents our astonishment at some of the possible ways for humans to understand the world, make sense of their environment and interact with it. *Resonance* is the recognition that there are a multitude of possible ways to live, to be human, and that we share something in common even with the most unusual of these. Confronting the material traces of these, provided the context is sufficiently appreciated, allows us some access into other peoples' worlds. Understanding these underlying concepts in contemporary museology allows architects to better appreciate how they might design in a manner that decolonizes the institution.

Kylie Message (2006) discusses a range of new approaches to museum spaces in the early 2000s. Addressing the redevelopment of existing museums as well as entirely new institutions, Message asks how these institutions add a layer of self-consciousness to their colonialist pasts. Retaining the principle of education for all from their positivistic roots in the nineteenth century, a question is raised regarding what form that education might take. Tracing the historical development of the contemporary museum through debates between figures such as Rosalind Krauss, Mieke Bal, Donna Haraway and Donald Crimp (Message, 2006:18) in a frame referencing Bourdieu's idea of cultural capital and Foucault's critique of institutions as power structures leads to a discussion of how museums produce value. This production of value is important in the cases we shall discuss later in the case of the hanok house, not as simple commodities, but as exemplars and representatives of a type. In the examples discussed by Message, the exhibits are not the only displays, but the museum and its processes are also on show to visitors, rendering the underlying mechanism of the collection transparent.

Writing in the introduction to *Object Atlas* (Deliss, Ed., 2012:7), anthropologist Paul Rabinow also discusses the *new* museum, particularly of ethnographic collections. These most fraught and contentious collections are intertwined with the discipline of anthropology, where an outdated idea of the ethnographer as cultural collector would be arranged and classified, displaying masks, pottery and often sacred items from a wide range of cultures. Rabinow acknowledges the colonialism at the root of the practice and notes that it is part of the institution's role to continue to show objects, but also to be open and honest about how they came to be there. The solutions are to be found in both *remediation* and careful curation, not only to acknowledge historic wrongs, but also to move towards a *correction*. Clémentine Deliss is director of the Frankfurt Weltkulturen Museum and instigated the exhibition documented in *Object Atlas*. The book documents the work of an international group of seven artists and academics who were asked to respond to the museum's ethnographic collection. This engagement is framed as a form of fieldwork in the museum, understanding it as a site worthy of research, modelled after Aby Warburg's *Mnemosyne Atlas* which considered the institutions of art display in a similar manner. This takes Message's work on the self-conscious and critical museum seriously, if potentially introverted. In common with contemporary practices of ethnography, the project overcomes some of its potential issues through a form of co-production, even if this is by creative response to the museum collections.

The precise nature of the engagement with museum objects is considered by Constance Classen and David Howes (2006). Arguing for a more holistic multisensory engagement which avoids the totalizing tendency of the gaze, they argue that one confronts objects on terms more appropriate to them by using their associated sensory registers. They argue that each object in a collection 'embodies a particular sensory mix' (2006:200); it does not make sense to exhibit it behind glass in a way which affords only one form of engagement. Whilst objects in museums are removed from their context and not available for use in their original ways, this process famously noted by Baudrillard (1994) might produce some unintended effects of distancing visitors from objects and the people who made or used them. As we shall see later in this chapter, Classen and Howes's preferred solution to this conundrum of the 'open-air' museum (2006:218–219) where an entire context is provided, including buildings, and landscape is, in itself, uncanny and problematic.

Several pertinent arguments regarding the nature of collection can be found in anthropologist Suzanne Küchler's work on malanggan sculptures.[4] A malanggan is a kind of funerary artefact made in the New Ireland region of Papua New Guinea. The name refers to a variety of practices of making within this remit and is one of the most commonly found items in ethnographic museums containing artefacts from Papua New Guinea. These artefacts are revealing of both the nature of life and death in New Ireland, but also of material culture and its consumption in the West as an attempt at capturing and collecting the work of an exotic faraway land. Whilst not explicitly architectural, the malanggan describes the processes by which decontextualization operates.

The objects fulfil a role as a kind of memorial, but their creation and use both give rise to and resist the collection and exhibition of malanggan outside of their context. Küchler resists giving a description of the object until later in her work. This is deliberate, as her agenda is not to objectify, but to truly understand this most objectified of practices. In practical terms, however, the malanggan tends to be a carved wooden object, the image being a kind of image memorializing a deceased person.

The relationship between the person and the malanggan is particularly interesting; the image can be said to act as a memory, a mnemonic device representing the deceased. The malanggan is carved with images of several symbolic patterns and forms. These include different kinds of seashells and animals associated with the individual.

The forms are largely derived from a range of sources, including nature, man-made items such as canoes and pipes, and mythical and symbolic references. This collection of symbols and motifs forms the palette for the malanggan sculpture, with any given malanggan representing an accumulation of co-existing symbols. Küchler identifies a further schema of *assemblages*, similar to the difference between a romantic narrative and a heroic one; these types of assemblage are held to have wider cultural significance and are easily recognized and grouped by residents of New Ireland.

Most important is the cultural practice in which the objects are embedded: both intentional and unintentional. The funerary rituals are accompanied by the making of malanggan, and the eventual destruction and disposal of the items. Firstly, the production of malanggan is not a lost art; the creation and use of the artefacts continues to this day. The rituals of the funeral dictate that the malanggan be dreamt; the appropriate forms and symbolism applied to the 'skin' of the wood. This is, however, not a memorial or representation in this literal sense. The material durability (2002:7) is not part of the intent, but it is allowed to die and become part of a cycle of renewal. Further details on this are given by Karen Sykes (2007) who gives an account of changing processes in the making of malanggan sculptures with explicit reference to ethnographic materials: in this case, film informing contemporary carvers with past practices. Similarly, Haidy Geismar (2009) studies the intersection of malanggan and photography.

The malanggan is itself, at the end of the funerary ritual, symbolically killed and abandoned in a nearby forested area. This is the crucial point about the malanggan, and what allows it to pass in to the hands of Western collectors, but also why they misunderstand and decontextualize the artefact so radically. By concentrating on the 'deceased' malanggan artefact, they are dealing with it as an object, finished and completed – entirely outside of its functional context. It is also no longer a malanggan at this point, as it has been killed; it is no longer alive and no longer a malanggan.

Clearly an artefact exists and is patently there, but the collectors are essentially collecting their own objectivity, collecting their perception rather than the item they *think they are* even if well informed. The market in these carved artefacts if further complicated by the lack of care the makers have over them. For a short period, they represent a deceased person and are then discarded as part of the renewal process, no longer serving any purpose and simply left to rot. There appears to be no problem with the preservation of the artefact in a far-off ethnographic museum, as it is no longer the malanggan (Küchler, 2002:167–168).

This changing status of the object assigns no value to it at this stage, but during use, they are subject to economic exchange of shell-moneys, and of high status. Despite the ritual associations, once the image is killed it is no longer important, and they are happily sold to the Western collectors on this basis. They are misunderstood, but perhaps not exploited any more.

There is a great deal of detail in the study of the malanggan as a ritual object and typical artefact of non-Western art defined by the conventional museum culture of Europe and North America. What Küchler achieves, however, is to find, within the treatment of this artefact by the makers and users as well as the anthropologists and collectors, a microcosm of the whole endeavour of non-Western 'art' should such a category even be possible or desirable. The aim of these items, whatever their ritual complexity and aesthetic beauty, is bound up in the relations between people and between the living and the dead.

We can find traces of the malanggan in the instances described below: both of the intentional and unintentional cultural displays exposed by exhibition and museum practices. When we exhibit, we are not only showing the artefact, but exposing the mechanisms by which it was acquired or accessioned, the understanding of both the original culture and the collector.

The disciplines of museum studies and anthropology both discuss the power relations between the original makers of objects and those observing them in the controlled environment of the museum. The examples which follow discuss how museums have been reconfigured to depict absences, to allow populations to present themselves to the world rather than being placed on display, and objects with sacred value returned to their places of origin. The first example is the Edo-Tokyo Open Air Museum in Mitaka, Tokyo where buildings have been moved and rebuilt as museum pieces rather than demolished during the rapid redevelopment of the city, allowing visitors to access their interior and to interact with them in a way that is simultaneously authentic and constructed. The second is a discussion of the hanok house in South Korea[5] – its adaptation and resistance to contemporary life and the symbolism of preserving 'Hanok Villages' in dense urban environments by collecting and transplanting buildings, uprooting them from their original location.[6]

This chapter addresses a range of issues to do with collecting and cultural display. This is complementary to Chapter 3, where we considered some of the private and hidden aspects of life – the intimacy of the home, where meaning is not intended for the consumption of outsiders and must instead by gleaned from our encounters. Here, domestic spaces are recategorized as objects of display. The deliberate display of architecture is the topic here, treating buildings as objects or artefacts. The choice to make a display is an interesting one and is demonstrative of a desire to communicate, but also grounded in a fraught relationship of colonialism, misunderstandings and objectification.

## Cultural display: Monuments and theme parks

Cultural display occurs most obviously in the museum, but it is also a feature of other sites. The term refers to the deliberate display of something as an image or representation of a culture. It might consist of wearing traditional dress as a marker of one's own nationality or the use of culturally specific codes to indicate association with ethnicity or another cultural group. Indeed, it would be difficult to find a set of circumstances entirely bereft of cultural display, but certain sites can be understood more clearly as sites where a primary concern is the deliberate projection of an image.

In her study of the Japanese theme park industry, anthropologist Joy Hendry gives a fascinating account of the way in which their culture industry chooses to display both their own indigenous culture and that of other countries, notably the West. The monograph has the title of *The Orient Strikes Back*, recalling directly the work of Edward Said. Said's famous text, *Orientalism*, discusses the ways in which the West has conceptualized the world outside of Christendom, particularly through the vague concept of the Orient. Said is a cultural historian and develops his concept of Orientalism as a way of describing the root of Western politics, power relations and conception of Otherness.

Said's analysis indicates that is something pervasive about the manner in which the West conceptualizes the East,[7] framed around often flawed understandings of historical events and religious faith which are described by Said as more of an implicit than explicit characterization. This is nonetheless a powerful element in Western discourse regarding the East. Indeed, Said's work remains very important in contemporary geopolitics, with misunderstandings and tensions arising between communities in what is an intermixed world. Trade contact and closer co-existence has been a feature of life in the East and West for centuries[8]: it is hardly anything new, however much it might be represented in populist politics as such.

*Orientalism* is presented by Said as a *system for understanding* (or rather misunderstanding and reinforcing preconceptions) the East by the West. Implicit in this are the collection of art and the cultural display of Others. Rather than allowing people to represent themselves, Western authors, by a system of agreed discourses and commonly held assumptions about white, Western superiority, would make their knowledge about the East available. This includes disparate territories such as the Middle East, Indian subcontinent, China and Japan. The attitude of Orientalism is imperialistic and colonial. There is a paternalistic aspect to this: a belief that other cultures have not progressed beyond a certain historical period and that their domination by Western powers is in the interests of the countries in question. As such, Orientalism is also a critique of *progress* as a dominant narrative, a version of which is used to justify Western dominance, ignoring the alternative ways of being human which are the subject of anthropology's project. This attitude to progress justifies attempts to subjugate, dominate and otherwise exploit other cultures, for we in the West 'know better' and are acting in their best interests: reducing the relationship to that of a parent and child. This is clearly unacceptable, but there are remnants of this attitude even in how we act today; this is what Said is looking to expose with his work: these remnants of imperialist thinking which must be challenged in favour of more complete understanding between cultures.[9]

This relationship is not one way, however, and Joy Hendry's work explores one instance of travel in the other direction. In her study of Japanese theme parks, Hendry finds an example of reverse Orientalism and turns her attention to the conception of the West by a culture in the East. This is the result of an interest in the Western world, but a difficulty in travel. The solution is pragmatic and fairly unique: that in the bubble economy of the 1980s, Japan created a large number of theme parks which went beyond the familiar examples of Disneyworld, but which attempted to replicate European cultures in the bounded heterotopia of a tourist attraction.

A distinction is made between the theme park and an amusement park, arranged around rides, rollercoasters and the like. The book's introduction (2000:19) lists several parks representing countries, including Canada, Germany, Denmark, Switzerland, the United Kingdom and Spain. There are also a number of mixed parks with zones representing different countries. The parks typically include replicas of significant architecture; displays of the culture and history of the country in question are housed in large public buildings such as a town hall, with broadly sketched cultural themes overlaid onto the park. *Glücks Königreich*, for example, has the works of the Brothers Grimm as a theme, the British parks are often themed after Shakespeare and the Canadian example is focused on the novel *Anne of Green Gables*.

The German themed park includes restaurants and pubs selling the appropriate food and drink, bookshops with translated German literature and souvenirs either made on site in the traditional craft workshops or imported from the country of origin. The staffing of the parks is by natives of the country in question, and their role is to act as hosts, to put on displays of dance or crafts, and to often take part in a large daily promenade; all of which follow the theme park formula established by Disney.

Other examples such as *Canadian World* focus on the recreation of fictional settings such as Avonlea found in Lucy Montgomery's *Anne of Green Gables*. The park is still based on a real-life model – Prince Edward Island – and populated with the details found in the book. The experience of the park includes a variety of locations from the novel and offers opportunities for dressing in costume and having photographs taken as a memento. The popularity of the books in Japan is based on a resonance with the character of Anne-chan as she is known. Her resilience against adversity is valued as an approach to life, and the women who are her biggest fans and for whom the park caters are, according to Hendry, nervous and excited about meeting the Canadian actress playing her.

It is easy to be cynical about these places, perhaps more so in the case of one based on a fictional place; but it is clear that there is something more interesting going on. Indeed, similar situations are documented in detail by Venturi, Scott-Brown and Rauch in their seminal work of architectural theory *Learning from Las Vegas* (1977). Such themed places are often omitted from mainstream architectural discourse,[10] but serve a need and a purpose, and are important manifestations of space and cultural display.

The integration of crafts and performance traditions into the parks is particularly important to note as a practice-based contrast with the object-based museum culture of the West. Many city museums in the UK, for example (and many more in countries with the strongest historic links with Japan such as the Netherlands), will have collections of Japanese artefacts arranged in cabinets and displayed as a group of items from a certain place, or a taxonomy of object types such as arms and armour, pottery and works on paper. The museum tendency is for decontextualization, for display of objects out of space and time – arranged according to an arbitrary scheme. Theme parks by contrast are spaces for performance by people from that region. The performances might be inauthentic to a degree, but they have some basis in convention, tradition, and the reality of the arts and crafts in question.

This opens a question of our position regarding the *real* and the *replica*. Japanese people, when interviewed by Hendry (2000:168), considered their carefully rebuilt replica of Shakespeare's birthplace in Stratford-upon-Avon in *Maruyama Shakespeare Park* to be more genuine than the actual house in England. This authenticity is based on the use of anachronistic crafts and materials, ensuring that the building was constructed as it would have been in the first place. More interestingly, as the house is not marked by the passage of time, it is understood to be closer to how Shakespeare would have experienced it.

The long list of theme parks visited by Hendry indicates another common thread, however. These parks, taken together, offer a *collection*. The approach is, however, practice based: the fascinations are with the ways in which life is organized, the craft behind the making of bread, beer or pottery. This practice-based approach avoids certain elements of the *objectification* process noted by Baudrillard, but perhaps organizes it in a different way rather than avoiding the pitfalls entirely. By taking it out of its original time and context, this approach runs the risk of objectifying a practice rather than an artefact. The interest is with historical places, cleansed of contemporary influence. This is troubling, as it has an attitude of denying the present: that the interest in other cultures is muddied by the co-existence of the present and the past. Whilst being based in practices and performances, then, the result is uncomfortable and at ill-at-ease with reality. This is also not how the Germans, Spanish, Canadians or British choose to represent themselves. This is how the Japanese choose to represent *them*.

This is the problem that is heightened when there is an unequal power relation between the various parties concerned. These European nations and their people can easily redress the balance and have an influence over how they are represented, but the issue is crucial when it comes to marginalized groups who are subjected to the gaze of the collector and the museum.[11]

Monuments have a common purpose of cultural display.[12] Where in Chapter 3, we were considering the subtleties of cultural display in the home, where we do not *deliberately* construct and place this on view for others to make sense of. Monuments are circumstances where we *do* deliberately make a display. The collection *The Art of Forgetting* edited by Adrian Forty and Suzanne Küchler deals with several examples of this building and sculptural typology. Tracing a history for the monument in the West from the Renaissance (of course, this history extends into antiquity), Forty and Küchler discuss the processes of sedimenting human memory in material objects (1999:2). This transfer of memory from human minds into solid things is a curious process, but one which extends the duration of those memories, granting them a kind of persistence if not permanence. This explains the shock when a monument is deliberately destroyed in war (an act recently included in the United Nations (UN) definition of a war crime), as it is an attempt to erase the culture of a people.

This means that monuments can function not only as a symbol of an event worthy of remembrance in perpetuity, but that in representing it, some of the actual living memory can be invested into the stone. The monument effectively enables us to forget an event and allow life to go on, symbolizing the event and activated at particular memorial times of year, but not to burden everyday life with the facts of something terrible. It this manner, the Cenotaph in London functions as a focal point during the remembrance services every November, but is effectively dormant the rest of the time.

Memorials are most often erected to mark military campaigns and political figures, extending to civic events more recently. The postwar period in the twentieth century wrestled with the complexity of the Holocaust: clearly an event in need of commemoration and memorialization, but one which continues to intersect with contemporary politics. Finding structures which could make sense of such terrible events was particularly difficult, and Forty and Küchler address several examples, arguing that a genre of *anti-memorial* emerges. The temporality of the monument typology is one parameter for these designs. Where the conventional monument attempts to arrest time, there is an address to the passage of time in Christian Boltanski and Jochen Gerz's approaches to Holocaust memorials, with monuments which lower themselves gradually into the ground or paving stones which have undersides bearing the names of Jewish cemeteries: 'the memorial is invisible, only known about' (Forty & Küchler, 1999:6–7).

There are other examples of these memorials by artists and architects which also engage with time and hiddenness: at the time of its construction it was noted that Daniel Libeskind's Jewish Museum in Berlin (Figure 4.1) was

**FIGURE 4.1** *Author's photograph of the Jewish Museum, Berlin by Daniel Libeskind.*

more effective and emotionally affective before the artefacts were installed in the display cases. The absence represented by the jagged geometry of the structure spoke volumes, particularly with its plan form symbolically extrapolated from the absent Jewish quarters of Berlin. From here, Forty and Küchler develop a position towards *forgetting* that monuments are a form of necessary amnesia (1999:16). Libeskind denies the building memorial status, instead discussing its role as a placeholder for a forgotten name or unwritten music.

Strategies employed by monuments as machines for forgetting include:

*Separation:*
The monument expresses a division between what is to be remembered and what can be forgotten.

*Tension between remembering and forgetting:*
This is often the source of drama in a memorial: when a memorial is active, it can act as an accusation to the mourners that they are not holding the memorialized individuals in their mind at all times.

*Exclusion:*
By leaving a scar or remnant of war damage, it remains apparent and excluded from the temporality and development of the city at large. This was proposed by Lebbeus Woods for the former Yugoslavia, where he proposed damaged buildings be repaired with visible scars.[13]

*Iconoclasm:*
The actual destruction of monuments of previous undesired eras, such as the examples from the former Soviet Union filmed by Laura Mulvey and Mark Lewis as *Disgraced Monuments* and discussed by Forty & Küchler (1999:10). The process of destroying and repurposing statues of Lenin after the fall of the Soviet Union shows alternative strategies for iconoclasm.

(Adapted from Forty & Küchler, 1999:8)

A useful example might be the *Fourth Plinth* in Trafalgar Square, London. This space operates like an iconoclastically destroyed monument, being periodically occupied by a work by a contemporary artist. The plinth, however, was never occupied. The intention had been to place a statue on it, but the funds for the construction of the square ran out before the planned military equestrian statue. The problem of what to place on the plinth became all the more fraught as public opinion on the celebration of generals and admirals fell out of favour towards more civic topics. Indeed, the very idea of public statues of 'great' figures is very complicated and contested, ensuring that filling this void was difficult. By establishing a programme of contemporary public art which could occupy the space for a limited period of time, the 'fourth plinth' avoids some of the issues of permanent monuments. Certain of the proposals, however, do still fulfil the function of monumentality and remembrance, if in a different manner to the conventional military narrative. Yinka Shonibare's *Nelson's Ship in a Bottle* occupied the plinth in 2010 before a public appeal funded its acquisition and permanent home at the UK National Maritime Museum in Greenwich; it memorializes global trade and colonialism by presenting a model of Nelson's ship *Victory* with masts created from canvas influenced by Indonesian Batik.

Other exhibits on the plinth included an egalitarian project by Anthony Gormley who literally gave a platform to some 100 contributors in *One & Other*. More interesting, however, is the work by Marc Quinn of *Alison Lapper Pregnant* in which the conventional language of the naturalistic representation of human form is applied to a non-traditional subject: a pregnant woman with physical disabilities. The white marble statue stood in stark contrast to the strongly militaristic male occupants of the other plinths, positioning her as being every bit as heroic and worthy of celebration.

Complicating the narrative around monumentality has its roots in postcolonial understandings of the world whereby the assumptions made by earlier generations of Western colonialists can still be found in our institutions. Decolonization is a process, one of giving voice to those denied it, of recognizing the persistence of ideologies which deny agency to non-Western societies and individuals in forming our worldviews. It is a process of making aware and redressing balances, and a project we are only just beginning.

## Collections of architecture

Whilst the traditional museum is an architecture of collection, several examples exist where architecture itself is collected. Many city museums attempt to show the past of their host city through reconstructions of historical buildings, but the *Edo-Tokyo Open Air Architectural Museum* in Tokyo (Figure 4.2) takes another strategy. It is an example of the genre of open-air museums as described by Hendry, but the experience of visiting the museum is marked by a kind of disjunction, haunted by a feeling that things aren't quite right: the houses and shops are provided with a context, but it is a constructed one. The museum acquires buildings scheduled for demolition and arranges them in a parkland setting, clustering some together as a typical street from the Shōwa era,[14] and separating others out for special attention as individual dwellings with gardens. The buildings themselves sit on the cusp between those which

**FIGURE 4.2** *Author's photograph of the exterior of the Edo-Tokyo Open Air Architectural Museum.*

would be preserved in situ and those which no longer serve their original function and would be demolished. They tend to be either the houses of significant figures (such as modernist architect Kunio Mayekawa, who trained under Le Corbusier) or representatives of important building types such as a public bath-house, koan police box and various retail outlets.

The relationship between architecture and its context makes an unsettling experience when visiting the open-air museum. Baudrillard's discussion of museum objects articulates this well and highlights the decontextualizing nature of collecting. It becomes clear that the transplantation of entire buildings represents a jarring fissure in our expectations for each structure. Small cues are present regarding the original relationship between buildings and the ground, their orientation and their positioning alongside other buildings. One store bears the marks of the Second World War bombardments whilst its neighbour is completely unscathed: as they originally occupied completely separate parts of the city. These cues become amplified over time to produce a deeper disquiet with the arrangement: the buildings are clearly authentic but their arrangement is not (Figure 4.3).

# MUSEUMS AND ARCHITECTURES OF COLLECTION

**FIGURE 4.3** *Author's photograph of the interior of the Edo-Tokyo Open Air Architectural Museum.*

Baudrillard's work *The System of Collecting* presents collection as an activity rather than a finished thing. The process of collecting things involves decontextualizing objects both spatially and temporally. Six key strategies are given:

1. Divesting the object of its function.
2. Loving the object.
3. Treating the object as a pet.
4. Placing the object in a series with others.
5. Assessing the quality of the individual object and selecting based on criteria.
6. Arresting and controlling the passage of time.
   (Adapted from Baudrillard, 1994)

The change in function is crucial to understanding the process the institution engages in when transplanting an entire building from its original context to the parkland setting of the open-air museum. More than simply a scaling up of the process of placing pottery or furniture in a gallery, the fundamental lack of portability of architecture is essential to the unsettling nature of the act. The object is not only stripped of function, but given a new one: it *becomes the museum* at the same time as it is placed within it.

Buildings which would have been private are opened up to small groups of tourists inspecting every aspect of their set-dressing. Much like the production design of a film, attention has been paid to every element of the fixtures and fittings to freeze each of the buildings in an appropriate period (Figure 4.4). Often, this periodization is fixed to one era: no traces of earlier or later periods are allowed to muddy the image we have. We see behind the scenes of domestic life and are permitted to wander from room to room whilst being cordoned off from furniture which might invite us to actually dwell or inhabit the space.

This underlines another issue: that one is transformed into the spectator of a spectacle in what would otherwise read as a viable piece of architecture.

**FIGURE 4.4** *Author's Photographs showing details of the Edo-Tokyo Open Air Architectural Museum.*

The buildings are *loved* by the collector, cared for and maintained such that there is no dirt, no *matter out of place* as Mary Douglas might express it. This establishes a distinction between *patina* and *dirt*, a category difference between the acceptable and unacceptable elements of wear and tear.

Baudrillard discusses the collected object as a pet: cared for, but controlled and neutered. The nature of the building is denied, the photographer's studio on site bears all the hallmarks of such a space, the equipment in place, studio lighting and backdrops, but it is not permitted to behave as a studio. The buildings belong to a similar period, in order to *evoke* 1920s and 1930s Tokyo; this series is important in giving some coherence to the collection. The mix of urban and rural structures accentuates the unsettling nature of the space, however: despite belonging to similar eras, the co-mingling of a farmhouse with urban and suburban modernism underscores the feeling that this place is not as it might wish to appear.

The buildings in the museum are exemplars, each carefully selected and curated. This erases much of the ordinariness from the architecture: the homes are those of famous poets and architects, not representative of the general population; the bath house preserved is both typical and a worth example: a Platonic ideal of the Japanese bath house of this era. Many other bath houses went un-collected, perhaps lacking the tile mural of Mount Fuji or the coherent composition of this example.

The root of the disjointed experience is how it attempts to arrest time: erasing traces of inhabitation from unwanted eras, the buildings are dressed to conform to a precise point in time and then held there. This is self-evidently part of the museum's narrative, but it is one which places the experience in this strange transition between exhibit and architecture. The museum as it stands attests to some of the ways in which we read architecture as we find it in the world: underlining the importance of context and temporality, the engagement with the wider environment and how it accommodates the passing of time, either by alternative occupation, remodelling, or even simply by containing some more contemporary objects and furnishings. As well as offering a window into Shōwa Tokyo, the museum sharpens how we view architecture in the wider world, and the importance of subtle cues to temporality and context.

## Seoul's strategies of architectural collection

A variation on the open-air museum is presented by the various strategies used by city authorities in Seoul to maintain groups of hanok houses. This traditional form of courtyard housing consists of a perimeter wall in masonry and decorated with geometric patterns, with timber construction for the interior and curving tile roofs. A unique system of underfloor heating has a long history in hanok construction, and the homes themselves are occupied, often adapted to modern needs (Figure 4.5)[15] evidenced by air conditioning units, utility company meters on the exterior and above-ground electricity supply.

Two areas which gather these together are Bukcheon and Namsangol (Figure 4.6). Bukcheon is a bustling mixed residential and small-scale retail area on a steep hilly part of the city. The tone of the area is quiet and low rise, with contemporary architecture carefully designed to work alongside the traditional. The low-rise element is particularly notable in Seoul, a city constrained geographically by mountains, meaning that the modern parts of the city are extremely high in density. The pressure on land as the country modernized leads to a large number of hanoks being demolished, and it wasn't until the 1990s that preservation strategies began in earnest. Now, there are three simultaneous strategies for preserving hanok living. The first is preservation of existing hanoks, protecting them and conserving them. Often, this conservation involves a similar strategy of dismantling and relocation to the open-air museum noted in Tokyo above. The issues with decontextualization are more complicated here, as the hanok houses are often relocated in a sensitive manner, alongside other similar structures in order to assemble a coherent district. Where these houses retain their function as dwellings, the villages are relatively successful – if turned into tourist attractions in their own right as picturesque photo opportunities. Some

**FIGURE 4.5** *Author's photograph of hanok adapted to contemporary use showing ventilation and utility meters.*

**FIGURE 4.6** *Author's photograph of Namsangol Hanok Village: an example of the open-air museum approach.*

examples are retained as museums to hanok living, however. This presents a similar set of circumstances to the open-air museum, rendering the buildings as exemplars by divesting them of their function as homes.

The second strategy is pursued at Namsangol: the preservation of hanok living by promoting and producing new houses according to an established standard. This is somewhat different to the strategies presented above and involves the creation of a historical standard from the remaining buildings. A series of discernments are then made as to what constitutes a true hanok and what falls outside of this definition: how many concessions can be made to modern living? This definition is provided in part by the Ministry of Land, Infrastructure and Transport via the National Hanok Competition[16] where a range of contemporary examples of hanok are publicized.

This distillation of the collected hanoks into a set of parameters or rules represents a further step in the architecture of collection, an attempt to reconstruct a historical form by keeping it in step with contemporary conditions. Part of this is similar to the development of *mingei* as an appreciation of folk art in Japan, with the aesthetic qualities of *mak* and *bium* described by Byoungso Cho.[17] *Mak*, in this instance, is a kind of crudeness borne of spontaneity, represented by the roughness of timbers and how they meet

**FIGURE 4.7** *Author's photograph of newly constructed house designed to look like a traditional hanok: detail of wall under construction. What is notable here is the manner in which the wall is decorated to resemble hanok construction rather than built using those techniques.*

stone foundations. *Bium* denotes a kind of emptiness, offering a description of the courtyard void at the heart of the hanok to Cho. The celebration of the raw materials, untreated and showing imperfections, gives traditional Korean architecture part of its aesthetic. This becomes codified in the new hanok (Figure 4.7), counter to Cho's discussion of the improvisatory nature of Korean arts more broadly: collection, even operating in the mode of reconstruction and new building, serves to ossify and freeze things into a series.

# Restoration and reclamation

The adoption of the hanok typology in an imitative fashion is significant as it relates to the nation-building exercise adopted by South Korea, in parallel to the reinvention of national spectacle at Gyeongbokgung Palace,[18] the 'restoration' of Cheonggyecheon Stream and the relationship of the new Seoul City Hall to its counterpart, a relic of Japanese colonial occupation. These three examples represent alternative forms of cultural display, but a deliberately constructed notion of culture designed to make a statement of unity with reference to past occupation. Processes of reclaiming culture need to be demonstrative and visible, as in the case of the new City Hall and the Cheonggye Stream Restoration project.

The Cheonggye Stream Restoration in central Seoul (Figure 4.8) sits on the edge of the Dongdaemun area and is a key element of the regeneration of the city centre. The stream, flowing from the north of the city to the Han River, was central to the garment industry, becoming polluted through the dyeing of cloths and other activities.

The stream was known for flash floods and uneven ground conditions, and was seen as a problematic area for some time despite embankment works from 1900 to harden the edge between the water and the city. In the 1950s, as part of the city's modernization project, the stream was culverted and replaced with a road at ground level, followed by an elevated expressway in 1965. The expressway was accompanied by the development of modernist mixed-use buildings for Sewoon Sangga, combining marketplace and residential functions by architect Kim Swoo Geun. In 2002, the former CEO of

**FIGURE 4.8** *Author's photograph of view of the Cheonggyecheon restoration.*

Hyundai, Lee Myung Bak, was elected mayor of Seoul, including the proposal for the restoration of the stream as a campaign pledge. The project is always referred to as a restoration, a term loaded with intent: the idea that the city had lost this river was an essential part of the narrative. The demolition was preceded by a citizen's walk along the closed expressway in 2003, a symbolic reclamation of the territory by people from vehicles.

The project, designed and constructed by a team of engineering firms, was led by Seo-Anh Total Landscape, with a 5.8-km stretch completed between July 2003 and September 2005. Notably, the excavation works revealed several Choson-era artefacts, including the Kwangtong Bridge from 1410. This is a crucial element of the restoration narrative and embeds the restoration project firmly in the public imagination as a form of national recovery. The remains of the bridge were treated almost as relics, afforded the importance of artefacts and sparking a national debate whether it should be rebuilt using the stones recovered, or if they should be placed into a museum. The decision was to use the stones in the reconstruction directly, with missing stones replaced with replica masonry.

The uncritical use of terms such as 'natural' abounds in architectural and urban design discourse, particularly when an overwhelmingly positive image is projected about the benefits of a project. The Cheonggyecheon is repeatedly referred to as natural, and the strategies surrounding the planting in the park are a deliberate move away from the picturesque and manicured traditions of landscape design and more akin to projects such as the High Line in New York. There is considerable artifice in the stream restoration, however. Not only is the planting carefully selected in order to be representative of native varieties, a simulation of nature, but it has to be managed and cared for by a team of gardeners (Figure 4.9) as well. This attracts a wide range of insects and bird life to the stream, but the water is largely reserved for ornamental carp. More concerning for the narrative of the natural state of the park is the water itself. The uncovering of the stream revealed that the flow was barely present. The solution here was in engineering: water is processed and cleaned from the Han River before being pumped up to the top of the stream. The topography of the stream still contributes to flash floods, however – a warning system is installed on the walls of the stream with sirens, announcements and flashing lights meaning that the park is evacuated during heavy rainstorms: a relatively frequent occurrence in Seoul.

The design itself is modest and conservative, carefully considered and managed throughout. Particular attention is given to the ground plane, where materials indicate the different phases of the scheme, which moves from its most formal language in the West to a less-defined character with deliberately overgrown planting in the East. Stepping stones are laid in the water for crossing at various points on the level of the park, and the stages of the linear

**FIGURE 4.9** *Author's photograph of teams of gardeners at work on the Cheonggye stream.*

development are further distinguished by variations in the water itself: fast flowing waterfalls and deeper, still water with a glassy surface.

A bold design decision is taken in the East section of the stream to remember the expressway itself, as three of the reinforced concrete piers are left in a state of deliberate ruin. This is closest to the remaining expressway structure, complete with abandoned ramp connections where Cheongge-ro (Figure 4.10), the 1960s expressway, would have connected to the network. The memory of the site is not, then, restricted to the ancient and mythologized recent past, but includes the radical urban planning decision of removing 5 kilometres of infrastructure.

The design of the new Seoul City Hall (Figure 4.11) is a useful case study in discussing the relationship between power and building as well as the retention of potentially toxic relics. As a manifestation of authority, a city hall or parliament building often represents the manner in which governments wish to be understood. It is in this regard that the intersection of the old city hall, built under Japanese occupation (notably in a style resembling European Colonial architecture); and the deliberately science-fiction aesthetic of the new structure by Yoo Kerl and iArc Architects is particularly striking. The duality of these structures, old and new, and the discussion of a contentious historical

**FIGURE 4.10** *Author's photograph of the East section of the stream, with expressway piers retained.*

structure underline the importance of meaning and association in architecture: the colonial administration is a potent site politically, but demolition is a denial of history. By transforming the original building into a public library, dominated by a highly engineered and future facing landmark, a clear political statement is made by the building.

The process of the rehabilitation of a colonial structure and eventual decolonization attempts through new images can be discussed through this building, an expression of dynamism from a city which is increasingly defining itself as a global technological hub. Such buildings are an expression of power and loaded with symbolism. The new Seoul City Hall has a clear and unambiguous relationship with its predecessor. The old city hall, partly demolished, sits on the adjacent site to the new building and was constructed by the Japanese colonial administration during its occupation of the country from 1910 to 1945.

The Imperial style of the Japanese architecture represents the adoption of Western-style architecture throughout the period of the Meiji Restoration; opening to Europe encouraged Japanese architects to construct buildings using similar technologies and forms, resulting in a variation on the kind of classicism so often exported by European colonial architecture. The building remains open as a public library, housing archives and rooms dedicated to the

**FIGURE 4.11** *Author's photograph of Seoul City Hall, with the old Japanese colonial administration building (now the central library) in the foreground.*

history of the city. A number of these rooms have been left as a deliberate statement of subverting authority and power: boardrooms are opened to public view with the conference table replaced by tabletop-style exhibits with animations and infographics informing visitors about the demographic change the city has gone through. The mayor's office is also open, with the desk and telephone providing photo opportunities for visitors.

The new building dominates, however. The slab organization is sculpted to resemble a large glazed wave looming over the old structure. The effect is as heroic as it is science-fiction in its aesthetic. The building is approachable at the same time: open to the public with a large public exhibition space on the ground floor framed by a lush green wall climbing the full height of the interior. The symbolism of the structure is clear: the statements from iArc Architects upon securing the commission in 2008 and its opening in 2012 continually define it as future facing, alongside openness and transparency as political ambitions, but the overbearing position of the new building sends a clear message: that this is a self-confident city aware of its colonial past, but defiantly looking ahead to future successes.

Both old and new buildings address a large public square, a rarity in Seoul. The presence of the governmental institutions here and along Sejong-ro has made this an assembly point for political protests over the years, to the extent that there is a near-permanent deployment of riot police equipped with batons, shields stacked nearby, and vehicles ranging from the semi-military equipped with water cannon through to coaches painted in police livery. The demonstrations are generally peaceful, but persistent, so tensions build up to flashpoint over longer periods of time, with protests often related to trade unions and labour relations, trade deals and military relationships with the United States, and most recently in 2017, enormous demonstrations and counter-demonstrations of between 500,000 and 1.5 million people spilling beyond the square demanding the impeachment of President Park Geun-Hye. The location is symbolic as well as practical: the focal point of public democracy is the city square and the city hall: protests here attract more attention and are taken more seriously.

There is a monumentality to Seoul City Hall, both old and new, and that function of architecture is often overlooked in contemporary debates. The notion had a revival of course in the work of Aldo Rossi, whose Architecture of the City develops a theory of monumentality as either propelling or pathological (1982:59). This is summarized by Peter Eisenman in his introduction:

> When a monument retards the process of urbanization, it is conspired by Rossi to be 'pathological'. The Alhambra in Granada is an example of one such part of a city functioning as a museum piece. In the city whose analogue is the skeleton, such a museum piece is like an embalmed body: it gives only the appearance of being alive. (Eisenman in Rossi, 1982:6)

According to this formulation, old Seoul City Hall was transformed from a pathological monument preventing the city from moving on to a propelling one, whilst the aims of the architectural competition were to produce a forward-looking structure; it quickly calcifies and runs the risk of being another pathological monument. This is prevented by the square and the relationship the building has with this public space. Attempts are made to privatize this, of course: often under the guise of special events and entertainment such as a large ice rink in the winter months. This seemingly innocuous insertion into previously public space runs the risk of privatizing the space more permanently as events fill the calendar, providing revenue and diverting the awkward spectacle of protest to other venues.

These examples, alongside newly commissioned (and problematic) structures such as Dongdaemun Design Plaza by Zaha Hadid Architects, are part of a long-term project to construct an image of Seoul as a viable 'world city'. Part of this process is the demonstration of Korean culture through the restoration of an old landmark and a forward-looking defiance of a potentially pathological monument.

# The urbanism of collection

Rapid urban development in South Korean cities resulted in the loss of much of the traditional courtyard housing stock, particularly as they are inefficient uses of the available land, unable to accommodate the increasing population density in cities hemmed in by mountains. The symbolism of the 'traditional' home is significant, and selected details are seen to be emblematic of the hanok: the windowless walls to the street, the substantial tiled roof (Figure 4.12), facing on to the courtyard, and sophisticated underfloor heating are all retained. The construction materials are designed to have the appearance of masonry and tile, but these are an affectation: decorative features applied to a carefully poured in situ concrete wall. Modern living also demands more space, so the hanok is larger, still appearing to be single storey, but in fact making use of the topography to accommodate garages for cars and other expansions of the house specification. The established rules of the new hanok (Figure 4.13) accommodate these innovations along with the use of modern materials in areas which are not seen: structures of concrete are acceptable for basements and even walls, so long as externally, these are decorated in the appropriate imitative fashion.

**FIGURE 4.12** *Author's photograph of roof lines of hanok house district.*

**FIGURE 4.13** *Author's photograph of modern hanok.*

The architecture of collection has two key implications as understood in this chapter: it has a direct relationship with colonialism, even where it is attempting to redress that balance in some way, it is with reference to the body of theory emerging from this challenge to Western dominance in academia and geopolitics more broadly. The second is that collecting is a way of organizing and bringing order to the world: a form of organization that might have unreal or jarring results, as it abstracts things from their context. Anthropology as a discipline has context at its heart: this is a kind of extreme contextualization, directly opposed to modernist tabula rasa approaches where the desire for starting from a fresh piece of territory erases something essential from the social fabric and cultural memory attached to a place. Collection and cultural display, for all the benefits of allowing for communication and understanding, are fraught with dangers meaning that care must be taken in order to allow the qualities of resonance and wonder to emerge without harm to the people we are being asked to identify with, ensuring that their voices are heard and that misunderstandings and assumptions are not made.

Not all collection is cross-cultural, of course, as we see in the example of the open-air museums and courtyard house typology. Such attempts to re-present our own histories are just as difficult to manage, of course. The underlying intention of such activities can be problematic, either freezing a living tradition at a certain point or constructing a false narrative, one which supports an agenda which might appear essential or positive at the time. The intentions become more and more apparent over time, as does the artifice driving the collection: meaning that the narrative, however useful it is, becomes suspect as a constructed fiction serving a purpose rather than historical facts which serve to contextualize peoples' lives.

## Notes

1. See Baudrillard (1994) and Lucas (2014) for more on this, particularly as it relates to the keeping of a sketchbook.
2. See Greenblatt (1991) for a full exploration of the themes of resonance and wonder.
3. One question architects often ask when presented with anthropologically based works is the status of the anthropologist within that context: are they more than mere tourists or postcolonialist adventurers? What is the value in an outsider trying to understand these events or objects which might be much more swiftly explained by someone who actually uses them in their everyday life? There are various forms of anthropology of course, but one aspect of the study is to position oneself as a curious outsider, asking naive questions in order to unpack the deeper details of what is happening.
4. Papua New Guinea, and the study of malanggan is not restricted to Küchler, of course: a wide range of anthropological approaches have been taken to both this region and these artefacts. Others have discussed malanggan in order to pursue alternative theoretical agendas. Marilyn Strathern (2001) uses the sculptures as a lens through which to view Western intellectual property debates, and Miyazaki (2010) develops this into a discussion of the familiar themes of gifts and exchanges. Janet Hoskins further uses the malanggan to develop the themes of agency and biography, drawing on earlier work by Alfred Gell.
5. See Hwangbo (2010) and Hwangbo & Jarzombek (2011) for more on these processes.
6. I have discussed museum studies, ideas of collection and the architect's sketchbook as a kind of museum in Lucas, R. 2014. 'The Sketchbook as Collection: A Phenomenology of Sketching' in Bartram, A., El-Bizri, N. & Gittens, D. (Eds.). *Recto-Verso: Redefining the Sketchbook*. Farnham: Ashgate. This chapter includes a detailed discussion of the Soane Museum, the Francis Bacon studio in Dublin, and contextualizes my sketching practice in the British Museum through the work of Baudrillard, Greenblatt and Elsner.
7. Both 'East' and 'West' are too wide ranging to be truly useful as categories given the enormous variety present in each region. Contemporary theory discusses the 'global North' and 'global South': indicators of the concentration of wealth in the Northern Hemisphere which are argued to be more useful, if similarly broad categories.
8. Indeed, Japan is a notable exception due to its long period of near isolation called *Sakoku*, lasting from the 1630s to 1853 when American Black Ships forced the opening of Japan's markets.
9. There is obviously a wider critique of contemporary architectural practice to be made within the framework of Said's theory: the export of architectural expertise from the West to the East such as detailed by Stanek (2012), the exoticization of non-Western works as a misunderstanding of their

context and the extreme decontextualization encouraged by contemporary competition-based commissioning for grand projects.

10   See Scott Lukas (2012) for a sociologically informed history of the theme park centred on American examples.
11   The most extreme example here is the ethnographic collection. It can be argued that outdated practices of display in such museums offer as much understanding as potential misunderstanding aside from the moral and ethical considerations of placing a group of people on display without their explicit permission or input.
12   See Rossi (1982) for more on his distinction between 'pathological' and 'propelling' monuments.
13   See Lebbeus Woods (1996, 1997) for more on his strategies towards scar tissue and other forms of 'radical reconstruction' in war-damaged architecture, particularly in the former Yugoslavia.
14   Japanese periods run according to the Emperor's reign; Shōwa Emperor Hirohito's dates are 1926–1989, and the era name often used as a short hand to refer to pre–Second World War Japanese architecture when European construction techniques were combined with Japanese detailing in an early example of critical regionalism.
15   See Hwangbo (2010) for more on the conservation strategies used for hanok houses in South Korea.
16   As documented in: Kim, Dan Bi & Lee, Jae Soek (Eds.). 2016. *Hanok, Korean Traditional Architecture: 2011–2016 National Hanok Competition*. Seoul: Architecture & Urban Research Institute & Kim Dae Ik.
17   Cho, Byoungso. 2018. 'Imperfection and Emptiness' in *Architectural Review* 1448, February 2018, pp. 44–50.
18   See Hwangbo & Jarzombek (2011) for more on this.

# 5

# Marketplaces and Sites of Exchange

## Introduction

This chapter discusses marketplaces through a number of theoretical lenses. As one would expect, theories of exchange feature strongly here, as these unpack the details of how people trade materials, goods and services. Anthropological accounts of exchange explore ideas of economies other than the dominant mode of capitalism, seeing that there are means of trade other than through monetary equivalence. Foundational to this is Marcel Mauss's influential study of *gifts*. Whilst conventionally thought of as acts of generosity, Mauss observed that gifts are often accompanied by obligation and reciprocity. By accepting a gift, you enter into a social relationship where, at some point, you will make an equivalent offering; should one refuse the gift, then the perception could be that social relations are being refused or rejected: a serious insult.

Such exchanges are the focus of the sub-discipline of economic anthropology instigated by the likes of Hart and Hann. A more general theory of practice is also explored here, but could easily be applied to any of the typologies under discussion. In economic exchange, the practices around trading are apparent and based on rules, making them an excellent example for the discussion of practice. Theories of practice turn their eye to the things that we do and the ways in which we do them. This set of theories explores how we know the world through the skills we use and how constellations of those skills constitute an embodied lifeworld known as a *habitus*. To a skilled negotiator, the world is constituted of opportunities, margins and negotiations: their skilled practices influence how they understand the world. Other collections of skills offer alternative understandings, such as that of the marketplace porters and couriers who know one market intimately, or the most efficient routes between markets and retail, respectively. For these individuals, the market is a spatial construct, understood at different extents of scale.

The spaces designed most completely around practices of exchange are marketplaces. These sites could be described as perfect images of the rules of engagement of that market, describing the tacit understandings and explicit rules governing position, extent, neighbours, competition and trust. Two examples are discussed: Tsukiji seafood market in Tokyo, which was decommissioned in 2018, and Namdaemun general market in Seoul, which borders a commercial retail zone on one side, and a business district on another, and a third border provided by one of the ancient gates to the city.

## Theories of exchange

Exchange is an important set of theories governing how we trade goods, according to various economic models such as barter and monetary exchange. This chapter focuses on marketplaces as a type, describing them as architecture characterized by their practised nature. Theories of practice constitute a relatively recent *turn* in theory where a large number of writers focus on a particular theory or method in order to explore what affordances it has for producing fresh understandings of familiar problems. Whilst this might seem to be a kind of academic fashionability, it is helpful to have a body of work which is operating in concert in order to reassess old assumptions about an issue and to express something useful about a topic.

The shift to considerations of practice is not a new phenomenon, having some of its origins in positions taken by Wittgenstein and then a wave of ethnographically informed work, including Pierre Bourdieu, Anthony Giddens, Jean François Lyotard and Michel Foucault. Each approaches the topic in a different way, but the editors of *The Practice Turn in Contemporary Theory* (Schatzki, Knorr Cetina & von Savigny, 2001:2) situate the concept as arrays of activity. This allows for a great diversity of opinions as to what constitutes an activity, as well as considerations of whether nonhuman actors can be understood to engage in activity and have practices. Practice theory underlines a dependence between activity and skill in the production of knowledge and understanding. Practices are seen as the activity of putting skills into use. This has implications for the body engaging in that action, returning theorists to physicality and embodiment. This places the human body itself at the threshold between skills and their application in the world, constituting a *habitus* as more than a collection of related practices, but instead an understanding of the lifeworld brought about through the exercise of a practice.

In order to understand exchange, a number of theories are helpful: Michel de Certeau and Pierre Bourdieu's pioneering work on practice and habitus; Marcell Mauss's foundational work on the gift as prototypical form of economic activity introduces ideas of reciprocity and obligation. Arjun Appadurai's work is foundational to material culture studies and brings the focus on exchange back to the goods at the centre of that transaction. Appadurai explores the implications of objects having careers, moving from one status category to another depending on their wider political, social and economic contexts. Further examinations of status are explored in Alfred Gell's work on marketplaces, where he diagrams and maps the overlapping structure of a marketplace. This sets the scene for Theodore Bestor's detailed examination of Tsukiji seafood market in Tokyo before decamping to a new site at Toyosu.

The chapter is completed with a kind of manifesto for the market typology, drawing a little on the spirit of Rem Koolhaas's famous *retroactive manifesto for Manhattan* in *Delerious New York* (1994). The marketplace is an important architectural site, one which has lessons for a kind of radical mobility and temporality in architecture. It is an architecture of interlocking habitus: collections of practices which allow the porter to understand the site differently from the vendor or the buyers. Theories of practice allow us to understand how each of us frames our encounters with the world through the skilled encounters we have with it.

A deeper understanding of these fundamentals of economic anthropology and gift economies is essential for a detailed understanding of our sites of exchange, informing the design of individual commercial units, department stores, malls or market buildings. Each has its own needs and requirements, but a detailed assessment of these is based on reciprocity and trust, practices and habitus, the embodied knowledge of assessing goods in a trade. As a sub-discipline, economic anthropology looks to understand the underlying principles of exchange. This has its own history – a concern held as long as anthropology in general – and is partly founded in an idea of seeking more just alternatives to the dominant models in use in the industrialized world. Contemporary economic anthropology responds to the substantivist work of Karl Polyani rather than formalist classical economics and articulated by anthropologists Keith Hart and Chris Hann (2011:55). Formalist approaches prioritize fundamental categories and elements of exchange, such as scarcity, utility and profit, found in conventional economics, tracing the appearance of these features in the cases reported through ethnography. The substantivist approach works back from the ethnography and the empirical data contained there. Substantivist anthropology conceptualizes economic activity as a socially produced system rather than as underlying laws or rules which can then generate a variety of approaches. Polyani reinforced a historical division between pre-industrial economies and their basis in reciprocity, describing how abstract 'market' of industrial societies operates to delocalize or disembed economy from its context. Hart and Hann's approach involves returning to macro-economics of global systems and nation-states in a discipline more commonly concerned with the small scale and specific. Money is discussed not as a commodity, but as *purchasing power* (2011:60), and is a token representing your claim; this is in opposition to the formalist approach of seeing money as a technological development from barter systems, a logical conclusion of a presumed intellectual development. Other aspects such as land and labour (2011:71) are expressed as 'fictitious commodities' in contrast to the very real foodstuffs or building materials which constitute an actual commodity.

## Exchange as practice

Certain key elements of Michel de Certeau's work stand out as being of particular interest for architecture: *Walking in the City* (1984:91–110) and *Spatial Stories* (1984:115–130). Here, de Certeau discusses the theoretical implications of how we walk around the city, how we engage with it and how we make our way from one place to another. He builds a theory of how we not only understand space, but also mobilize *any* skill, any set of understandings and set them into *practice*. This is a theory of practice less specific than the understanding of professional practice in architecture (or any other similarly validated profession).

de Certeau is interested in developing an understanding of the spatial practices we engage with in the city. People engage with different spatial practices according to their circumstances, and each city presents a set of conditions determined by its population, typology and morphology, terrain and climate. This gives rise to secondary conditions, including density, where the interaction between high population and limited terrain makes for a city of towers, with more people housed in less land. This creates a set of conditions which determine the practices required to live and work there.

Rural or wilderness settings also alter our engagement with space fundamentally. The basis of our understanding of the space changes, as does the nature of social life possible in that space. Rather than ironing out the differences, as a map might render the countryside in a continuity with towns, villages and cities, there is a fundamentally altered basis for understanding the countryside which has its roots in the openness of space, the increased exposure to the elements, the life going on around and many more issues. A useful diagram to contrast with the map might be the urbanist and botanist Patrick Geddes's 'valley section' drawing (Figure 5.1) which depicts various practices and how they relate to the landscape: from miners in the hills,

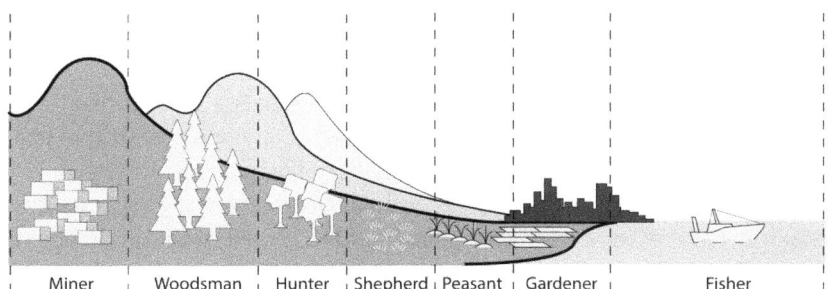

**FIGURE 5.1** *Author's redrawing of Patrick Geddes's drawing 'The Association of the Valley Plan with the Valley Section'.*

through woodsmen and hunters in forests, and towards shepherds and farmers before arriving at the central market town lower down the valley. The section ends at the coast with fishing activities by the dock.[1]

There is, of course, no single way of understanding the countryside. A farmer, for example, sees this environment entirely differently to a tourist or a rambler. The farmer sees a landscape which they have stewardship over and for which they are responsible. The farmer is aware of the seasons, the harshness of the winter and the productivity of the land. The tourist and rambler might have similar awareness and some overlapping interest in seeing the country as a *landscape*, that is to say something distant and unspoilt[2]: to be appreciated at a distance as something visually pleasing: as something *to be preserved*.

The city is also subject to alternative *spatial practices* depending upon one's reasons for being there. These spatial practices refer to the concrete ways in which people engage with their environment not merely different perceptions; each habitus constitutes an entirely different way of understanding the city through one's actions there. de Certeau argues that 'every story is a travel story – a spatial practice' (1984:115); he argues that we organize our daily routines into narrative structures when relaying them to others, giving form to the day and organizing our perceptions in retrospect.

We can see here that there is a direct relationship to wayfinding and navigation here,[3] but the key thing to understand is the most clearly obvious: that practices are the things that we do and the way in which they are done. The spatial practices of a night-shift security guard (and I speak from some experience of this due to a stint when I was a student) are rather different from a regular commuter. The city is understood and *enacted* differently by this group of people, who sleep at different times, travel at different times and inhabit the city in a different manner. de Certeau speaks of geographies as plural here, and this is a good way of understanding the spatial practice: as a *geography in process*, one under construction.

In simple terms, using the bus or metro is a practice distinct from that of walking around the city. Each comes with a particular understanding of space, a way of interacting and getting practically from one place to another.

In a slight reversal of the language we would conventionally use, de Certeau speaks of '*space as a practiced place*' (1984:117). Normally in architecture we would speak of *place*[4] as the practised, as the experienced and lived space, which is overly geometric. Restating the idea according to our own conventions that *place is a practised space* makes a good deal more sense. de Certeau continues in this vein to develop an example from the work of phenomenologist Maurice Merleau Ponty (1984:117): a distinction between *geometric* space and *anthropological* space. This multiplicity of spatiality is of interest architecturally: that our experience, memory, dreams and aspirations as well as more pragmatic factors such as class, occupation, gender identity – all contribute to the *space* we experience.

The geometric understanding of space does not account for the possibilities of other perspectives and limits the scope of understanding experiential and socially produced spaces. de Certeau critiques this as a 'univocity' in the dominant formal and Cartesian readings of space. His point is that such an understanding is too limiting and that there is always a multiplicity at work.

The notion that both *space is existential* and *existence is spatial* lies at the heart of de Certeau's applicability to architecture. If spatiality is elevated to existentialism, then we are speaking of it as nothing less than a mode of *Being* expressed through *spatial practices*. These practices operate in groups called *habitus*. This is fundamental to understand the importance of the wider environment, of context and site. Where we are and how we act there is intertwined with our very core, our existence.

For de Certeau, space has a mobile character and is constituted of movements rather than being static and fixed as in the description of *geometrical* space given by Merleau-Ponty. This all reads as something of a critique and attack on Cartesian geometry, coordinate systems and the delineation of form: all things which architects employ on a regular basis. The critique is, however, to move away from *only* understanding space in this way. Purely geometrical understandings of space are too often presented as inherent scientific facts when they are one of many ways to understand the environment we live in. Architects can continue to use this shared understanding where it is useful, mindful that other spatialities co-exist and can offer just as much to the design process.

For de Certeau, space is constituted of directions, speeds and timeframes. Space is composed of the practices we engage in there. Environments are more than merely abstract forms which we negotiate, but are instead co-produced by our socially informed interactions with them: spaces, according to de Certeau, are a bundle or knotting of practices – *practices* of mining or other material gathering, *practices* of making, *practices* of distribution, *practices* of use, and *practices* of disposal. Even where an item is at rest, it is only there as a result of practices. As shown later, the marketplace is a rounded example of architecture as practice, with informal arrangements iteratively designed in order to maximize economic benefit for the vendor.

## Habitus and the temporality of practices

The collection of groups of practices is discussed in detail by Pierre Bourdieu in his 1980 work, *The Logic of Practice*. His work is complementary to de Certeau's and seeks to find an underlying structure to the practices described. Bourdieu finds this to be the *habitus*, which are:

> systems of durable, transposable dispositions, structured structures predisposed to function as structuring structures, that is, as principles which generate and organize practices and representations that can be objectively adapted to their outcomes without presupposing a conscious aiming at ends or an express mastery of the operations necessary in order to attain them. Objectively 'regulated' and 'regular' without being in any way the product of obedience to rules, they can be collectively orchestrated without being the product of the organizing action of a conductor. (Bourdieu, 1990[1980]:53)

Habitus can therefore be understood as a meta-practice, an organizing principle for a set of activities. This organizing principle, as Bourdieu calls them *structuring structures*, can be used to *transfer* practices from one circumstance to another. This transferability lies at the heart of an approach which renders activity in one sphere applicable to another. One example can be found in the example of the Papua New Guinea *malanggan* discussed in Chapter 4 with reference to the work of anthropologist Suzanne Küchler. In certain malanggan, there is a representation of knotting and pleating on the surface of carved wooden sculptures. These representations have a degree of accuracy denoting the experience of the carver in making knots. The *habitus* of knotting is applicable both to the literal tying of ropes and to the carving of a sculpture. More than a motif, the knot is a form of *practice* and *understanding* which can be transferred from one circumstance to another. Habitus complicates theories of practice which might at first appear to speak in such self-evident and everyday terms as to be useless. The opposite is true, however, as practices are so fundamental and basic to our being, forming a fundamental theory of how we act in and upon the world over time. The ways in which an understanding from one circumstance, one practice, can influence another is central to habitus. These are the constituent parts of our multiple *ways of living* and as such can be said to lie at the heart of anthropology's project as a discipline.

Bourdieu notes that approaches to habitus and practice are *not* a process of obedience. These are not social rules, but are instead ways in which we have been encultured to act. This is another important distinction, for there are other terms for the social norms and constraints which are artificially imposed, for example, by religious belief, capitalist economic pressures or other large social structures. Habitus is a collection of unconsciously enacted practices which define everyday life: learnt behaviours which allow us to navigate broad societal organizations. This takes practice into the territory of collectivity and practices as behaviours which we might not have full control over. Practices can enforce normative expectations, controlling our actions through subtle influences rather than explicit laws and constraints (Bourdieu, 1990[1980]:54).

Habitus is therefore historical and can enforce a set of practices in a manner much more powerful than explicit social constraints and laws. Bourdieu's term *dispositions* is key to understanding this: that habitus is a set of attitudes and ways of being, moving and interacting with the world. Habitus is implicit rather than explicit; we reinforce our past by re-enacting past practices, framed within an overall structure of habitus. While Bourdieu discusses examples of habitus and practice which fall into the category of ritual, he contrasts these activities with economic exchange and gift giving. The manner of this distinction is expressed in terms of the temporality of the practice. Where rituals can be understood to have an a-temporal quality, outside of the everyday lived existence of people and presented as an eternal present, there is another quality to the time spent in everyday and non-symbolic exchange practices.

Exchange practices can refer to economic exchanges, gender-based exchanges such as marriages, and also to gift-giving and other status-based exchanges. Gifts are one of the most theorized exchanges in anthropology, seen as a fundamental category from which we can learn a great deal about other forms of exchange (Figure 5.2).

A distinction can be said to lie in the quality of the reversibility or irreversibility of a practice. Exchanges are cyclical and move in a direction from one phase to another, eventually returning to the start. To short-cut this as a simple reflection, however, would be to heighten the nature of obligation in the gift-giving practice. The implications of returning this gift to the giver are deep, containing elements of offence caused, of a lack of acceptance, and it would be difficult for a friendship or other relationship to survive the return or refusal of a gift on the wrong terms.[5]

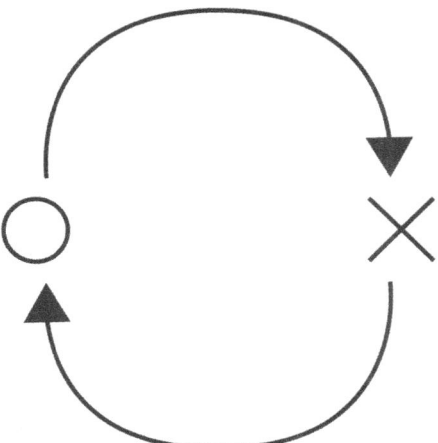

**FIGURE 5.2** *Diagram of cyclical gift giving and of reflective obligation.*

This is presented by Bourdieu as an activity that is a collective denial of objective reality. Gifts are given to represent relationships, as a way of forming or strengthening the social bonds between individuals or between groups of people. We subscribe to this alternative reality when engaging in gift-giving practices, maintaining an artifice that gift exchange is a selfless act with no motivation other than an altruistic expression of love, friendship or solidarity. We see in the next section that this is a kind of social fiction, and that gift giving implicates us in a series of reciprocal exchanges and that gifts often come with an obligation to respond in kind at some later point. This sounds very cynical of course, but it is the role of social theorists to question and understand such processes by which we construct our social identities.

The collection of skills possessed by an architect constitutes a habitus, framing our encounters with the world around us. Training of the architect's perception allows the architect to understand examples of architecture in terms of their underlying planning, materiality and historical context. Other skills would include drawing, another practice of observation which informs our knowledge of the world even when we are not actually drawing. Arranging space conceptually through conventions such as plan and section gives us a way of organizing and arranging our perceptions.

## Reciprocity, obligation and the gift

Marcel Mauss's classic account of *The Gift* (2002[1954]) is one of anthropology's best-known and most debated texts. He uses the model of gift giving as a way of exploring broader economic exchanges, finding gifts to have a fundamental social function of reinforcing connections between people, of producing bonds of reciprocity and obligation.

Reciprocity is one of the most important concepts discussed by Mauss and describes the manner in which one person giving a gift might, at some point in the future, expect one in return. There is, then, despite the altruism of gift giving, an obligation built in to the act: the expectation that the receiver will return the favour at some point in the future.

Reciprocity exists in other forms of exchange, of course. More direct monetary and economic exchange comes with rules and tokens for the exchange in question (money), but the play of altruism and obligation in gift giving is particularly interesting. Mauss argues that, in gift exchange, an unreciprocated gift damages the standing of that individual (2002[1954]:83).

According to Mauss, exchanges are a way of placing people on an equal footing. Writing on the *Rules of Generosity*, Mauss notes that in the case of the Andaman Islands, gifts are used as part of marriage ceremonies. The exchange of gifts ensures that the families joined by a wedding are made equivalent, with gift giving replacing direct communication from the point of the wedding onwards (2002[1954]:25). This ability of a practice to stand in for another shows an interchangeability of activities, a mechanism by which symbolism can emerge.

We can see these examples of anthropological research reveal some of the complexity possible within gift exchange. Rather than consider this as an extreme or exotic example, it is important to consider it as an example of the diversity possible in human relationships, even where those relationships have familiar parameters and elements. Gifts are given in a wide range of cultures, but those exchanges are considered differently in each case. Anthropology, by virtue of giving us such interesting examples, illuminates the variety possible across such simple practices.[6] What is clear is that there are different gift-giving cultures within any region, dependent on factors including but not limited to ethnicity, religion, social class and even location.

Mauss finds the tradition of *potlatch* (derived from the Chinook word *potshatl*) found in various Pacific Northwest indigenous societies (also present in a different form in Melanesia) to be one of the most revealing and pure forms of gift exchange. Typical potlatches involve vast banquets held in the honour of another clan. The hosts of the celebration gain status by making an extravagant gesture in honour of their guests. This is a conspicuous expenditure of wealth, demonstrating the surplus you have to spare for such a celebration. Mauss takes the term and applies broadly it to this *form* or *genre* of exchange regardless of origin and expresses gift economies as extending beyond the bounds of material objects.[7]

This develops into a concept of *a system of total services*.[8] Mauss holds that there is no such thing as a natural state of barter or exchange in humanity and that all such practices are socially specific and constructed. The potlatch is a coming together of families or clans in which there is a vast display of goods, services, honour and rituals. One function of the potlatch is to redistribute status across a social group. Importantly, hunting rights can also be given in potlatch, representing the rights individuals have to use the land for their own sustenance. These goods and services are literally *given* and performed in honour of the guest group. The law of reciprocity *demands* that the guests must later strive towards an equal display, be that a feast, a gift or a performance. This can get out of hand, and sometimes resulting in violent clashes which, importantly, *are not regarded as outside of the exchange, but wholly part of it*.

One of the most extreme forms of potlatch involves the destruction of goods by the hosts in honour of the other clan, perhaps even involving the killings of chiefs and nobles (2002 [1954]:8). This extreme competition is one of the justifications given for outlawing the practice in Canada in 1884 (a law only repealed in 1951), but the suppression of indigenous culture had a broader intention of bringing communities into the societal norms established by European settlers.

In unpacking the Melanesian form of potlatch exchange, Mauss addresses the risk in not reciprocating fully or properly: that participants lose status in the form of social capital and prestige (known as *mana*).[9] With potlatches occurring to mark important life events as well as to mark a trade festival, it is clear that such exchanges are a part of life which structures time and experience; these are events which must be prepared for. Once one has gained social capital through potlatch, there is a constant risk of losing it, so goods and services must be given away.

It is important to link these gift-giving activities back to the idea of *practice* discussed above. Mauss's work predates the theories of practice discussed, but this theory elaborates upon the theory of the gift. Practices of gift giving are varied and are temporal practices where the direction of travel cannot be reversed so much as placed into a self-perpetuating cycle of repetition. Gift-giving events require common subscription; they must remain *observed* as celebrations, or the practices will die out.[10]

> A considerable part of our morality and our lives themselves are still permeated with this same atmosphere of the gift, where obligation and liberty intermingle. Fortunately, everything is still not wholly categorized in terms of buying and selling. Things still have sentimental as well as venal value, assuming values merely of this kind exist. We possess more than a tradesman morality. There still remain people and classes that keep to the morality of former times, and we almost all observe it, at least at certain times of the year or on certain occasions. (Mauss 2002 [1954]: 83)

Mauss notes that one element of the gift which is of crucial importance, and often criticised or problematized, is *extravagance* (2002[1954]:88). Making a show of generosity to the potential embarrassment of others has the effect of belittling the receiver, or at least making them feel awkward at receiving something of such high value or effort with a potential worry over how they can afford to reciprocate. This also denotes self-aggrandisement on the part of receiver, for they can nurture a belief in their own superiority confirmed and corroborated by such behaviour through an internal process of justification in which the receiver considers that they have performed some vague undefined service towards the gift giver which makes them worthy of such excess.

Writing on Art, Anthropology and the Gift, Roger Sansi discusses some of the implications of the gift in Mauss and later anthropologists' work. The idea that 'one gives one's self while giving' (Mauss, 2002:227) is interesting in the context of not only art (which Sansi is writing about here (2015:11)), but also architecture. The public-minded architect might well think of their work in part at least as a gift, due to the personal investment in the process of design. This giving leads to an idea of the 'particle person' discussed by Marilyn Strathern (1988), later elaborated into Alfred Gell's notion of distribution of agency (1998:103). If we give something of ourself via a gift, then our selfhood becomes scattered across the people and places it has been given to. The power problematic raised by Mauss and Strathern is never far away, however, and a 'gift' of architecture may instead be an imposition, underlining the status of the architect as professional and expert, indicating hierarchy and power, with an obligation to the receiver to maintain and care for this work. Sansi suggests some solutions might lie in the work of relational art practices (2015:101), where a genuine generosity takes the place of the obligation-laden gift.

## The material culture of exchange

Another important aspect of exchange lies in its material culture. As part of an agenda-setting collection, anthropologist Arjun Appadurai describes *Commodities and the Politics of Value* (1986:3–63) and the ways in which objects in exchanges can have a different status at various points in their biographies. Appadurai's work traces objects and their trajectories, looking at how they operate in a social context at each stage of their careers. The most useful aspect of his analysis is the commodity phase of objects (1986:13):

1. The commodity phase of the social life of any thing
2. The commodity candidacy of any thing
3. The commodity context in which any thing may be placed.

## MARKETPLACES AND SITES OF EXCHANGE

This schema conceptualizes the object as being able to move between states, at one time available for sale as a commodity, another time so laden with symbolic meaning or association with personhood that it is not. This is where theories of exchange come into contact with material culture studies: that the notion of commodity is itself not fixed. If commodity is considered to be a phase, rather than an inherent quality, then it opens up the question of how and when it becomes a candidate for exchange, and what the context of this exchange is. Appadurai therefore discusses commodities as being 'things in a certain situation' (1986:13).

The most spatial element of this is the *commodity context*, speaking directly to the ways in which different spaces of exchange operate. The expectations of an auction house, marketplace, supermarket and department store are all quite distinctive from one another (Figure 5.3), such that the same goods might be for sale in each. The qualities of the interaction between vendor and buyer are mediated by the context, variously arranged to allow negotiation, display, demonstration or comparison with similar products.

Appadurai draws on the work of Georg Simmel to discuss the inherent value of exchange practices, noting that the act of engaging produces that value; it does not reside in the thing itself. It follows, then, that this socially produced value is subject to various forms of politics: of display, authenticity,

**FIGURE 5.3** *Author's Photographs showing the architecture of various forms of economic exchange: Namdaemun Market, Wako Department Store, Prada boutique.*

knowledge, expertise and connoisseurship, of supply and demand (1986:57). As such, the project of economic anthropology is not so much to overturn Marx's work on political economy as to add ever greater nuance to it.

## Tsukiji market, Tokyo

Anthropologist Theodore Bestor's ethnography of Tsukiji fish market in Tokyo explores the daily life of this institution and contributes theoretical insights to some of the broader aspects of the anthropology of marketplaces.

Crucially, the market is established as a set of practices (Figure 5.4) which interact with one another, from the porters who move the produce from one area to another to the skilled cutting of expensive tuna, the actual buying and selling of the fish, and the integration of the food into Japanese life, with the influence this has on which cuts and colours are perceived to be the most desirable.

Tsukiji has elements both of a globalized marketplace and of the specificity of Japan, even Tokyo. As the largest seafood market in the world, produce arrives here from across the globe and is bought and sold for domestic as well as overseas consumption. Bestor describes this not as international or global, but as something else entirely: as *trans*national, as surpassing and moving entirely beyond the notion of sovereign states and towards a complete statelessness. The economics of the market is only briefly touched upon in the account of the market (Figure 5.5), which, like any other endeavour, is constituted of people and practices.

Bestor traces the tuna fishermen off the New England coast (Bestor 2004:301–320) to this fish market in Tokyo. His focus for this work is the controversial trade in Bluefin tuna. The species of fish in question is

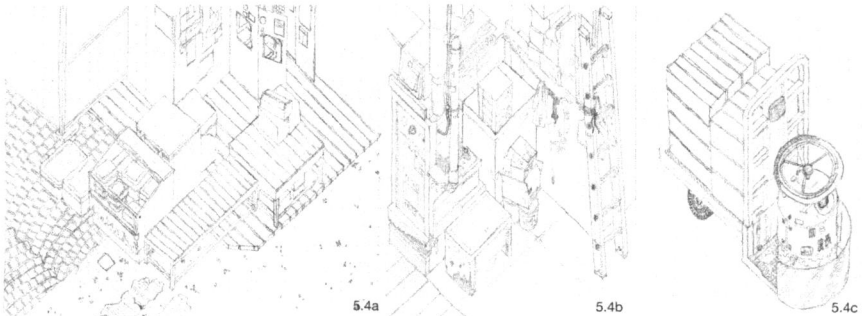

**FIGURE 5.4** *Drawings showing front (a) and rear (b) of Tsukiji market stall and turret truck (c) used for transportation of goods within the market.*

**FIGURE 5.5** *Author's Photographs of Tsukiji market.*

large, powerful and fast; they migrate thousands of miles every year, and the quality of the fish has strong cultural associations for those who pay the highest prices for prized specimens (particularly during the first auction of the new year, where the often inflated price is an indicator of the confidence of the market). This study is an example of how intimate knowledge of the workings of an institution is essential to understanding how to design for it. One could approach Bestor's anthropology of this site as a deep form of site analysis, allowing for design interventions or a whole new market[11] to be designed on the basis of the detailed account given. Understanding the roles of everyone working there in an integrated fashion from the porters to the sellers to those cutting the fish or testing quality all contribute to a more complete picture of the site. Where available, the work of anthropologists can be used to gain a deeper understanding of the specific cultural and social aspects of a given place.

The theoretical implications of Bestor's research can be applied to different places. For example, following the path of a commodity around the world, looking in to how it is sourced, caught, freighted, assessed, sold, bought and consumed, gives us a picture that moves beyond our easy assumptions and towards a full understanding of the economics, cultural and social significance of any practice, place, event or material. These are the forces which indirectly influence the architecture, either in its initial building, or how it becomes adapted over time.

Bestor suggests that there is a direct connection between the practices of Japanese food preparation and consumption and the ways in which the market operates (2004:176), influencing global seafood consumption through their dominance of the market. Downturns in Tokyo can have an effect as far away New England or Cornwall. This extends to the value attached to certain types and degrees of quality of fish such as the absolute regularity of size, shape and colour required for produce consumed during wedding banquets. Practices are more than merely the things that people do and the peculiar ways in which they do them, they are deeply ingrained and encultured ways of life, understanding and knowledge of the world embodied in some of our most fundamental interactions: these are echoed in other practices, embedded in connoisseurship, trading patterns and value judgements.

The ethnographic research conducted by Bestor is framed around a long-term engagement with the site of Tsukiji market and a range of the people who work there from porters to company bosses, locals who visit alongside tourists to the high-class restauranteurs who require the very best produce. The food culture of Japan and of the world at large is presented in microcosm by Tsukiji market. Bestor details the various agencies and actors who have a role in Tsukiji, including the governmental organizations and regulators through to shipping companies, various strata of buyers for the local and overseas markets, wholesalers and many, many more.

Practices include the cutting of the fish, specific forms of finger counting used in the auctioning of fish and the assessment of produce necessary for the top-level buyers. The market operation generally begins at 4 am (although some supporting activities begin at midnight), with the grading and arrangement of produce for the auctions which begin at 6 am (2004:177), described in a multisensory fashion with the lively soundscape of Styrofoam and bells, the mass movement of turret trucks and people, the flopping of live fish and attempts by crabs to escape their tanks.

Bestor describes parts of his research method as open ended, exploring the market for days on end in order to establish its geography. He expected to find organizations akin to neighbourhoods (2004:272) where the space was organized not according to the produce for sale: no section for tuna or for octopus, or where the high end Ginza buyers might all go. This was not the case, however, and the distribution of stalls appeared at first glance to be entirely random. Every 4 to 5 years, the stall locations are subject to a lottery and assigned randomly (Figure 5.6) rather than according to a rational system grouping dried fish, frozen fish and wet fish in subsections, or even separating fish from shellfish and other seafoods.[12] In Tsukiji, there is such a heightened

# MARKETPLACES AND SITES OF EXCHANGE

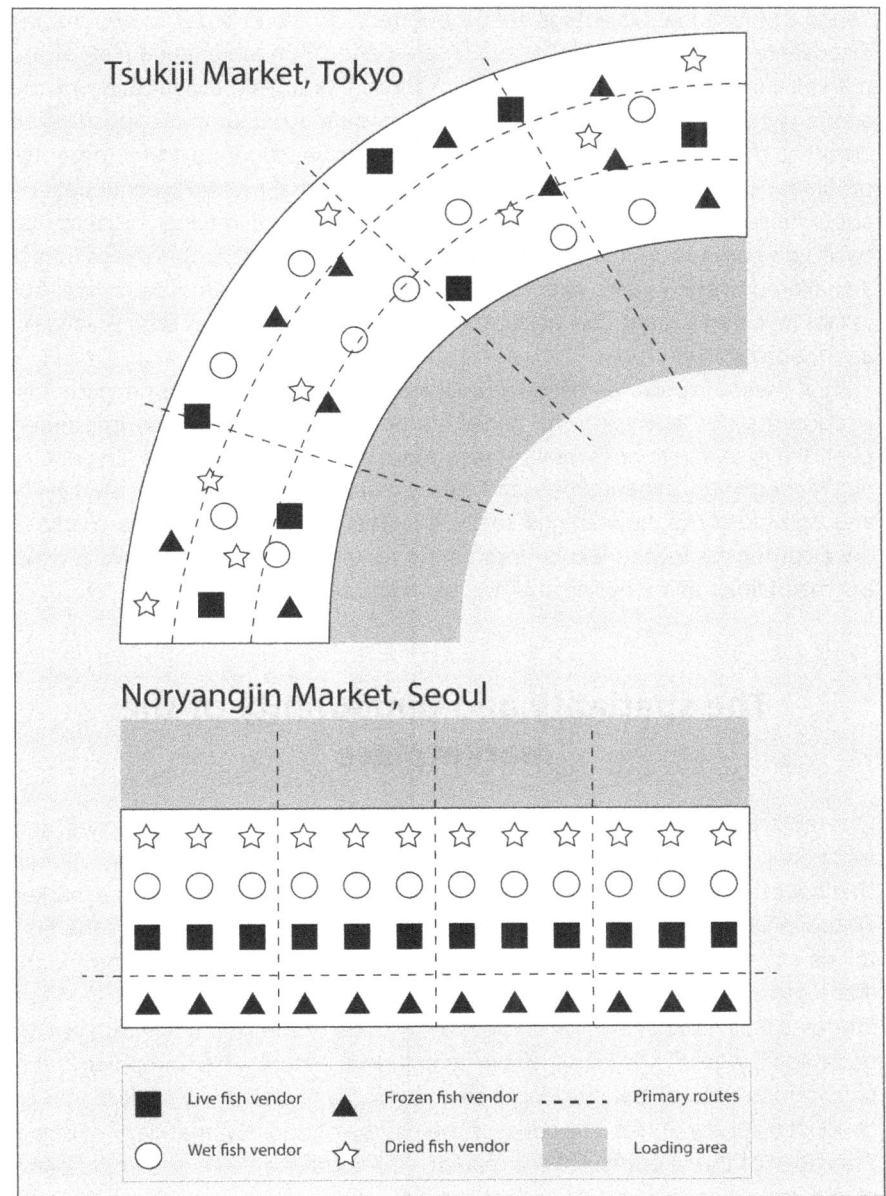

**FIGURE 5.6** *Contrasting layout of Tsukiji market (Tokyo) and Noryangjin market (Seoul).*

sense of locational advantage that the lottery is held in order to ensure any disadvantages aren't in play for too long a period. The fan-shaped plan of the market and high-pressure environment force this on the organization of the space, where peculiar plan forms, location near to columns or positioning closer to the market entrances can have a massive influence on the potential profits for each stall holder. Bestor himself admits that he had preconceptions about family relationships built over generations or a rational organization based on some technical specifications – the revelation that there was in fact a shake-up every 4 years seemed so illogical in terms of his expectation, but in fact revealed a great deal about the operation of the market both practically and theoretically.[13]

It is these discoveries based in everyday practices that become incredibly important when analysing the social life of a site. It takes a fully immersed period of research to understand these aspects of the marketplace: an enquiry not loaded with expectations and preconceptions, but open to the reality and complexity of how things really are. The latest phase in the market's development at Toyosu will be interesting to see how much of Tsukiji's ways are maintained and what new practices might emerge.

# The spatiality and temporality of the marketplace

One anthropologist who began to combine more graphic approaches and traditional ethnography was Alfred Gell. In the essay *The Market Wheel: Symbolic Aspects of an Indian Market* (1999:107–135), Gell describes a market village in Dhorai, central India. The temporality of the market is one of the first things mentioned by Gell: in common with many markets across the world, it is a site which is sometimes a market and sometimes not (1999:107). What interests Gell most of all here is the weekly cycle of the site. It is worth noting once again one of the aims of the longitudinal nature of anthropology: the physical features of the site could be surveyed in a day or two. Were you to conduct a survey of this site but over the course of one day, that day not being the Friday of the operation of the market, you might well miss the entire point of the exercise. This is a fairly flippant way of making a serious point. Each place will change over the seasons, from one day to the next, one week to another. By examining a place over a longer period, anthropologists gain more than just more data: there is a substantial difference in the kind of data given by a temporal approach to a site.

Importantly, Gell uses plans to describe and understand the site of the market. He uses diagrams to outline the actions of various vendors in the market, depicting a matrix of sellers from jewellers to dry goods salesmen and the three main constituencies of customer: *tribal*, *local Hindu* and *non-local Hindu*. His charts depict the complexity of these relations, which groups trade in money and which ones deal in barter goods, credit or services. Further context for the market is described diagrammatically, with other local markets mapped out across the course of the week, making it instantly clear that the regional marketplace reserves certain days for certain markets. It is clear that Dhorai does not operate in isolation, but is part of a network which operates as a total system.

Gell uses diagrams not only to explain the social relations to the reader, but as a way of revealing some of those interactions and correspondences (1999:121). The market represents broader societal interactions in a microcosm, the purchase of goods serving as a focused unit of analysis. He is careful not to extrapolate too much, but rather to use this instance to corroborate material he has gathered from other social contexts in the area. There two social structures are at play in this marketplace: one to do with social status and one to do with the hierarchy of the values of different kinds of goods, arranged in concentric zones (1999:121–122).

Gell's analysis considers the way in which jewellery retains its value and can be re-sold, keeping its status and exchange value, perhaps even rising over time. This inherent value of precious metals and stones gives this centrally placed stall even more status within the market, greater than other luxuries, which can be similarly expensive, but are not a 'permanent store of value' (1999:123).

The zones of the market, then, are numbered from the centre out to the periphery as follows:

1. Jeweller
2. Luxury goods (refined or processed)
3. Consumables (unrefined or raw materials)
4. Non-luxury cloth and dry goods
5. Vegetables and local crops
6. Low-prestige crafts and middlemen.

Two forms of axis are also presented:

*Radial*: Choices between the zones themselves are between fundamentally different types of value.

*Circumferential*: Economic choices within a given zone are made on the basis of value for money.

The maps and diagrams Gell develops not only describe his findings, but assist him in arriving at them. They represent abstractions of his long-term and sophisticated observations of the dual concentric and axial arrangements of this marketplace. The same can be true of any site analysis conducted by an architect sufficiently open to these overlapping practices of description. The ways in which architects engage with a site can be understood as a set of skilled practices appropriate to the profession. These practices are collected together, grouped as a *habitus*.

Writing in a more explicitly architectural frame (Mooshammer, Mörtenböck, Cruz & Forman, 2015; Mooshammer & Mörtenböck, 2015 & 2016), the market as architectural typology is rehabilitated and described as a global phenomenon estimated to represent up to 50 per cent of economic activity worldwide. Marketplaces are described as 'a locus of multiple forms of agreement' (2016:9) and as the most public of spaces. This has both a civic and an economic dimension, a site for negotiation. A feature of these spaces, operating as heterotopias (see Foucault, 1986), is that they do not function in isolation: markets, even the most informal, are networks of spaces, connecting sites of production with those of consumption, and linking one marketplace with another. As such, they are spaces of communication, of transmission. These unofficial and informal architectures are often ignored by architectural history and theory, falling outside of what we consider to 'be' architecture: their impermanence and flimsy materiality suggesting that they are something completely different from the received canon of architecture. They are, however, sophisticated reading and rewriting of space as a set of social relations. Designed by non-specialists with limited means and permission, they are nonetheless sophisticated articulations of spatial conditions arranged around exchange, communication and transmission. Bringing these marketplaces into the orbit of architectural debate requires a fundamental shift in our discipline, too often embedded in the neoliberal economy alone through mechanisms such as competition and commissioning, professional validation and indemnity insurance; the informal marketplace integrates some of the latest technologies (2016:18–20) in unexpected and innovative ways, makes efficient use of materials and occupies space with the lightest of touches. It exists at the threshold of the legitimate and illegitimate, the permitted and the illegal.

The benefits of the marketplace are sometimes hidden. Writing on his concept of black urbanism, Abdoumaliq Simone (2010:227) discusses one example of young women who make deliberate detours on the way home from their jobs as housekeepers and nannies in order to expose themselves to the opportunities represented by the market. This is characterised as a spontaneous decision to diverge from their usual routes and to move into spaces where they had few or no existing social connections. There were risks to both their employment status and their safety in these sojourns, but the diversion was understood to be worthwhile as opportunities might be available there. This built social capital in their discussions with others,

## MARKETPLACES AND SITES OF EXCHANGE

building a cache of experience that allowed them to be valuable sources of knowledge about their city.

Simone's theory of black urbanism develops with a focus on the contentiousness of language; it is notable that Simone deliberately conflates the sense of black as a racial denotation with illegality of the 'black market'. He posits this very illegality and, more correctly, informality as a way of organizing and understanding this form of encounter with the city. His argument is that the conflation suggests alternative or unconventional forms of regulation in these circumstances rather than an absence of regulation or legal frameworks. Rather than focusing on legitimacy, Simone's approach to urban economies is to look at how interactions are actually practiced and performed (2010:280).

## Namdaemun market as model

Namdaemun market in central Seoul is a general market selling a wide range of goods, including street food, clothing, and kitchenwares (Figure 5.7). It consists of around twenty-five buildings and the grid of streets connecting them. The buildings have blank façades, windows blocked out or covered

**FIGURE 5.7** *Author's photograph of Namdaemun market field site.*

with typography as the maximization of selling space dictates. The buildings have ground-floor units which open to the street selling traditional medicines, luggage and other higher value goods. The interiors are arranged thematically, with one building devoted to clothing for children, another for cookwares and another for wedding fabric and jewellery. These buildings are open for most of the working week, but take breaks on the first and third Sundays of the month. General hours of operation are midnight to 7 am for wholesalers, and then 7 am to 5 pm for most other retailers. The grid of streets varies most from one day to another; most days the main streets are crowded with the white enamelled steel carts provided by the city government and an ever-decreasing number of informal ad hoc structures. There are more of these impromptu occupations of space on the days when the general market is closed, taking advantage when there is space available. The market is crowded with shoppers, vendors, couriers and porters; each of whom has a role to play in what looks to be chaotic initially, but is instead a series of overlapping and highly ordered spatial practices. The informal aspects of this market wouldn't normally be the topic for architectural discussion, but further enquiry finds that Namdaemun market not only fulfils any criteria one might set for what constitutes architecture, it challenges our preconceptions and establishes an architecture of temporality, mobility and practice which is every bit as radical as the 1960s counter-cultural architecture of Archigram or Claude Parent.

This chapter closes with elements of the project *A Graphic Anthropology of the Namdaemun Market* with the aim of understanding and knowing about this complex network of occupations, multiple and contingent architectures. The method itself is an application of architectural knowledge production to a socially produced context: making drawings in order to find out more about it, focusing my attention as a researcher. Drawing is an embedded praxis as an architectural researcher, essential to the conduct of the discipline and capable of producing notably alternative forms of knowledge to other practices such as ethnography. Celebrating the informal and ephemeral architecture allows us to understand it architecturally as an initial step towards producing new architectures which learn from these contexts.

A wide range of writers inform this position, which finds a basis in anthropologist Tim Ingold's (2013) discussions of alternative knowledge traditions and the idea of Knowing from the Inside. What does it mean to know from the inside of architecture or urbanism?

Inscriptive practices can be understood as forms of knowledge production equivalent to the academic text and reveal different aspects of a phenomenon to other forms of research methodology such as statistical analysis or interview and questionnaire-based data. Sections (Figure 5.8) through the alleyways tell us a great deal about how space is made efficient, how surfaces are used to display and store goods, and the use of materials such as castors and

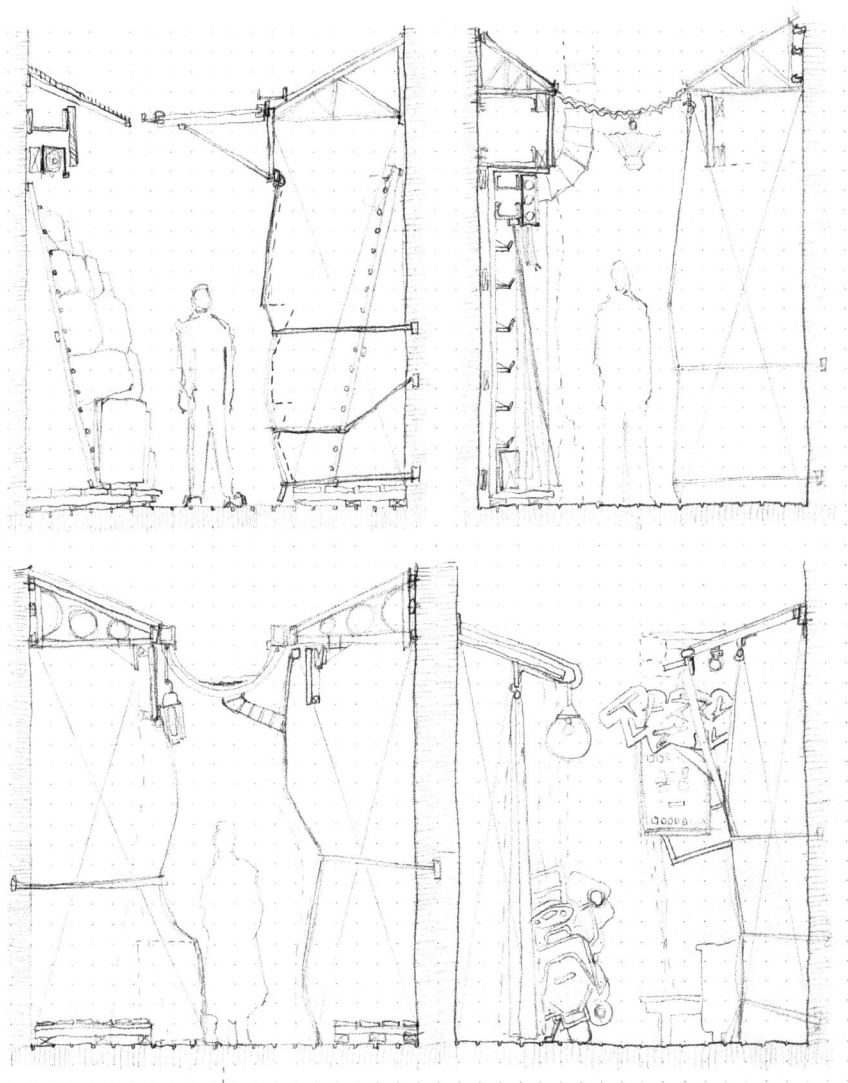

**FIGURE 5.8** *Section drawings of Namdaemun market.*

tarpaulin not normally associated with great architecture. The sections show occupation by vehicles; the use of posts and drains to clamp interventions in place; bridging between buildings in an iterative fashion, design as a series of add-ons.

Namdaemun market is different on each day of the week, following a pattern of occupation which is not only cyclical but also arranged according to the ebbs and flows of people, the demands of crowding and preferences, responsive to the weather and the working day of customers from the nearby business district and governmental centre. Some days the streets are clear of carts, other days the maintenance activities of the market are apparent for extended periods as vendors arrange their carts and goods carefully whilst others have already begun trading. This exposes the arrangement of spaces as something to be remade every day (Figure 5.9): spaces are recreated according to a pattern which has been established already through trial and error, resulting in the optimal design for the selling of the goods in question, be that hats, sunglasses, luggage dumplings or socks.

This represents a challenge to conventional thinking on architecture. The aim of looking at markets such as Namdaemun is to remind ourselves of the qualities of some of the most engaging spaces our cities have to offer. There are indications of tentative trajectories moving in this direction. Cedric Price (2003), Archigram (Cook & Webb, 1999) and others of 1960s counter-cultural architecture movements insisted on the mutability and responsiveness of architecture, but in a manner which recalled the interior of an airliner or directly referencing the space race. Similarly, recent discussions of agency in and of architecture, seeking to recover a social element for architectural

**FIGURE 5.9** *Author's photograph of pallets being dragged about to respond immediately to market conditions.*

# MARKETPLACES AND SITES OF EXCHANGE

debates, have problematized the relationship between people and the built environment. A more effective model for this architecture of response and control, of immediacy and iterative change is in the marketplace: a space largely outside of the purview of professional architects.

In parallel to this, the market must be packed away at night. The spaces that are frequently made are just as regularly unmade. Markets are highly regulated spaces; the units which occupy ground-floor premises have a defined area of pavement in front of the store. This is a permitted spillage, where goods are carefully arranged in a stepped arrangement, making goods visible to passers-by, and with a constant monitoring by the vendors who make this space their own territory. Notably, neighbours assist one another even when they are in competition for the same trade, monitoring each others' external space when required (Figure 5.10). This reciprocity indicates that the market is orderly, not a site of conflict, and that keeping it in good order ensures safety for everyone's livelihood.

This spillage must be packed away at night: a permeable edge that retreats back into the store or is covered over with a protective tarpaulin secured with tough canvas strapping and bungee cords secured by padlocks. In this way, even the most formal structures demonstrate an ebb and flow, encroachment

**FIGURE 5.10** *Author's photograph of external spaces monitored by neighbouring stall holders.*

and retreating on a daily cycle. Once packed away, the shutters go down and the halogen spot lighting is switched off. Surfaces are occupied and returned to the public real on a regular cycle, transformed through protective coverings which communicate when a stall is open for business and when it is closed.

The modular carts are also put away every night (Figure 5.11). The clattering movement of a quad bike trailing a long caravan of white modular carts, some secured with blue or green tarpaulin, occurs late in the evening – hooking the carts together and collecting them together at a parking area close to the entrance to the market zone. Informal carts are the responsibility of their owners, as they exist outside of this system.

All too often we focus on the making of architecture and not enough on its dismantling. Clearly there are a great many imperatives behind a refocus on the undoing of spaces. This has recently been catalogued by Stephen Cairns and Jane M. Jacobs in *Buildings Must Die* (2014)[14] which rethinks the multitude of ways in which a building can be undone. Once again, the elemental nature of the market is instructive. Small elements can be replaced as and when required, adapted with small but important improvements which are specific to the needs of each vendor. The interplay of repeated cart modules and their adaptations offers an important lesson for architecture.

The market is one of the most engaging spaces in this, and other cities. It is sensorially and experientially rich, representing a series of overlapping habitus: the market known by the motorcycle courier is different to that of the van driver, the manual porter and the foreman of the portering company. The other groups in the market also have their own habitus: their own collections of practices which overlap in some places but not all. The vendors have practices of gaining attention through vocalizations and eye contact; they have practices of surveillance – both of their own pitch and that of their neighbours. The

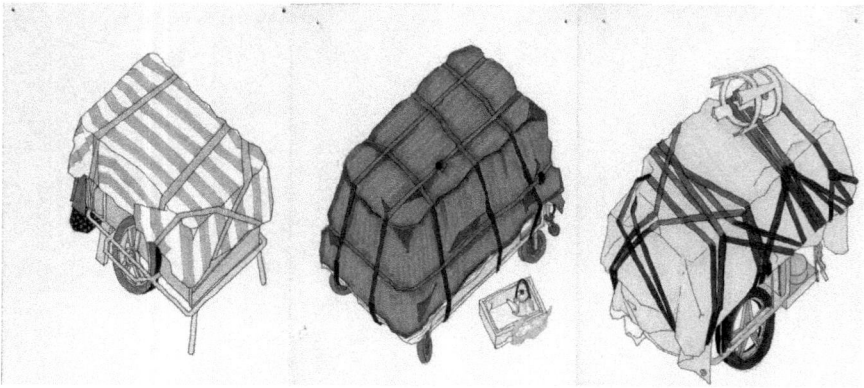

**FIGURE 5.11** *Axonometric drawings of Namdaemun carts packed away.*

vendors have practices of display, ensuring that their stall is displaying goods as effectively as possible, attuned to the cost of the items: some cheaper goods are piled high in order to demonstrate an abundance, where goods intended to be seen as more expensive are curated more carefully: selected and pared back.

The nature of space in the market is more embodied and sensorially rich than a Cartesian model would suggest. In James Gibson's model of space,[15] a triad of surface, medium and substance is presented. The cyclic and flow of architectural elements in the market can be understood as a medium. There is also the medium of the air itself, heavy with oily street food smoke; the viscous medium of the crowds who visit the market; and the medium of the vendors with their carts, material to be manipulated. The air is heavy with food carts' pungency and thermal qualities (welcome bursts of heat in harsh winter, unbearable in the humid summers); crowds thicken and disperse; the carts migrate across the site: each according to their own schedules (Figure 5.12). The quality of the air changes suddenly as food is flash fried or a stacked dumpling steamer opened up; the crowds pulse over the course of the day, condensing around lunchtime and 5 pm; the carts operate with a separate daily and weekly rhythm which converses with that of the monolithic buildings.

It would be misleading to claim that the market is made without the intervention of architects or designers. In the first instance, a distinction must be made between *professional* architects and others who might also define and design space. Whilst there is something engaging in the title of Rudofsky's influential study, Architecture without Architects (1987), the subtitle is often forgotten: *a short introduction to non-pedigreed architecture*. Pedigree is a problematic term of course, but rather than arguing that those who make space in the market do so without architects, it might be

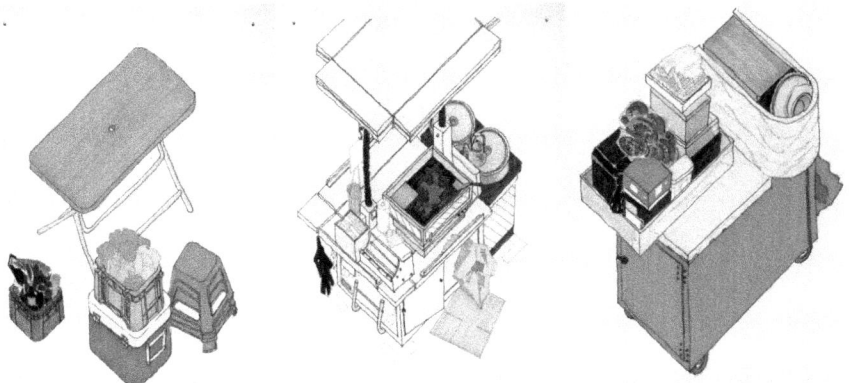

**FIGURE 5.12** *Axonometric drawings of Namdaemun carts in open state.*

more interesting to consider them as architects on different terms to those prescribed by professional bodies across the world. The profession has good reason for legislating who is considered an architect, given the range of skills and breadth of knowledge required. When architecture fails, it can be costly and dangerous, so the security of validation is important.

Architecture, at its root, is the definition of space. It is impossible to argue that the market vendor does not do this – perhaps on a smaller and more informal scale, but architecture can be said to be present. Spaces are articulated and defined: even the most informal stall has a front and back, a zone for the vendor and one for the buyer (Figure 5.13). Often in informal stalls, a sheet of cardboard is placed on the ground, marking a territory as well as offering some thermal protection and a softer surface.

Articulation is a term commonly used in architecture, used to refer to the modulation of a surface in order to render it as communicative or meaningful. Classically, this is described as a façade which presents itself as a diagram of the forces travelling through the stone, distributing the weight of the roof down to the foundations via the openings of windows and doors. This

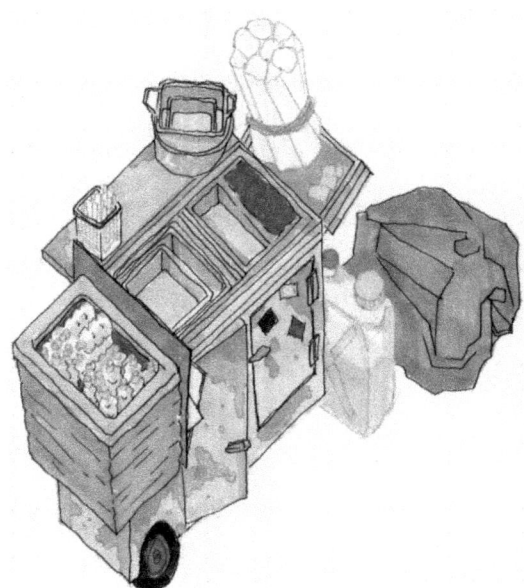

**FIGURE 5.13** *Axonometric drawing of Namdaemun cart showing the definition of front and back through simple means such as facing direction, position of ingredients and cutlery implying the territory of the vendor.*

is rather different with the market stall, mobile cart, alleyway restaurant or store unit with spillage onto the street. Each surface is mobilized in order to communicate in a direct manner: surfaces are supports for goods, displays of wares available for assessment of quality, bartering on price, ordering what is not available at present, and purchase. A more appropriate model might be Venturi, Scott-Brown and Rauch's influential study Learning from Las Vegas (1977). The study of Las Vegas with its neon signage, vast parking lots and shed-like constructions is not at first glance the most promising, but it elaborates a theory of signs and signification in architecture through the analysis of banal architecture, famously reducing all architecture to two categories: decorated sheds and ducks.

Surface is crucial to this communication and definition of space.[16] Surfaces are used to tell people what to expect from a place, as a way of attracting customers. At a different spread of scales, this is precisely what happens in Namdaemun market.

People transform themselves into surfaces, from the courier company representative who wears a webbing gilet decorated with large logos of the portering firm he represents (Figure 5.14). This gilet has numerous pockets for mobile phones, order books and other essential paraphernalia. Older manual porters wear heavy timber A-frames strapped to their backs, being loaded up with one heavy box after another until the strapping secures the load. A contortion of the body takes place as the porter pitches forward before finding the correct angle to allow him to carry his load to another point of the market. Once again, the individual is transformed into a surface for the convenance of goods around the market. Some informal vendors define a territory on the ground with fabric or cardboard, arranging bowls and stock around them within arms reach as they simultaneously define space and engage in food preparation practices. Each of these spatial practices is architectural in nature, contributing to the definition and utility of each space, creating opportunities for transactions. This establishes an architecture on alternative terms and by alternative means. This architecture affords the opportunity of an iterative redesign every day: a responsive user-centred construction where the vendor can assess and reassess the layout and positioning of the cart relative to context and buyers on a daily basis.

The modular cart is an interesting case in this regard (Figure 5.15), as it offers something of a control for that experiment. The white enamelled steel carts have storage, can be plugged in to power networks, have an unfolding canopy and platform for selling from all mounted on robust castor wheels.

Indeed, even the positioning of the cart is altered from one day to the next. Where conventional architecture considers context carefully, reacting in a considered manner to the surrounding environment – built or otherwise – the market cart does so within a very specific context and at an accelerated

**FIGURE 5.14** *Author's photographs of portering equipment and of portering company organizer.*

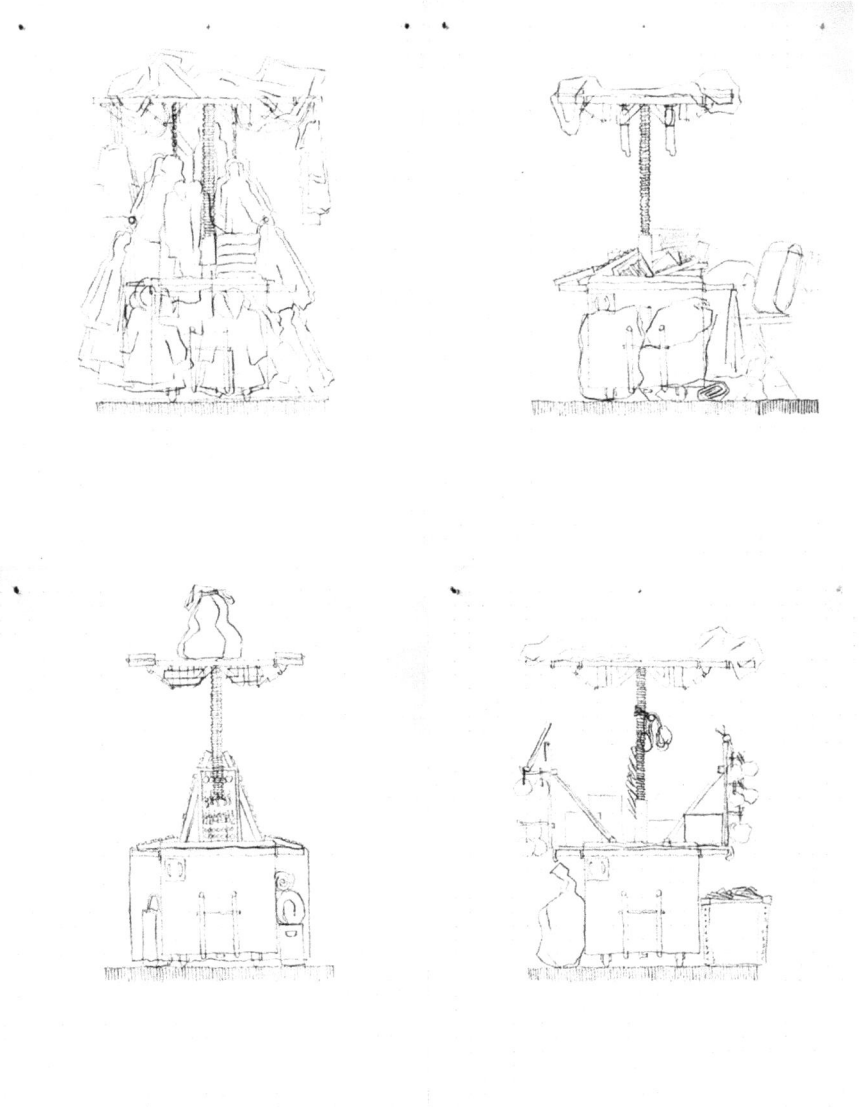

**FIGURE 5.15** *Elevation drawings of modular Namdaemun carts showing variations.*

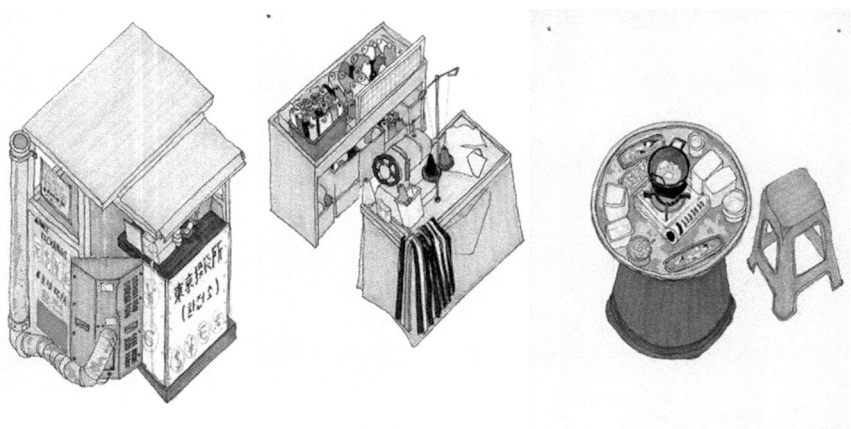

**FIGURE 5.16** *Axonometric drawings of informal Namdaemun stalls and lunch table.*

pace. There is some competition for certain places in the market; some stalls (Figure 5.16) always manage to keep the same pitch whilst others find a different spot from one day to the next.

In terms of the arrangement of goods and even the vendor in relation to the cart, a number of models emerge. Some focus all attention on projecting one selling surface: orienting the vendor and buyer in a direct manner; some allow the buyer to browse over a longer period (particularly where many variations of the same object are sold) whilst others increase the pressure of the decision: encouraging the buyer to make a snap decision.

Both the informal and the modular carts have a fraught relationship with infrastructure. The truly informal carts interact with the modular carts and the formal market buildings in a variety of ways – which challenges the idea that a market is either formal or informal (see Mooshammer, Mörtenböck, Cruz & Forman, 2015), as Namdaemun if simultaneously formal and informal. This definition can be articulated in terms of the relationship with infrastructure. The clearest relationship lies in the monolithic multi-floor buildings which constitute the bulk of the market. Following a blank-façade department store typology, the interior of the market buildings is arranged with row upon row of individual businesses loosely arranged according to the goods on sale. These buildings might be understood to be infrastructure: a framework which can be occupied by a diverse range of market stalls.

At the other end are the truly informal and ad hoc assemblages of the informal stalls. These often pitch up at the fringes of the market zone, just outside of the permitted areas so as to avoid paying rent whilst still taking advantage of the critical density of occupation. This is a fraught and somewhat parasitic action on the formal market, but offers essential additional trade, so is largely tolerated so long as the prime pitches of paying vendors are not compromised in any way.

In between the two is the modular cart. This has some of the formal flexibility of the informal cart – but within limits. The modular cart, crucially, needs power to operate[17] – and these power points are distributed around the permitted areas of the market and not beyond. Despite the mobility of the wheeled cart, it is limited by the need for electricity to power the lighting and also to enable the mechanism which raises the roof of the cart. Whilst it is clear that these were offered as an improvement to the experience of the market for both vendors and buyers, there is an ulterior motive at work: to limit the market to a certain zone, to limit its spread.

Speaking more to Gibson's *medium* than surface, the idea of flow is crucial to architecture when considered as a social construct rather than physical, stable object: as merely substance. The three categories must interact, and it is surface which accommodates the various interacting flows of people, traffic, goods: the back and forth of social interactions. The study of the marketplace and its architecture is then a study of its use of surface, the various transformations of surfaces and the technologies used to convert a surface from a blank, unusable sheer wall into a display for goods. Such technologies are simple at times: steel wire grids mounted inside frames, trestle tables which are quickly demountable, platforms on castors, plastic sheeting and parasols.

Far more interesting approaches to surface and the complexities of articulation possible in contemporary architecture are pursued by architects such as Kuma Kengo, in his recent pursuit of the anti-object (2010). He presents several strategies for achieving this effect: flowing out, erasing, minimizing, unravelling and breaking down into particles. The above might be characterized as approaches towards the role of the surface where Gibson discusses the viscosity, cohesion and composition of a mediating membrane between medium and substance. There are clear parallels to be drawn with the anti-object as an attempt to move beyond the orientation towards form found in later modernist architecture.

The experimental rearrangement of the constituent parts of a market stall is a work in progress, one which responds to social and physical context for economic gain: every decision has an implication which can be assessed over a short period of time and either repeated the next day or adapted for further improvement. This iterative reconfiguration is a design process: one which has an alternative temporality to that of the conventional architectural office, but a design practice nonetheless.

That is why it might be disingenuous to speak of Rudofsky's *architecture without architects*, but more honest to speak of professional and unprofessional (certainly not amateur) ones. This is not intended as pejorative or judgemental, but rather a statement of the context within which a practice is conducted: the primary concern of the market stall holder is measurable and immediate improvement to sales, and their skills are limited to relatively straightforward and small-scale arrangements of prefabricated elements, but these do define and adapt space to their needs. The professional architect has a wider set of skills which allow them to operate at a range of scales,[18] a variety of building typologies which require considerations of engineering, construction detailing, waterproofing, fire escapes, circulation and daylighting amongst many more considerations. The fundamental aims of adapting and defining space remain, however.

The architectural historian Niklaus Pevsner famously declared that 'a bicycle shed is a building. Lincoln cathedral is a piece of architecture.' (2009:10). This statement has had a disproportionate influence on the development of architecture: the declaration that some structures do and others do not constitute architecture is, to Pevsner, not founded on the presence of a professional architect – but rather on the intentionality which can be discerned from the building. By making architecture a judgement, a reification or status for such structures, he is placing some things outside of the realms of architecture. Intentionality is notoriously difficult to ascertain, of course. The designer of the bicycle shed might have considered the economy of means and honesty of a simple structure whilst the builder of the cathedral might have simply been working to an established model: following a pattern.

It is more fruitful to consider in what circumstances either structure could be considered to be either architecture or building, to ascertain this as a quality which might have shifting considerations rather than an absolute and enduring definition. To those who use informal architecture such as bicycle sheds and market carts, these are important ways to articulate space. They mediate between substances, media and surfaces in a meaningful way, give affordance for appropriate actions and provide a frame for social interactions of various scales and temporalities.

You might share the space of a bicycle shed with a large number of people – some of whom you meet regularly as you keep similar hours, others who you never meet but still maintain a social relationship with. The market stall is similar: a social situation is constructed and managed through a range of formal and informal architectures which cooperate and predate on one another, which support and compete, which afford and deny – all to different degrees at different times.

Namdaemun and other urban marketplaces are important pieces of architecture. This requires a leap of faith in expressing the architectural qualities of the iteratively designed market stalls which interact with the more robust infrastructure of monolithic buildings. This is an architecture steeped in spatial practices, in habitus. As such, it is a prototype for an architecture which can cope with rapid changes, an architecture as focused on dismantling as it is on construction. This non-professional architecture is often accompanied by a narrative of being perpetually at risk, and this is certainly the case in the nearby Dongdaemun flea market, displaced by the arrival of Zaha Hadid Architects' Dongdaemun Design Plaza.

I would argue that there is a capability for adaptation and change if interventions are more modest. Constraining the market by introducing the electrically powered modular carts leads to a different kind of creativity where the module sparks a myriad of responses; informality co-exists with formality and an architecture founded on practised space is capable of moderating its activities and reacting to newly introduced conditions. This agility of the marketplace is one of the key qualities which conventional architecture might usefully learn.

# Notes

1. See Welter (2003:60–65) for more on Geddes's valley section drawing.
2. See Ingold (2011:38) for a critique of landscape as scenery and (2011:126) for an explanation of his preferred term of *weather-world*.
3. See Ingold (2000:231–232) for more on the distinction between navigation and wayfinding.
4. Notwithstanding the direction of 'place-making' literature as an instrument of planning and development policies rather than a philosophy of how we understand and co-produce our environment.
5. Bourdieu discusses this irreversibility of gift exchanges (1990[1980]:100–101), noting later that such exchanges are symbols which stand in for relationships, making these manifest.
6. Joy Hendry's work on Japanese gift-giving culture is a case in point here, where the same factors of reciprocity and obligation are under discussion, finding their way into the corporate sphere as well as private lives; one interesting factor is the use of *furoshiki* wrapping cloths and the importance of how a gift is presented, wrapped and unwrapped (1993). As noted in Chapter 4, Inge Daniels (2010) describes how Japanese gift giving tends to avoid permanent gifts for some occasions, as the obligation to keep an item can be problematic in terms of storage, meaning that edible gifts of food are more considerate.
7. See Chapter 7 on the Sanja Matsuri festival that other kinds of competitive engagement with feasting take place as a form of status: the degree of enthusiasm for the event, participation in the embodied practices of carrying heavy portable shrines and the quality of celebratory street parties around the neighbourhood associations.
8. Mauss (2002[1954]:6–7).
9. Mauss (2002[1954]:11).

10   Mauss (2002[1954]:83). The recent Ben Wheatley film *Happy New Year Colin Burstead* (UK, 2018) is a good exploration of this, in which one relatively successful and wealthy member of a family makes a show of hosting a party at a country house. The undercurrent of envy by his guests is expressed in various ways, notably distaste for the extravagance and excess.

11   The market moved from its site at Tsukiji to Toyosu, in the north of Tokyo Bay in October 2018. This controversial move has some of its roots in the need for land for the 2020 Olympic Games and a desire to upgrade facilities from their idiosyncratic state. The move was delayed for some time due to controversies over the brownfield land designated for the market, as it failed several key tests for the presence of unwanted chemical contaminants during construction work. A remnant of the old market remains on site, serving the function of tourist attraction, a role the market was uncomfortable with, occasionally banning intrusive visitors who interfered with the smooth running of the market.

12   This is in contrast to markets such as Noryangjin in Seoul, another large market, which has a clearer division of stalls according to categories of live seafood, wet (fresh) fish, dried and fermented goods, and frozen and refrigerated produce. This allows a consolidation of the services required for large fish tanks or large refrigerators.

13   A secondary market exists during the lottery period where the positions gained can be traded, providing a windfall for minor traders if they are lucky enough to land a corner plot. They can either choose to take advantage of that newly prominent position or accept payment from a larger stallholder for the position. This subverts the principle of the lottery, and gives a sense of consistency in the market, and demonstrates how intangible aspects of the market can end up becoming commodified.

14   See Cairns & Jacobs (2014) for a taxonomy of the various ways in which a building can be demolished, dismantled or otherwise undone.

15   See Lucas (2012) for an exploration of the implications of Gibson's (1986:22–28) triad as an alternative to architectural notions of space.

16   See Lucas (2020) for more on the reading of South Korean markets through the lens of James Gibson's theory of surface.

17   See Lucas (2017a) for more on how the market limits its extent through the power requirements of the modular carts.

18   This scale is both physical and temporal: with the professional architect having a tendency towards the 'permanent' or at least enduring structure.

# 6

# Routes, Walking and Wayfinding

## Introduction

Architectural spaces are most often activated by the routes we take within and around them. Notwithstanding variations in terms of mobility or mechanisms such as elevators and escalators, walking remains a dominant mode for understanding space. The modification of these routes through festivity is one way in which social activities can reinscribe space, rewriting the city according to an alternative understanding.

Walking is also related to wayfinding and navigation, the processes of making sense of a wider space and plotting a specific route through it. Several schools of philosophy and creative practice have contributed to this understanding of the everyday process of getting from A to B, how meanings can become sedimented in those routes and what purposes certain paths have over others.

Alternative practices of walking illuminate how such an ordinary activity can vary: the predetermined itineraries of tourists or the skilled collecting strategy of some hillwalkers. There can be a great deal of nuance in exploring these distinctions, but the way one walks when exploring or lost is substantially different to when we know our way and use those routes every day. Some qualities of movement are explored with reference to the activation of Japanese cities such as Kyoto during New Year festivities: the city is occupied differently as celebrations bring residents out onto the streets for temple visits on New Year's Eve followed by shrine visits on New Year's Day. Here, we have destinations driving a peripatetic knowledge that is reserved for this time of year, late at night.

# Rhythms of walking

Phenomenological approaches to our experience of space are well established in architectural discourse, articulated in the work of writers and practitioners such as Steen Eiler Rasmussen (1962) and Juhani Pallasmaa (1996). Phenomenology is a branch of philosophy concerned with how we grasp the external world. As such, it has held sway over anthropological discourse for some time, with debates extending the reach of the theory in order to discuss how perceptions alter the understanding of reality, with different concepts of the world arising from sensory data. One area where this comes into sharpest focus is in the discussion of walking, a simple practice for most able-bodied people; it is nonetheless subject to a great many variations. This chapter draws on the peripatetic sociology of Jean-Francois Augoyard (2007) and other theorists who have challenged ideas of how and why we walk.

Architecturally, routes through buildings have been understood through the medical metaphor of circulation[1] and through ideas of promenade. Each of these conceptualizes movement through the building in different terms, either as a flow, somewhat akin to fluid mechanics which depersonalizes and abstracts the building users to an extent, or as a deliberate display: where one is deliberately looking to be seen. There are more metaphors for our movement through the built environment, but these two are most pervasive in architectural thinking, giving us ideas such as Space Syntax[2] and agent-based modelling, and flânerie[3] and the Situationist dérive. Sensory data provide further nuance, sharpened by night walking practices[4] and gendered understandings of urban wandering.[5]

As noted in Chapter 5, theories of practice help us to understand how space is experienced in a substantially different way when the purpose of that walk is circumscribed by a set of skills or rules, such as in the procession of clerics and lay altar servers in a Christian church as opposed to the general congregation. The ceremonial procession marks certain points of a service, organized according to a tight script. The congregation has a much more open script, with certain cues taken from the priest. Our focus in this chapter is how walking practices activate spaces in different ways, coded according to the *sacred* and the *profane*. This distinction is found across conventional architectural discourse, referring primarily to religious space; it is easy to extend the consideration of the 'sacred' to secular activities such as attendance at a gallery, where a tension between the conventions of hushed crowds slowly shuffling around the works and contemporary guided tours and engagement through family-friendly activities.

A significant attempt at a similar understanding of the movement inherent to urban life was suggested by philosopher and critical theorist Henri Lefebvre (2004). He states the intention of the book was to 'found a science, a new field of knowledge: the analysis of rhythms; with practical consequences' (Lefebvre, 2004:3). His work insists on the quality of movement as being rhythmic in nature, whether at the glacially slow pace of a rock, or the relatively swift movements of humans and other animals. These rhythms are composed of linear and cyclical elements – of time, space and measure. This whole ecology of movement is useful for overturning the static, the idea that things can ever be wholly fixed or permanent. The analogue of the rhythmanalyst is the psychoanalyst, and Lefebvre playfully outlines what this character might do (2004:20).

The social nature of such rhythms is given the name *dressage*. Similar to the comportment demanded of horses in show events, this dressage is another set of spatial practices in which we conform to a set of commonly understood norms. Rhythms are culturally specific and social. The movements of everyday life differ from one corner of the world to the next. Take, for example, the preference for bowing in Japan, where the depth of bow is representative of relative social status, perfunctory bows to maintain politeness without over-exertion are also developed and robotic androids are programmed to bow in order to endear themselves to the public. There is a slightly awkward overlapping between the social function of bowing and the adoption of Western hand-shakes in order to ease business transactions with representatives of foreign companies. All of these factors are of anthropological interest, but deeper patterns of space use conform to the same concept of *dressage*, where we are encultured into behaving in a particular way, using space in a certain manner.

Fundamentally, rhythmanalysis is a philosophy of the body, as this is the unavoidable measure which one must work with: our concepts of time and space are founded in our own being. An extension of phenomenology, then, the rhythmanalyst listens to their own body (2004:67). In order to focus on rhythms, Lefebvre does away with the *thing* in Chapter 1: material culture must be jettisoned in order to allow the researcher to focus exclusively on rhythms.

This chapter analyses how space is activated through ritualized activity during the New Year celebrations in Kyoto; the difference between sacred and profane use, and what varieties of space are possible.

Movement is a crucial element of how we understand space by moving around in it. This might seem startlingly obvious, but there is a great deal to say on this topic, as the way in which we move in space is often omitted or codified too deeply by the design process in architecture and urban space, erasing the social and reducing people to the data of where they are going, but rarely *how* or *why*. In order to understand movement, a series of strategies must be considered, from social science-based approaches to the recording and writing of notations. Each of these approaches carries with it a series of benefits as well as difficulties, but what are the opportunities afforded by an approach to movement in the built environment?

It is helpful to add that this topic can also be understood in the context of work on the senses (Lucas & Romice, 2008; Lucas, 2009a, 2009b). If we open our concept of sensory perception out to include movement as a form or special case of proprioception[6] and tactility, it is clear that this holistic and haptic approach to space can inform our approach to design, considering the potential routes through, stopping points, programmatic uses and appropriations. The question we seek to answer for each situation is: what is the *quality* of movement within this space?

## Categories of walking

Jean-François Augoyard's[7] study *Step by Step* focuses on the experience of living in French New Towns, in particular the everyday walking routes taken by residents of l'Arlequin New Town on the outskirts of Grenoble. His aim was to develop a peripatetic social science, a position towards everyday life by walking with people, interviewing them as they go about their business. Augoyard takes his cue from the work of Michel de Certeau's *Critique of Everyday Life*, and it is worth examining the ordinary and banal that we must focus on in this case. This idea is also central to the project of this volume, where we are looking to understand the built environment not through unusual and spectacular events,[8] but rather to focus on the regular, almost banal life of the city and building. We make a large number of assumptions when thinking about the everyday, largely based on our own experience of life as establishing some sort of 'norm' from which situations can be seen to deviate to one degree or another. This is perfectly natural and often informed by our broader social group, including family and friends. From the point of view of architectural design, such assumptions are insufficient: design processes must be based on observation and informed research rather than prejudice, presumption and normative ideas of 'good' and 'bad'.

It is interesting to note Augoyard's use of a concept as simple as the *step* as an organising principle (2007:3). This is an example of how you can take on a straightforward idea as an organizing principle or unit of analysis. Here, the daily routines of respondents are of interest and reducible to a set of steps, one foot after the other. Taking a step is a simple idea, but one which propels the subject forward, questioning the idea of a direction, the divisibility into discrete steps, the space between steps. By walking with respondents, a sociality of walking is understood explicitly. As we see later, the companionable context of walking makes a huge difference to how we understand space.

A dog-walker understands the city in a way distinct from a rambler, a parent with push-chair, a wheelchair user, a lone flâneur or a courting couple. All of these walking practices are distinct from one another, and individuals can, of course, move between these categories relatively easily. The underlying structure of walking is important to the study in this case, and Augoyard's work expresses this as a taxonomy or categorization of alternative ways of moving through this same space.

People have a *relationship* with their habitat. This is clear and worthy of interrogation both from the point of view of the researcher seeking to understand the nature of this human engagement with space and from the point of view of the architect who wants to modify, improve and alter the terms of this exchange. Interestingly, the impulse to *make people say something* of this relationship is stressed by Augoyard, and this is one of the most difficult practical problems in social science research practices: how to elicit a response that is accurate and informative of how people really live. In a way, this can be understood to be a little like observing particles in quantum physics, for as soon as one looks at or scrutinizes a phenomenon, the very nature of that thing can have altered substantially through the process of being observed.

Augoyard begins by considering several categories of paths, noting that 'the city is a furtive object, it seems, one that conceals itself' (2007:7). His general approach is to collect categories, variations on a theme which elaborate and add nuance to how we understand an issue:

- Arteries: the most obvious, main routes.
- Impasses: frustrations and blockages to the way we want to go.
- Side-streets: short-cuts and minor routes taken for various reasons.

Certain qualities are under-represented in the literature on walking, and one such aspect is being lost. Whilst procedures of wayfinding are often discussed, the negative connotations to being lost often lead to it being treated merely as a condition to be avoided, that we are perpetually looking to escape from. Lostness offers a curious counterpoint to these theories of navigation which neglect to consider that there is as much interest in how we move when lost and finding our way as there is when we are in full command of our location (Lucas, 2008a, 2008b). In my own work, I addressed this with a series of drawings about getting lost in the Tokyo subway. During my first visits to the city in the early 2000s, my language skills and lack of familiarity rendered large stations such as Shinjuku and Shibuya as puzzles and labyrinths (Figure 6.1). Rather than depict my process of finding my way, the intention for the project was to unpick what it meant to be lost, to celebrate that condition as underlying any exploration of space: it was a process of finding out about that place.

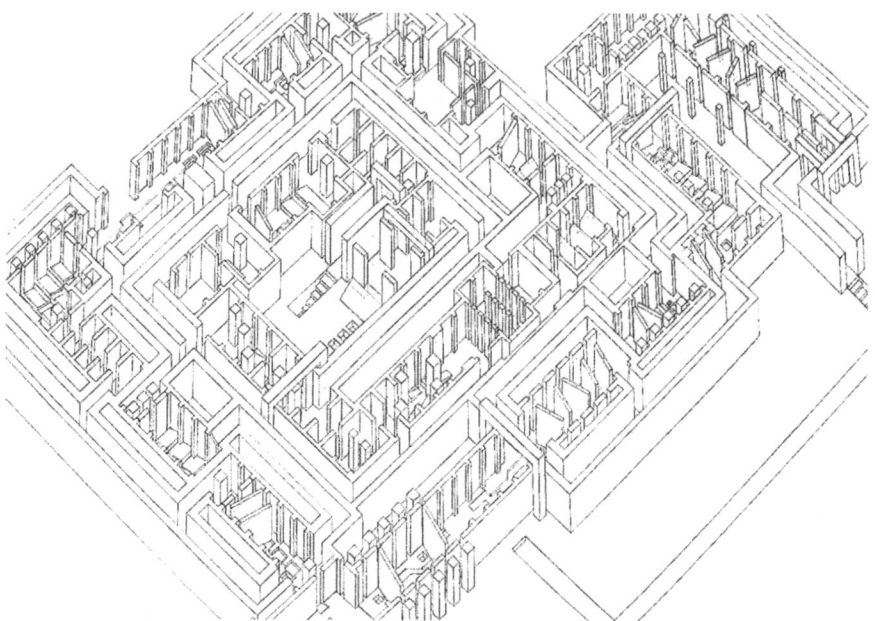

**FIGURE 6.1** *Getting lost in Tokyo labyrinths.*

With the aim of understanding the nature of lostness, I began working with process diagrams (referred to as the flowchart diagram), Laban movement notations, axonometric drawings, alternative maps of the city and oblique photographic references. The project was explicitly anthropological in nature, but auto-biographical rather than ethnographic in the participant-observation sense. One aim was to interrogate the process of making drawings[9] themselves, but I was also describing my walking practice in Shinjuku Station. The notations made use of Laban conventions, but expanded on the repertoire of that mode of representation somewhat by focusing on my intentions and relationship with the flow of people. Part of the process of making lostness visible was to break the experience down into episodes, a narrative layer which was expressed diagrammatically by the flowchart. This allowed episodes to have a discrete identity, and to be caught in loops, potentially repeating as I made similar navigational missteps in different locations. The structure of the project allowed me to explore what it meant to get lost and to lost that condition when in an unfamiliar place: a project I would be unable to make now that I am much more familiar with the context.

We shall see below that many of the aspects covered by Augoyard in his taxonomy of walking can be found here: the doubling back upon oneself, the alternative routes taken, the blockages presented at times. The research question for Augoyard was to ask:

> In the collective space that is the city, what part is frequented, appropriated, and effectively inhabited (in the active sense) by each inhabitant? (Augoyard, 2007:7)

His concern is for what he terms *inhabitant malaise* and the sources of this almost medicalization of disengagement (2007:9–12), noting that changes can result in inhabitants' maladjustment to their environments. The reasons for this might be a lack of engagement during the design process or a lack of information about new facilities which have been introduced. In sum, however, the inhabitants of space in Augoyard's example could find themselves ill equipped for their modernist environments (a reversal of the usual critique that the architecture is failing the inhabitants). Blockages to the enjoyment of the urban environment are related to the ways in which inhabitants occupy and understand the urban space they live in. If a change is too radical or swift, for example, it becomes difficult for people to inhabit that space: the rules implied or constraints applied are just too far removed from their understanding of how to live that people already have. This means that the environment fights against the desires of the inhabitants, causing dissatisfaction and misuse, particularly where the environment has a strong agency and attempts to channel the movements and activities of inhabitants.

More positive examples of similar environments might be found elsewhere. Whilst the high-rise apartment typology is problematic in some cities, others such as Singapore have, with small adaptations to the type, created examples which are much more liveable. The Housing and Development Board (HDB) block developments (Figure 6.2) are a form of publicly owned housing with high density as appropriate to the context. The ground floor of the development includes several important features, however. Often, a garden area is provided in a central courtyard, deep enough in plan to allow light in; the gardens are well maintained and make use of the space above underground car parking. The garden includes fitness facilities designed with the needs of older residents in mind, and a community centre is also situated on site. More important still are the food courts called *hawker centres* in each block. Filling a similar niche to street food, the hawker centre is an arrangement of relatively informal and low-cost food outlets serving the HDB housing above. This is a social space for gathering with friends, family and colleagues, passing time and simply occupying the public realm.

Another innovation is the inclusion of leftover space, un-programmed voids at ground level. These spaces serve an important social function as they can be used by residents for life events such as weddings or the wake following a funeral. Firms dedicated to providing temporary furniture and facilities for these events support this activity, meaning that the relatively small footprint of the typical HDB apartment is less of an issue when a

144                    ANTHROPOLOGY FOR ARCHITECTS

**FIGURE 6.2** *Author's photographs of HDB housing blocks in Singapore including hawker centres and flexible social space.*

large family gathering is called for. Each of these activities integrates into the daily routines of inhabitants of HDB blocks: walking to and from the car park or transit stop includes chance meetings, running into people at the hawker centre. The maintenance of the gardens means they are well used, with covered walkways protecting residents from weather that can, at times, be ferocious. These are modest, unspectacular buildings, formally similar to large-scale housing developments in other cities, but their functioning is enhanced by both the inclusion of some shared space and their continued maintenance, ensuring that they remain in good shape. The relative success is as much social as it is architectural.

The Singapore example relies on a set of shared spatial practices, ways of using the space allotted to the development. If, as in the case of Augoyard's respondents, the inhabitants have had a long period of disenfranchisement from spatial understanding suggested above, the problem is compounded and more difficult to resolve, as there is no real set of spatial practices to refer to in the first place. The intervention of city users in the production of their environment is presented as a solution to this, be that in the boldest sense of the actual planning, designing and building of a space, or the more subtle production of space that comes through extended inhabitation.

Political factors also have a great deal to contribute, of course. This extends to the management of expectations; and also expressed in terms of the political forces, inhabitants are often subject to rather than in control of. The technology and process of architectural production often leave the power relations of inhabitants out of the equation: sometimes as the architect has no control over this, but also sometimes out of a complete lack of concern. Consider, for example, the statement of the author George Orwell, who argues that *every act is political* (2013 [1946]) and that the statement of something as apolitical is in itself a hugely political statement. This gives us the idea that walking can be a political act, either in terms of how we occupy and make ourselves present in space or in terms of what spaces are provided for walking, where it is denied, and who might be excluded.

Augoyard asks us to look at the everyday details of the lives of people in ordinary circumstances (2007:23), as this is where we spend most of our lives: in the banal spaces of travelling to work, buying groceries, getting some fresh air. What emerges from this is an examination of *spatial practices*. Spatial practice is a term which encompasses more than merely 'movement' but represents an attitude and approach to life: how Augoyard's respondents and interviewees understand space directly through their engagement with it. This is not a notion of space which is abstracted from this practical everyday engagement, but firmly grounded within it: this everydayness *orients* the entire approach.

By constructing walking narratives with informants, people are able to articulate what they do, how they do it and why. This idea of narrative, of storytelling, is an important structuring and ordering practice, one which concentrates on the experience of space, always moving away from rationalization and simply understanding the alternative experiences possible within any given space. This is absent minded and disinterested (2007:25), but no less significant for that. I have argued similarly elsewhere (Lucas, 2008a) that by walking, one can *rewrite* the city, not accepting a given script but performing one's own score there.

This draws a relationship between walking and language: of reading and then rewriting an environment as well as to consider the different *rhetorics* and *poetics* possible from such an understanding. Augoyard, once he collects these narratives and pure experiences shared with his interviewees, seeks to define a set of *figures of spatiotemporal expression* (Figure 6.3). This structuralist approach of categorization suggests a catalogue of some of the possible understandings of this walking space. This approach is similar to the one we see in Augoyard's subsequent work on soundscape[10] and uses some rather convoluted terminology. The qualities he finds are, however, very powerful in discussing the narratives he elicited from residents.

*Exclusion*: the denial of permission, or other form of discouragement from an area.

*Paratropism*: a practice of substituting one path for another, perhaps as an alternative due to building work.

*Peritropism*: a series of variations in path grouped together as a set, to vary your route to a regular destination.

*Polysemy*: the process of simultaneously reading and writing an environment, opening the possibilities for alternative understandings of a well-known space.

*Ambivalence*: vague or undefined spaces we tend not to notice or care about, possibly omitted from the narrative account.

*Staggered polysemy*: interpretations of a site such as the perception of fear at certain points on a defined path or awareness of social constraints.

*Bifurcation*: a clearly divided space can have this effect, with one condition on one side of a barrier, a completely different feel on the other.

*Metathesis of quality*: these are definitions that are atemporal, such as a space defined as 'nice in the mornings', and still taken as a route at other times.

*Symmetry, dissymmetry and asymmetry*: these qualities refer to the way in which a journey to a destination and back again can display the same path in a different light.

Adapted from Augoyard, 2007:23–114

Augoyard continues, describing other effects in encyclopaedic fashion. One manner of understanding the findings of his study is that by walking, people are appropriating space. By appropriation, we understand the way in which people can take possession of a space for themselves, making it their own through continued use, understanding as a form of practice, and by making adaptations, naming things or through familiarity. A famous example of this is Iain Borden's work on *Skateboarding Space and the City* (2003). Borden explores the embodied nature of skateboarding as an extreme engagement with the city, heightening the perception of kerbs, railings and benches as well as the development of skate park architecture from early practices of skateboarding in abandoned infrastructure and empty swimming pools. Key to his argument is the notion of appropriation, both in how a skateboarder uses the city and also in how particular structures end up part of the repertoire of skateboarding. Walkers are engaged in a similar process, developing a kind of ownership over certain parts of their cities.

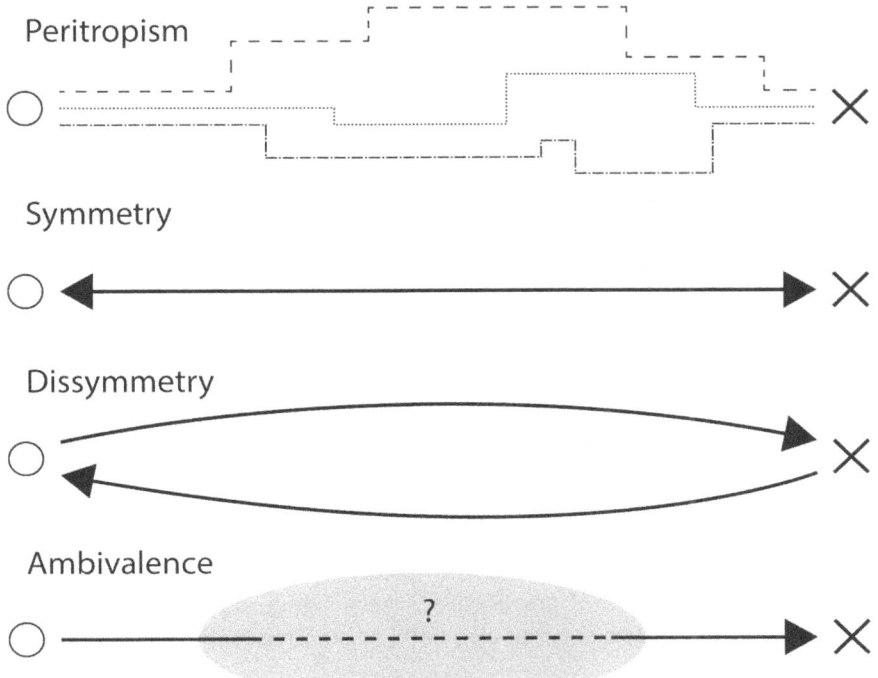

**FIGURE 6.3** *Diagrammatic renderings of Augoyard's qualities and forms for everyday walking.*

Naming, numbering and other forms of appellation are the most basic forms of appropriation highlighted. By naming something, either with its established name, or one of our own inventions, we gain agency over that thing. The process of naming aids in differentiating and marks out a theory of movement in urban space that is driven by destinations and waypoints as well as routes. These elements are commonly understood and named in order to gain some control over the environment in our discussion of daily events: 'Something happened at this place on the way to work'. Augoyard sees *inhabiting* as something mobile and temporal: it unfurls over a period of time and is explored in an ambulatory fashion. Inhabitation is too often understood as static and fixed to a particular position, but the approach taken here challenges this, expressing movements as part of this extended notion how we can inhabit the urban environment, particularly where routes are established through our own explorations.

## Cultures of walking

As one of our most fundamental forms of movement, walking seems to be simple and obvious with little more to be said about it. Our task, however, as designers and researchers, academics and practitioners, is to be a little more critically engaged: asking questions of such assumptions. Walking is every bit as culturally specific as any other practice we engage with. It is also one which is central to our experience of the environment, be that man-made, artificial or a combination of the two.

This deceptively simple form of ambulatory movement is tackled in a collection of essays edited by anthropologists Jo Lee Vergunst and Tim Ingold (Ingold & Vergunst, 2008). There is some history of this in the discipline, from an essay by Marcel Mauss (1947) where the concept of *Techniques of the Body* is introduced. Mauss's work was left incomplete, however, and there was an interruption in anthropological consideration of the topic between the 1930s and 1960s, when Pierre Bordieu began once again to consider the theory of *practices*. As noted in Chapter 5, Bordieu gave us the idea of *habitus*, the collections of practices which constitute our very being in the world. And this is also a concept also pertinent to Chapter 3 on the home and practices of dwelling.

What is clear, however, is that there is a theory of practice: of *simply doing things*. This is more stating of the obvious: walking is important, the majority of people *can* walk and there are variables in *how* we walk. This raises questions of what these differences and points of commonality are precisely, and why is it important to think in any detail about how people walk?

Other than physiological variations in the placement of feet or movement of joints, there is a question of what the human factors are in influencing how we walk. The differences between individual walking and that of a couple, or a group are instructive: that within a similar setting, the group size and dynamic informs the manner of walking. This might be expressed as an interruption to the walking practice by conversation, or the need to negotiate aspects of the walk such as maintaining a similar pace. These factors could be argued to be separate from the walk or an essential part of the habitus in question: walking in a group requires one set of skills, subtly but significantly different from walking as a couple or as an individual. Walking is often celebrated as an ideal way of getting to know a place or for being fully immersed in the environment of hills and mountains. The directness of engagement with the ground offers us some hints: in an essay, the Japanese architect Isozaki Arata (1986) describes the *floor orientation* of Japanese architecture, noting the surface qualities of tatami mats and cultural practice of removing shoes before entering the interior of a home. This is because of the material of the floor, which is not robust enough for outdoor footwear. Similarly, cities afford certain kinds of movement through their historic and contemporary ground conditions: cobbles assisted in the movement of heavy goods by horse and cart, but did not suit the automobile sufficiently, so tarmac became the norm. Meanwhile, paving stones make the city walkable for pedestrians, often demarcating zones for traffic and zones for people. This is in stark distinction to the various ground conditions found elsewhere: tangled roots and fallen leaves on a forest floor, viscous mud capable of sucking one's boots clean off in fields after rain, scrabbling up gravel and stone where the solid nature of the material underfoot is often deceptively brittle.

A series of case studies are presented by the researchers who have contributed to Ingold and Vergunst's work. Some, such as Katrin Lund and Hayden Lorimer (2008:185–200), consider the nature of 'collecting' hills in the form of 'Munro Bagging'. This is a way of talking about hillwalking as a prescribed set of achievements, where one is given a list of large hills and mountains in Scotland, each over a specified height.[11] Walkers then keep track of the Munros they have climbed, and these form a part of a collection, metaphorically bagged by the walkers. This forms a reference point for conversations between fellow walkers. The prescribed list, varying difficulties and idea of a shared experience allow walkers to compare and discuss their experiences on a level ground (so to speak).

There is an interesting play of individual experience and cross-comparability in this practice. Lund and Lorimer note that few walkers would self-identify themselves as 'Munro baggers' as this is seen as derogatory and reductive of the practice of hillwalking to a tick-box exercise. This noted, however, many will admit that this collecting impulse is a part of their walking.

> Today, as a semi-formalized and nationally arranged mechanism that enables people to organize the way they climb mountains, Munro's tables have no obvious rival. As a community with a shared recreational passion, walkers-cum-collectors are richly diverse and self-differentiating. Long before academic analysis intervened, 'Munroists' had their very own politics of identity and position. (Lund and Lorimer in Ingold & Lee Vergunst (Ed.), 2008:187)

Walking, then, can be understood as a social practice, even when conducted individually or in small groups, as the route or object of the walk can be understood as literal common ground. The specification and listing is essential to this form of walking, providing that reference point to which walkers can append their own stories, be they extreme weather conditions, unusual occurrences or comparisons with other walks.

The codification of these walks forms what Lorimer and Lund call a 'performed presentation of geographical knowledge' (2008:190). This form of knowledge, it is argued, must be engaged with physically and practically – backed up by published guides and maps – but experienced in the environment. The hill articulates the environment in a particular manner, constructed from markers and milestones as well as offering sight lines, preferred views and the feeling of simply being as high up as one can go.

Lorimer and Lund argue that the knowledge produced by Munro baggers cannot be understood only as individual *or* collective, but must always be understood as *both*. This is the key to such a specified script of movements. Similar practices could be found in dance, where notated or recorded performances of well-known ballets offer a reference point to the fresh performance of a ballet. Tourist itineraries, similarly, have a reference: a notation against which performances might be measured. This suggests that aspects of script and re-performance of a predetermined itinerary are built in to the notational practices surrounding Munro climbing, particularly those related to movement. It is worth noting, then, that the Munro guides are a form of simple notation in themselves, offering a script akin to that of fine-tuned Laban notations, but made up of different types of information: only that relevant to the climbers. The nature of the notation becomes apparent in terms of temporality, stretched over the entire career of a hillwalker or mountaineer rather than a few hours of defined theatrical performance.

Walking has long been understood as an aesthetic practice, and the interplay of notation or cartography with the practice or act of walking offers one of the opportunities for creativity within this.

## Hatsumōde – New Year festivals in Kyoto

A peripatetic takeover of the city is common to many festivals, and the festive state of the city often reveals it in a heightened state: the city at its most urban, a kind of super-normal state. Studying this state of the city reveals the importance of walking routes and the power of simply occupying spaces which are not normally used, or being present at unusual times of day. New Year celebrations are one such occupation, where normally serene and quiet religious spaces become hubs of celebratory activity. In line with the dual religions often observed by Japanese people, Buddhist temples are visited to see the New Year in, and a Shinto shrine is visited on New Year's Day, but some shrines also have activities in the lead up to the turn of the year.

As an important national holiday, New Year (the calendar year is celebrated alongside the lunar New Year in Japan) is accompanied by decorations celebrating the zodiac animal of the year to come alongside arrangements of *kagami mochi*, two large round pounded rice cakes stacked on top of one another and decorated with a daidai citrus fruit, paper streamers, and placed on an elevated wooden tray; the chewy mochi are to be eaten lightly grilled on 11 January. Other decorations include *kadomatsu* or 'gate pine' arrangements of three cut bamboos placed outside the entrance to buildings, further decorated with sprigs of pine tree or plum tree (Figure 6.4). This threshold marker starts to appear from mid-December until mid-January and is intended to welcome the *Toshigami*, Shinto *kami* who bring in the New Year. The temporary nature of the decorations, which are designed to be consumed in part, along with the marking of the threshold again marks this festival out as distinctly architectural in its sensibility.

The New Year's Eve traditions celebrated in Kyoto and other Japanese cities take possession of the city in a manner different to festivals such as Sanja Matsuri,[12] but the city is still occupied by the people of the city in a wholehearted manner. The relationship between home and the temple and shrine is strongly expressed: a bringing of the city and wider community into the domestic sphere.

Associations with particular shrines and temples often conform to family or neighbourhood lines – with no hard rules about which you would give priority

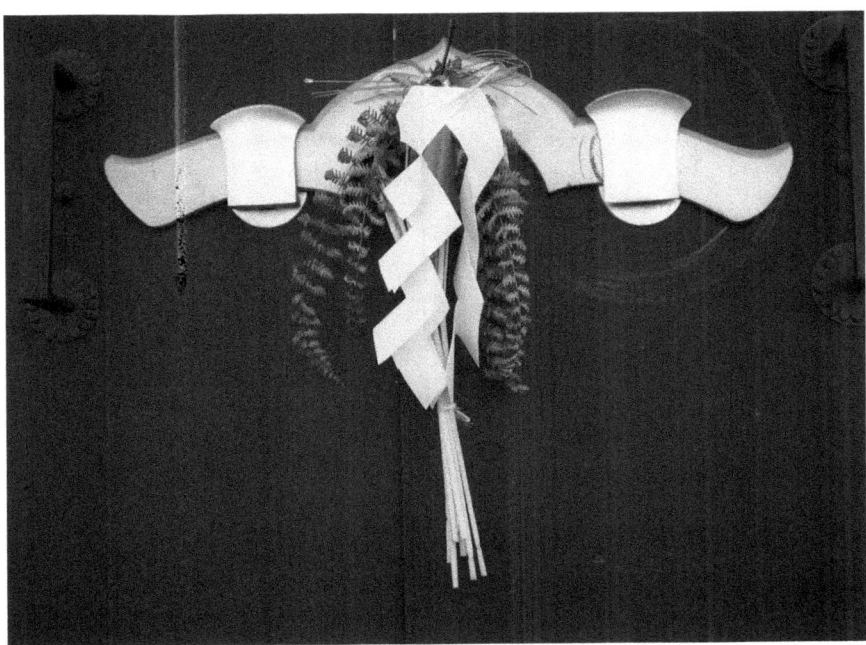

**FIGURE 6.4** *Author's photograph of Kadomatsu decoration.*

to. Some of the larger temples gain more attention due to their scale and prominence, but the smaller temples also garner more visitors than usual and are celebrated for their atmosphere of intimacy, even authenticity.

Streets that are normally deserted at this time of the evening in winter are full of revellers walking from temple to temple (Figure 6.5). This activation of space outside of the norm is one component of the festive city.

Okera Mairi (おけら参り) is a tradition particular to the Yasaka Shrine. Sacred fires are lit at the shrine, large braziers are tended carefully by feeding them the wooden tablets with wishes and prayers written on them, the burning of these prayers sends them up to the heavens to be fulfilled. Short 20–30 cm lengths of bamboo rope are sold by hawkers – rakish characters who are tolerated by the shrine, but operate as a secondary economy making profit from a sacred practice much like the street food market which springs up within the sacred precinct during celebrations. The ropes are lit at the fires, then spun in the air and carefully protected from the wind to keep them burning (Figure 6.6). The purpose is to take the fire from the shrine back home and light the hearth for cooking the first meal of the New Year. We might relate this to Banham's (1969) and Heschong's (1979) concepts of architecture as environmental control and modification, where he maintains that architecture

**FIGURE 6.5** *Author's photograph of Kyoto street during New Year celebrations.*

**FIGURE 6.6** *Author's photograph of Yasaka Shrine, Kyoto with braziers, street food sellers and amazake.*

is as much about the maintenance of thermal conditions as it is about form and space. Associating this important source of heat with the local shrine is a significant and architectonic act.

Also at the Yasaka Shrine, monks give out sweet non-alcoholic sake called *amazake* in exchange for a nominal donation. Delicate porcelain sake dishes are also received as a memento. Other parts of the sacred precinct are occupied by street food stalls selling a wide range of hearty and informal foods, including rich noodle stews, fried chicken and charcoal grilled fish.

Temples observe the tradition of Joya no kane (除夜の鐘), tolling a large bell (Figure 6.7) 108 times to represent the number of earthly desires and passions which assail humanity and prevent us from reaching the state of Nirvana. Each ring of the bell dispatches one of these desires. Worshippers can queue to take a turn at certain temples to ring these enormous bells for themselves. Waiting on the hill of Kodai-ji Temple in Gion is something of a test of endurance, with the extreme cold just staved off with hot drinks of tea and sake, and crowds huddled around open fire braziers. Going through such modest hardships is seen as an integral part of the experience to some revellers.

**FIGURE 6.7** *Author's photograph of Bell at Kodai-ji.*

Visiting temples and shrines in the middle of the night is an altered experience from the normal run of daytime visits. More time is spent waiting for various small events which punctuate the festival, and the environmental conditions make for a completely different sensory experience: the bright flickering fires against inky night skies, the hubbub of excited revellers punctuated by bell ringing and engaging with various activities such as the lighting of ropes: these practices all alter the narrative or rhythm of the visit, marking it out as a special experience.

The New Year's Day shrine visit is called *Hatsumōde*[13] (Figure 6.8) and follows similar patterns of local versus major shrines as the New Year's Eve activities – extending even to returning to hometowns away from the cities and towns where people have settled. The year is inaugurated by drinking sake from a barrel (in the case of hotels this might be a full-scale barrel, homeowners often opt for a barrel-shaped container to be filled from a bottle with magnetic top for ease of 'breaking'); this is broken open with a mallet and cold, crisp sake drunk over breakfast.

Fortunes are a traditional part of shrine visits, but take on added importance at New Year. *O-mikuji* Fortunes are printed on paper and drawn randomly. Randomization is achieved by pulling a stick from a hexagonal container and taking the corresponding numbered fortune from a small drawer (sometimes

**FIGURE 6.8** *Author's photographs of Hatsumōde at Fushimi Inari Shrine.*

a vending machine takes the place of this process). When a positive prediction is received, it is tied to specific places in the shrine such as purpose built frames or the branches of pine trees. These will eventually be disposed of by the shrine. *Ema* are small wooden boards of various types (most often shaped as irregular wide-based pentagons and with decoration on one side specific to the shrine). These are written on by worshippers bearing prayers and wishes and are also hung at specific places in the shrine, to be burnt by the priests and attendants at important dates in the shrine's calendar. Clusters of both Ema and fortune slips are a feature of most shrines. Whilst not restricted to New Year, both *o-mikuji* and *ema* are an important part of *Hatsumōde*.

There are a great many more details to the festivities, from the display of food as a ritual offering (to be consumed later at a banquet and largely representing the generosity of local businesses) to the purchase of amulets and the details of the shrines and temples themselves. What is important to our purpose here, however, is to observe the manner in which festive activities change the nature of the space: underlining that space is socially constructed.

The intersecting path made by revellers who identify with particular shrines and temples for various reasons crosses over with a discussion of the secular versus religious nature of the events which dominates much of the literature on Japanese ritual. Shinto and Japanese Buddhism operate within daily life in a manner which frustrates easy categorization as religious activity. This celebration involves crossing the city in different ways to usual, occupying the street at times of day normally reserved for night trades of delivery, transportation and security. The festive decoration of thresholds and symbolically connecting the domestic to the religious makes for a study which opens the space of the city up as a pedestrian activity: in both senses of the word – utterly banal and ordinary; and as something to be experienced on foot.

## Notes

1. See Forty (2004).
2. See Hillier & Hanson (2008) for more on this.
3. See Careri (2002), Ingold & Vergunst (2008), Tester (1994), Gros (2015) and others for material on aesthetic wandering.
4. See, for example, Dunn (2016) and Beaumont (2015).
5. See Elkin (2017), D'Souza & McDonough (2008) and Rendell (1996).
6. A term referring to our perception of our own bodies.
7. The English translation of this 1979 work was not published until 2005, when Augoyard had become better known through his leadership of the Cresson Institute in Grenoble with Gregoire Chelkoff, with important work on the intersection between architecture and sound design in *Sonic Design* (2006) and a broader focus on the study of ambiance.
8. Notwithstanding Guy Debord's critique of contemporary life as being precisely focused on *spectacle* in *The Society of the Spectacle* (1994). Our intention is to rehabilitate the ordinary and our interest in this as architects. Many of the sources for this can be found in contemporary anthropology.
9. This is addressed in *Drawing Parallels* (Lucas, 2019a), where I discuss the particular case of the axonometric drawings.
10. See Augoyard & Torgue (2006) for more on this.
11. Hills over 3,000 feet, or 914 metres, are in the group of 284 Munroes. The practice is named after Sir Hugh Munro, a mountaineer who listed them in the 1880s.
12. For more on this festival, see Chapter 7 of this volume as well as Lucas (2018b).
13. For further details on Hatsumode and its place between cultural and religious tradition, see Ozawa De-Silva (2014) and Porcu (2012).

# 7

# Theatre and Festival: Performance and Liminal Space

## Introduction

Various forms of art and social event can be understood as performances, suspending the implicit and explicit rules of everyday life in order to enable roles to be adopted. Most often, we would associate this with the formal theatre space, where a clear distinction is made between the performers and the audience. This separation gives rise to a great many theories in anthropology and architecture, not least of liminality: of threshold spaces.

At their simplest, thresholds are openings between one spatial condition and another: a door from outside to inside, for example. The rules of behaviour in interior spaces are quite different from those outside, be that in the country or the city. Different standards of behaviour are expected in each place. Similarly, definitions of interior space multiply, with the bedroom, bathroom and kitchen of a typical Western home being understood to enable activities of sleeping, washing and food preparation. If spaces can be understood to have these alternative qualities, then the borders between them are significant.

Applying theatrical and performative metaphors to how we present ourselves socially can also have architectural implications: the ideas of staging explored by Goffman, for example, take account of how we project a constructed self in social situations. This is not a falsehood so much as an effective character designed for each interaction, reserving some of our deeper feelings for more intimate encounters.

This chapter addresses some of the ways in which these border conditions can be widened and exploited, from the subsidiary stage and complicated fictional space of a Kabuki theatre to the days of misrule in an urban festival in Tokyo, physical or social liminal conditions allow us to inhabit spaces in substantially different ways, representing one of the fundamental elements of architecture as a discipline. Some of the potentials of the *graphic anthropology* method are presented via the accompanying illustrations, ranging from architectural and diagrammatic to painterly and notational explorations of the festival.

## Spectacle and society

The theatre, one of our oldest forms of public building, is long associated with entertainment as well as a civic function. Theatres offer opportunities to study sites which are arranged around a spectacle in an unapologetic manner: vision is controlled and directed, acoustics harnessed, the flows of people around the site carefully managed. The two main constituencies for the theatre space are the performers and the audience, both of whom have their own spatial practices and who experience the building in substantially different ways.

Narrative and spectatorship theories give us some insights into this context, where the identification of the audience with the event being watched can lead to the tribalism found in football stadia or discomfort felt at violent cinema. Deliberate cultural constructions found in theatres and stadia of every type can be deconstructed using anthropological theories, interrogating the deeper meanings and cultural implications of the artworks and performances we create as people. Theatre and performance are implicated in some of the methods of anthropology, particularly within visual anthropology, where lens-based practices of documentary photography and filmmaking are used to explore the lifeworlds of respondents. This becomes complicated when a presumed audience is included, as the work runs the risk of objectifying the Other, making them subject to gaze in a colonialist manner rather than allowing people their own voice.

This can be overcome with careful negotiation, however, and demonstrates that there is complexity even within the dominant modes of investigation found in contemporary anthropology, that any act of representation can present the Other as exotic in dangerous ways, aestheticizing and romanticizing this otherness and denying their humanity and agency. Similar problems can occur when architects choose ways to interact with their clients or communities: community engagement is too often a form of validation rather than genuine enquiry.

## Social drama and liminal space

A key writer in the anthropology of performance is Victor Turner, who moved the discussion away from a pure discussion of symbols and what they stand for, and towards an appreciation of how the performance is produced, appreciated and reproduced. Performance represents a set of conditions apart from the everyday instances examined elsewhere in this volume, but the process of producing meaning from stories is an important and widespread human activity, resulting in drama and literature, musical traditions and cinema, video games and all manner of other outlets. Turner sees a connection between ritual activity and performance with many forms of theatre having their roots in religious practices (1987:24).

This interconnectedness between ritual or sacred action and the more banal stuff of life is crucial to work on performance and can be understood as a kind of hyper-ordinariness which establishes the paradigm for cultural performance and its part in the lives of the audience. The extent of this co-dependence and co-construction between audience and actors[1] brings it into contact once again with Ingold's ideas about the co-construction of people and their environments. Turner finds this co-construction to be mediated through a threshold condition: the *limen* which he draws from earlier work on folklore by Arnold van Gennep (1961), giving the famous 'rites of passage' in three distinctive phases:

1. Rituals separate members of the group into smaller clusters and place them in an indeterminate context, described as *limbo* by van Gennep.
2. This is a new context where marginality and liminality feature most strongly – a space between the sacred and the profane that can be inhabited during the time of a ritual practice. This indicates that ritual practice mediates the two worlds by means of an extended threshold condition.
3. This space requires a performance to be maintained.

Turner speaks of genres having a common structure temporally, including festivals as well as more explicitly dramatic performances. Rituals and other performances are not, as in the popular imagination, inflexible practices. Turner notes how they have elements which maintain the liminal state alongside features that are variable and open to spontaneity or improvisation (1987:26).

> The prejudice that ritual is always 'rigid,' 'stereotyped,' 'obsessive' is a peculiarly Western European one, the product of specific conflicts between ritualises and antiritualists, iconophiles and iconoclasts, in the process of Christian infighting. (Turner, 1987: 26)

Whilst perhaps stating the obvious, it is worth underlining this as a principle with architectonic implications: that adaptation is certainly a part of the ritual's nature: it always responds to its context, be that physical, cultural, social, political or economic. The instability does not preclude study of the ritual or performance, whichever *genre* it belongs to: perhaps there is a scope or trajectory to discuss rather than pinpointing a singularity of the performance.

Turner develops the concept of the *social drama*, a useful framing device for the performances in architecture, whether organized according to dramatic principles or as a way of describing other prescribed actions within space. The social drama is structured as a process, a series of phases beginning with a trigger event which breaches the status of normal lived life (1987:34). This is followed by a state of crisis, where people are asked to become involved. In discussions of ritual, this is referred to as an agonistic phase, but a similar structure is followed in conventional fictional narrative, where an unexpected event propels the narrative, and conflict is essential for the interactions of characters to be revealed. Further phases redress or reconcile these elements followed by a reintegration to a harmonious whole.

> Genres of cultural performance are not simple mirrors, but magical mirrors of social reality: they exaggerate, invert, re-form, magnify, minimise, discolour, re-colour, even deliberately falsify, chronicled events. They resemble Rilke's 'hall of mirrors,' rather than represent a simple mirror-image of society. (Turner, 1987:42)

If we are to understand formal performances such as theatre to be mirrors held up to social realities: ones which distort and accentuate as Turner notes above, then the architectures which have grown around these activities are important to understand. The architecture of various forms of theatre has sedimented ideas of how to organize narrative and social realities into a coherent form. As we shall see later, there are variations and options within dramatic performance, playing with what is apparatus and what is the content of the story. Anthropologists take this metaphor further: discussing the idea that much of social life can be explored using a theatrical analogy. Erving Goffman in particular develops a scenographic metaphor for how people present themselves to others in everyday encounters. We adopt a persona appropriate to the social context, a kind of mask, and maintain physical and social versions of the front- and back-of-house one finds in a theatre.

Turner is best known for his development of liminality in anthropological theory. This has a bearing on architecture, not only due to the use of similar terminology, but the importance of the underlying concept: the passage from one state to another. Finding the root of the term in Germanic languages, threshing is the activity of removing grain from their husk, often with a vigorous motion. It has come to mean a process of revelation, where the hidden is made manifest (1987:92). Turner describes everyday living as *opaque*, where meaning is present but hidden away: the social drama by contrast is *transparent*. Meanings are apparent and clear, often having a bearing on those everyday activities which might become more fraught if they were regularly loaded with meaning. He argues that relationships and their origins are revealed during times of social drama but are otherwise dormant.

The concept of the social drama is helpful in articulating the deeper possibilities of threshold. Dramatic performances are one way of manifesting many of the social bonds and structures that are normally hidden: this movement from opaque to transparent, exposing the underlying order. Cultural performances are not neutral: they are produced within a community, are a response to underlying conditions and can be either reinforcements or rejections of accepted norms. Often, social dramas serve to reinforce normative positions within each society, reiterating the existing social order even as it offers an outlet or 'day of misrule' where the poorest members of society might find themselves in a position of authority for the day. This performance is controlled and limited, a way of saying that you can be different, but only on this day.

More than simply exposing social structures, the social drama refreshes subscription to its rules and strictures. The regularity of the performance is important: continuity and persistence of an event is an essential part of its operation. This regularity or repetition exists even in the example of a secular ritual, such as annual academic graduations. Normally, the majority of participants only ever graduate once, but the presiding officers and academic procession maintain continuity of the event, ensuring the continuity of the social drama.

## Diegetic space and liminality in Nō and Kabuki

Writing about the design of a theatre for Nō[2] performances, Japanese architect Kuma Kengo focuses on the thresholds between offstage and onstage areas. In common with other Japanese dramatic traditions, the stage includes additional areas which are in-between the fully offstage and onstage. Frequently designed as a promenade or narrow pier extending from the stage to an entry point, it is the site of additional performances. In the case of Kabuki, these performances serve as introductions to a character, building anticipation for how they might add to the narrative unfolding, but they also allow for breaking the fourth wall: direct interaction with the audience and subtle undermining of the main stage. This is in essence an architectural illustration of Turner's discussion of liminality: the extension of the spaces between backstage and on-stage as a kind of physical interval allows for subsidiary performances to take place:

> Ordinarily, a theatre stage is intended to represent the world. The stage space being delimited, rules of perspective are often exploited to create the illusion of depth, so as to better imitate the real world. The baroque stage is a representative example of this type of theatre. The Nō stage, by contrast, was originally an open space, with no walls. It was not meant to be a representation of the world, for the world clearly existed on the other side of the stage. (Kuma, 2010:88)

Theatre in the round has a place in the Western tradition of course, but the manner in which the actors arrive on stage is very different: in both Nō and Kabuki, there is an interstitial space where actors promenade exaggeratedly before arriving on the main stage. In Nō, this is a bridge-like space, and the combination of elements indicates that Nō is a reflexive theatrical form: the stage is not a complete substitute reality, but a place within a wider world: there is action continuing beyond the stage.

This can be discussed in terms of diegetic space, a term common to film theory[3]. Diegetic space refers to the space of the performance, whilst extra-diegetic space is a territory outside of that action, implied by some cues within the drama. Crucially, extra-diegetic space is essential in some cases to validate the action of the drama by suggesting that it does not take place within a vacuum and that there are other lives and other places intersecting with this one. This is often the case in fantastic narratives where world-building is an essential part of the story. The tale loses authority if the audience cease to believe in the world it is set in, so cues and indications are used to show where other lives and stories might be taking place.

Christian Metz[4] was one of the pioneers in bringing semiotic theory to bear on film. The term 'diegesis' is used by Metz to mean the narrative content as signified. In cinema, the diegesis is the sum of the denotation of the film – the narration, the fictional space, and time, and the story as it is received by the spectator. As such, the diegesis is an imagined construct based upon the narrative; it is the imagined space outside of that narrative. Diegesis is an implicit system, one which is increasingly implied as the film progresses (with the start of the film requiring establishing shots to sketch the parameters of the narrative space); we can make more assumptions as we know the world of the particular film more.

Diegesis can be further defined in opposition to other terms. The time of diegesis is not necessarily identical to that of the discourse of the film, for example, Stanley Kubrick's *2001: A Space Odyssey*; its diegetic time spans millennia, whilst its discourse takes place in a couple of hours. The term 'diegesis' is useful primarily in terms of avant-garde film, where the dramatic narrative is not necessarily present; where little actually 'happens', but where a meaning is posited through diegesis. In this manner, the term is also more relative to architecture, which does not necessarily have a dramatic narrative, only an implied one. Architecture is employed in the activity of 'world-making'[5] as diegetic film is. Architecture can imply an other-worldliness, a sense of realm. The sum total of the architectural experience as it is received by the viewer implies a whole world outside based on or against these principles.

In Metz's discussion of the *autonomous shot*, he describes a single shot, distinct from its neighbours. Metz gives a catalogue of such shots which stand apart from the general flow of the film. The *non-diegetic* insert is an inserted shot which does not contribute or concur with the diegesis of the overall film, such as with Eisenstein's *Montage*.[6] The *subjective insert* is a shot within the diegesis, but one which is entirely subjective such as a dream or hallucination. The *displaced diegetic insert* is a shot which is spatially or temporally displaced from the context. Finally, the *explanatory insert* is one in which materials such as maps or newspapers are abstracted from the fictional space for the purpose of further explanation.

There are issues with this categorization, which is perhaps too absolute. The limitation of autonomous shots to short insertions is particularly problematic, whereas much larger segments of film may be shot in this way. Diegesis and diegetic space are helpful in constructing ideas of narrative space, however, and form a useful framework for the physical architecture of theatres and other spaces of performance and exhibition.

Erving Goffman's procedure of *frame analysis*[7] provides a further analysis more specific to theatre, this time of the Kabuki tradition where instead of masks, actors wear striking makeup in stories related to samurai legends. Writing on the theatrical frame, Goffman notes its complexity in Kabuki theatre, where certain events might break the 'fourth wall' convention, bringing the actors into contact with the audience via direct address. Broadly speaking, Goffman's theory of frames elaborates on the ways in which different constituencies participate in the same event. Performance provides a strong divide between these different groups: between the performers, the audience, and the front-of-house staff, all of whom experience the same place but through alternative filters or lenses.

Theatres are an ideal case study for how events are framed through examination of the various interests and roles of different participants. Whilst it is clearest here, it is a simple operation to extend this argument to other architectural types: domestic, institutional, commercial or religious buildings. Each is subject to alternative ways of dwelling and being according to the positioning of the building user. Goffman argues that we read our context through the dominant or *primary* frames at times: so the visitor to a religious site which belongs to a tradition other than their own might frame or interpret their encounter through their own faith, finding analogues for the kinds of religious practice they engage with. In a similar fashion, a trained architect often tends to frame their appreciation of a religious building through a professional scaffold: the thresholds, decoration, circulation, light, space and atmosphere, all as abstracted architectural qualities. Architecture, as a profession or training, can then be understood as a set of frameworks which might overlap and complement other frames. This dominant frame is the *key* in Goffman's terminology, and it becomes the reference point for other frames.

Goffman addresses this by describing the lamination of multiple frames (1974:82): we might apply several forms of understanding simultaneously. The separation of events by frames is, here, on the basis of intent. A rehearsal is different to a performance, even where all of the moves and actions are the same: as they are framed differently – once as a practice run and embedding material in the memory, and second as a performance unique to the audience present at the time.

The Kabuki-za Theatre in Tokyo (Figure 7.1) brings these elements of framing, diegesis and liminality together. The lighting is left up, not dimmed as I would expect of a Western theatre production. Despite the classical nature of the theatre, there is some audience participation in the form of encouragements

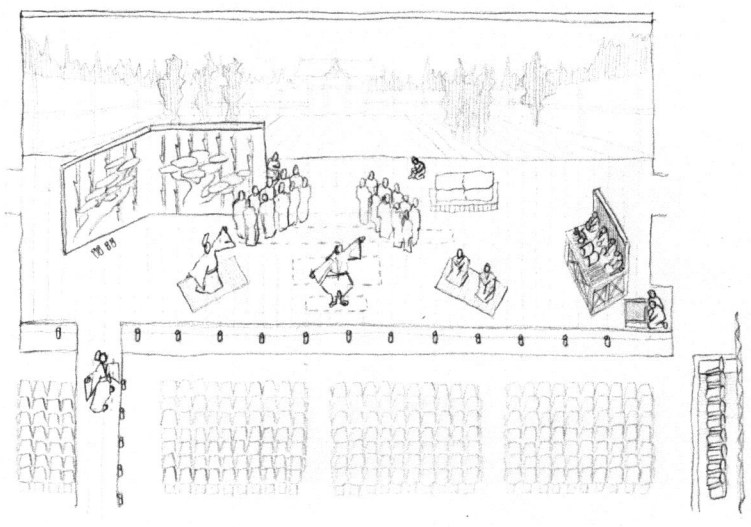

**FIGURE 7.1** *Sketched plan-oblique drawing of the Kabuki-za stage.*

shouted out from the crowd. The play is organized as discreet acts, and these are so separated as to allow for the sale of tickets for a single act as well as for the entire performance.

Japanese cultural codes are used as part of the stage setting, so that the act of removing footwear can effectively stand in for the transition from outside to inside without any flats or other scenery required to depict this passage from one place to another. This allows the stage to remain a contingent structure: determined by the actions of the actors rather than over-specified. The suspension of disbelief common to performance is present and correct here: the audience must subscribe to the story world and understand its rules, shortcuts and conveniences. This is most immediately apparent in the form of stagehands (Figure 7.2), dressed head to toe in dark clothing, who rush silently on and off stage with various props and pieces of scenery. They crouch and remain still and silent when required, but there is no darkness for them to recede into, and the audience is simply expected to understand that they are at once a part of the performance, but not a part of the story.

This speaks to the discussion of diegesis earlier and the various elements of narrative theory. The prop hands are part of the overall apparatus of the theatre (Figure 7.3) but are not part of the diegesis: they have no role within the story. This same presence of non-diegetic figures occurs with sound effects and musicians, who occupy a corner of the stage in full view of the audience. The Kabuki performance exposes its workings, is honest about the elements

**FIGURE 7.2** *Pictorial notation of the interaction between stagehand and actor.*

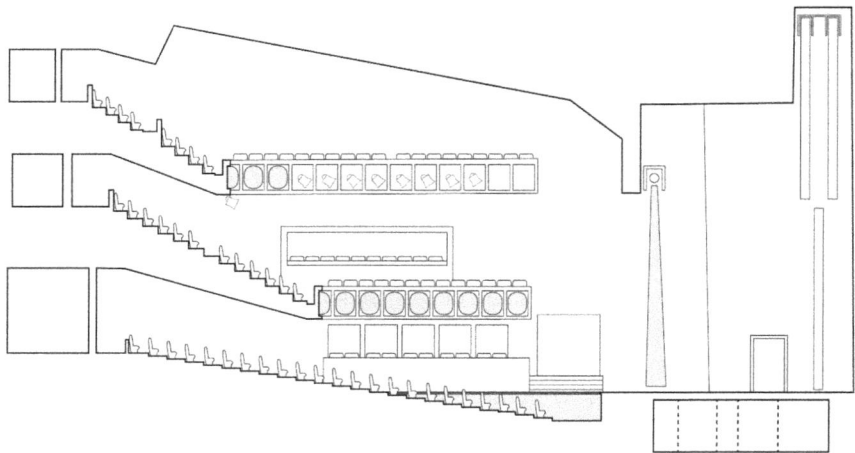

**FIGURE 7.3** *Schematic section of the Kabuki-za theatre auditorium.*

required to enhance the narrative, and expects the audience to understand who is part of the narrative and who stands outside of it.

The striking makeup and costumes of the characters are accompanied by a deeply affected and artificial way of acting. This is far from naturalistic, with dialogue half sung, half declared; movements are enhanced by the structured fabrics of formal kimono as well as various props and stools which allow more dramatic poses to be taken and maintained, rendering the actors as a kind of detailed diagram of a character.

The performance is, then, operatic in character: elements of dance, drama and music come together in a controlled and carefully separated way: elements are allowed to stand apart from one another in a manner that recalls the montage theories of filmmaker Sergei Eisenstein. The lead actors use high, warbling vibrato at times; a controlled crack in the voice is part of what Roland Barthes terms the grain[8] of this performance.

> It is this displacement that I want to outline, not with regard to the whole of music but simply to a part of vocal music (lied or mélodie): the very precise space (genre) of the encounter between a language and a voice. I shall straightaway give a name to this signifier at the level of which, I believe, the temptation of ethos can be liquidated (and thus the adjective banished): the grain, the grain of the voice when the latter is in a dual posture, a dual production – of language and of music. (Roland Barthes, 'The Grain of the Voice' (1977:181))

The space of the stage and auditorium is diegetically sophisticated.

*Off-Stage:* Drum, Flute, Percussion, and audience participation calls.

*On-Stage but non-diegetic:* Prop-hands, String Instruments, Narrator

*On-Stage and diegetic:* Sound Effects.

*Diegetic Space:* Actors on stage.

*Interstitial Space:* Actors' promenade into auditorium.

The main diegetic space of the stage is differentiated according to the ground plane. Shoes, cloth and mats are all used to define spaces. The promenade from the stage is a particularly interesting element and has some similarities into the staging of large arena shows by rock bands. The parallel nature of this space allows an actor to attempt to upstage their colleagues by overacting and making a great deal of their entrances and exits from stage via this deck, lending a comedic air to proceedings.

The complexity of the stage in Kabuki is instructive as it exposes many of the hidden workings of other theatrical forms. The same parameters might be at play, but Kabuki uses the stage in a transparent way, simultaneously in our world and that of the narrative. There is a shared conceit between the audience and the performers, that we are able to ignore the presence of stagehands and musicians, that the entrance to a building is indicated only by a place where people remove their outdoor shoes, and that energetic performances can sit between these two spaces in an extended threshold.

## How Sanja Matsuri makes Asakusa

A more elaborate example is the Sanja Matsuri and how the Asakusa district of the city maintains its strong sense of identity in part through the enactment of the annual festival. It is an example of how performance and ritual are flexible, adapting to the needs of the participants. It also serves to illuminate a broader idea of what constitutes architecture and urban design by including temporary installations, mobile structures and the bodies of people as factors in the built environment. This festival is a community-focused activity with a key contribution played by neighbourhood associations. The festival might appear initially to be a spectacle, an extraordinary event, but I argue here that in fact a heightened ordinariness lies at the heart of the festival similar to what has been observed by Henri Lefebvre:

Festival differed from everyday life only in the explosion of forces which had been slowly accumulated in and via everyday life itself. (2014:222)

Festivals contrast(ed) violently from everyday life, *but they were not separate from it.* (2014:227)

Asakusa's identity is distinctly *shitamachi* or low town (as opposed to the *yamanote* of the ruling classes in the centre of the city, these wards now enclosed by the route of the famous Yamanote Line train). This identity is maintained, much in the same manner as one would clean, tidy and repair one's home: the festival is a similar activity restoring social bonds through participation in a large celebration.

Neighbourhood Associations (abbreviated to NHA) have a role in the organization of the festivals. The associations are semi-official organizations which serve a variety of roles within Japanese society. In Tokyo, the NHA tends towards the larger size with membership of over 200 households being the norm (Pekkanen, Tsujinaka & Yamamoto, 2014:20; Bestor, 1990). In their present form, urban NHAs have their roots in a drive to help rural migrants integrate into urban life as well as in urban sanitation associations which became a necessity after several outbreaks of disease in the 1920s (Schmidtpott, 2012:125–147). With very high levels of membership (over 90 per cent in recent surveys), there is some dispute about how democratic these associations are: the leadership is unregulated and circulates around vested interests such as local landowners in some cases. The NHAs have a range of roles including fire and crime prevention, assistance for elderly residents, and the organization of festivals. They support themselves through subscription fees (generally modest and in the order of ¥500 to ¥1500[9] per month, unless a major fund-raising drive is in operation, such as for the construction of a new *Mikoshi* or portable shrine) and grants from local government for some services rendered. Schmidtpott (2012:134) details these, noting that from the 1920s, the NHA duties would include social obligations such as formal congratulations or condolences for births, marriages and deaths, and the farewell and welcome-home parties for military personnel. This was not all, however, and the NHA also had a more pragmatic remit to look after sanitation and fire prevention measures: making the associations something of an extra-governmental organization. Our main interest here is the role of the NHA in the organization of public festivals (Figure 7.4), where they acted as a conduit to mediate the needs of the shrine and the police and fire brigade who would ensure public safety.

Whilst the shrine associations are also involved in the organization of festivals, the majority of the organization falls to NHAs. This is certainly the case with Sanja Matsuri, for which NHAs outnumber shrine associations

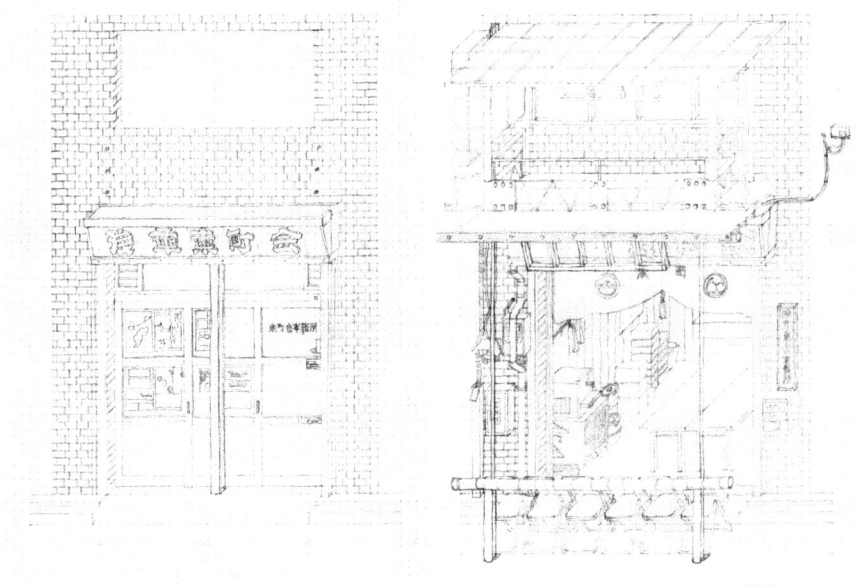

**FIGURE 7.4** *Oblique drawings of NHA outside of (a) and during (b) festival.*

significantly. One event of the Sanja Matsuri calendar occurs on Friday evening whilst preparations for the main *Mikoshi* parade are taking place. Groups of youngsters are assembled by each association at their headquarters, and they are given a number of money envelopes. These groups then visit each of the neighbouring associations in turn in order to hand over this offering and to pay respects to their counterparts. This introduces the youngsters from one neighbourhood to the elders of another and establishes a network of neighbourliness through the exchange of a gift which is expected to be reciprocated.[10]

This is described by Pekkanen, Tsujinaka and Yamamoto as social capital, after the work of John Helliwell and Robert Putnam (1995). Social capital is discussed in terms of networks of people which must be maintained over time and is built up through the conduct of social activities – such as the festival in this case. Whilst participation in other aspects of NHA work might be brought into question, the festival brings many of the more recalcitrant neighbours out onto the streets. Reciprocity and trust are key to this, something which, without becoming too heavy handed, could be symbolized by the manner in which the *Mikoshi* are carried around the streets of Taito ward. The contemporary activities of the NHA, like the 1920s list noted above, read as a list of how one might wish to achieve social cohesion (Pekkanen, Tsujinaka & Yamamoto, 2014:61), encouraging face-to-face interactions and cooperation without monetary gain. By assisting in the organization of festivals, sport, neighbourhood maintenance and crime prevention, the NHA ensures an important role for itself not only in the community, but *as* the community – a benign and beneficial presence in conducting public goods.

It is notable not only that managing the festival is consistently reported to be amongst the most important of the functions of the NHA, but that it also sits alongside activities such as looking after the needs of older residents, ensuring that waste is recycled, parks are kept in order, and fire prevention measures are up to date. Different aspects of the social and physical well-being of the neighbourhood are combined within these organizational structures.

Sanja Matsuri is an annual festival held by the Asakusa ward of Tokyo, one of the oldest districts of the city, as it is the site of the fishing village which grew into Edo, later established as Tokyo by the Tokugawa shogunate. Asakusa is the key *shitamachi* district, a working-class downtown area which has a character unlike the rest of the city (Jinnai, 1995; Lucas, 2009a). It was once the entertainment district of the city, the legendary floating world celebrated by authors including Ishiguro and Kawabata or artists such as Utumaro and Hokusai. That the district maintains its identity is in part due to this annual Shinto festival which celebrates the founding of the Asakusa-jinja[11] circa 628 CE, when fishermen found a bronze statue of the Kannon Bosatsu, deity of mercy, in the Sumida-Gawa, which was thrown back three times before they kept it and decided to build a shrine for it. Senso-ji is commonly held to be Tokyo's oldest temple with the current structures dating from 1649 having survived such events as the Great Meireki Fire of 1657, the Great Kanto Earthquake of 1923 and the firebombing of Tokyo during the Second World War (Cali & Dougill, 2013:63).

The festival is held over three days in May, taking over Asakusa ward (one of twenty-three in the city) with a series of processions and celebrations. Central to this is the complex of Senso-ji and Asakusa-Jinja. This sacred precinct contains both the Buddhist temple and a Shinto shrine – a common state of affairs in Japan where multiple belief systems coexist both for individuals and amongst the populace at large. The classic division is between Buddhism's governing the rituals of birth and death, and Shinto's dealing with the everyday (Ashkenazi, 1993:16–22). This is of course a simplification, but a useful one.

The route (Figure 7.5) to the sacred precinct is Nakamise Dori, a long pedestrian street occupied by low-rise shops and food outlets, all housed in corrugated metal buildings decorated according to the seasons (such as zodiac figures for the lunar New Year, cherry blossom in April). This *shotengai*, or shopping street, is a common feature of Japanese towns with distinctive characteristics and challenges as documented by Stephen Robertson (2014): in

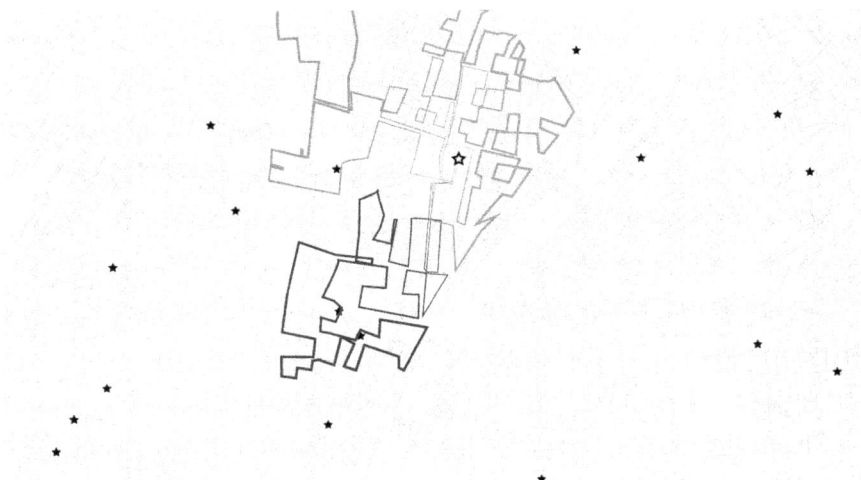

**FIGURE 7.5** *Sample route map for Sanja Matsuri on sunday; these are modified slightly each year.*

this case ritual goods, traditional crafts and foods are sold alongside the latest cartoon character memorabilia and tourist wares. The street is punctuated by large gates bearing enormous lanterns and fierce statues representing thunder and lightning. In the days preceding the festival proper, street food stalls are set up in the area around the temple and shrine, lending a festival atmosphere to the precinct. Such vendors travel from festival to festival, as many small towns and city districts hold events according to staggered annual and biennial calendars.

The festival begins with a procession on Friday afternoon. This procession walks up Nakamise Dori and consists of representatives of various Asakusa trades and traditions. Crowds gather and are corralled by marshals bearing the logo of the festival: three fishing boat prows in a circular *mon* (the family crest or coat of arms would be the closest European equivalent – see Ikuya (2001) for more details). Key participants in the procession include Shinto priests (*kannushi*[12]); lion dancers and *shukahachi* and *binzasara*[13] musicians; floats with drummers; representatives of the fishermen singing in traditional dress and straw boater hats, geisha and their attendants; dancers dressed in spectacular heron costumes (heron having particular associations for the fishing culture in Japan, where some towns still employ trained birds to fish for them) (see Figure 7.6). The procession winds around the front of Senso-ji towards Asakusa-jinja, which has a modest open air stage for the various music and dance performances that take place in sequence whilst festival marshals prepare for the days ahead. This initial part of the festival is orderly

**FIGURE 7.6** *Author's photograph of procession showing (a) neighbourhood association members; (b) musicians and dancers; (c) geisha; (d) heron hooded dancers.*

and solemn: the route is prescribed and has a measured, slow pace unlike the exuberance of the days to follow.

Before the main events begin on Friday, the three main *Mikoshi* (portable shrines) are prepared. The *Mikoshi* resembles a Shinto shrine in miniature(Figure 7.7) and is constructed from lacquered wood decorated with brass fittings, ropes, bells, lanterns and paper streamers. These are carried on long beams by teams of bearers. The *Mikoshi* range in size from the small children's version, through a standard size used by each local neighbourhood, up to the larger shrine *Ō-Mikoshi*. Thursday night sees the *kami* installed in the large *Ō-Mikoshi* in an elaborate ceremony including plunging the shrine precinct into darkness.

These larger *Ō-Mikoshi* belong to Asakusa-jinja and represent the two fishermen brothers and one landowner, who have taken on the status of *kami*[14] themselves, named:

*Hinokuma Takenari no Mikoto*
*Hinokuma Hamanari no Mikoto*
*Hajino Matsuchi no Mikoto*

# THEATRE AND FESTIVAL: PERFORMANCE AND LIMINAL SPACE

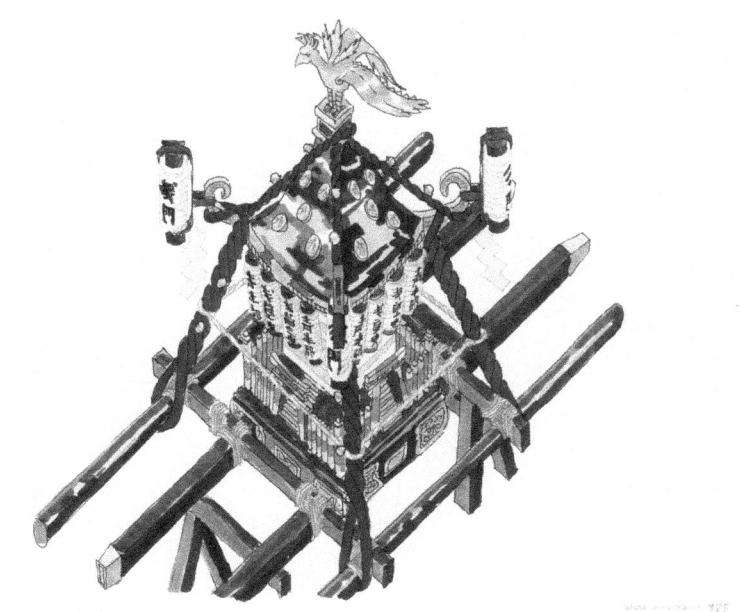

**FIGURE 7.7** *Axonometric drawing of an example of a neighbourhood* Mikoshi.

Asakusa's *kami* are unusual (although not unique; their status is particularly appropriate to this locale) in that they are three working-class or merchant-class people elevated to this status, known also as *Sansha* and *Sanja gongen* in an overlap between the Buddhist and Shinto religious traditions. Images of the three fishermen were sculpted by one of the monks and it is these artefacts that persist as the *kami* today. Locals who are members of the Matsuri organizing committee attend to the *Mikoshi* ahead of the installation of the *kami* into the shrine. This preparation (Figure 7.8) consists largely of practical measures such as attaching lighting, repairing wiring, polishing and other maintenance. All the while a larger group in festival dress of *happi* coat (coloured and decorated according to the district of Asakusa which they represent) gather in preparation for lifting the heavy structure for its procession around Asakusa. This gathering is boisterous and jovial in nature, a mix of men and women, old and young, representative of the neighbourhood.

The *Mikoshi* are often described as divine palanquins and resemble mobile pieces of architecture, their lacquered roofs decorated with large medallions inscribed with the *mon* symbol of the neighbourhood or expressing the formal rank of the enshrined *kami*, above a highly ornamental inner shrine structure depicting mythical beasts, often with miniature steps and *torii* gates, topped with *Hōō* birds (similar to phoenixes) and broad-braided ropes called

**FIGURE 7.8** *Author's photographs of street-side maintenance and preparation of the Mikoshi.*

*himo fusa* bearing multiple *suzu* bells (Figures 7.9 and 7.10). The *Mikoshi* are only considered fully sacred during festival times and are merely stored in a convenient place when not in use (one, for example, is stored in a glass display case in Asakusa subway station when not in use).

The priest arrives from the shrine, dressed in full traditional costume with gauze hat and lacquered wooden clogs, carrying sprigs of evergreen *sakaki* (Ashkenazi, 1993:31) which have been blessed at the main shrine. His role is to install or perhaps invite the *kami* into the shrine, meaning that this *kami* is now residing within the *Mikoshi*. He blesses the portable shrine and the gathered crowd, exchanging pleasantries with the organizing committee, who are attending to the *Mikoshi* from an open ground-floor retail unit. Throughout the Matsuri, such houses or units are used as resting or stopping points and are referred to as the *Mikoshi-shuku* (Ashenzaki, 1993:58). This is significant, as the festival is intended to ensure good trade for Asakusa ward for the coming year. This is a practical and pragmatic intention for the festival, and its location reflects these aims.

The neighbourhood gathers around the association office (sometimes a permanent feature, sometimes an appropriated space such as an empty store or garage). Those who are participating in the parade are dressed in the neighbourhood's colours and are drilled by the most experienced to lift the *Mikoshi*. This is no mean feat as some are reported to weigh in the region of 5000 kg. There are cries of

# THEATRE AND FESTIVAL: PERFORMANCE AND LIMINAL SPACE 175

**FIGURE 7.9** *Drawing of the various parts of the* Mikoshi.

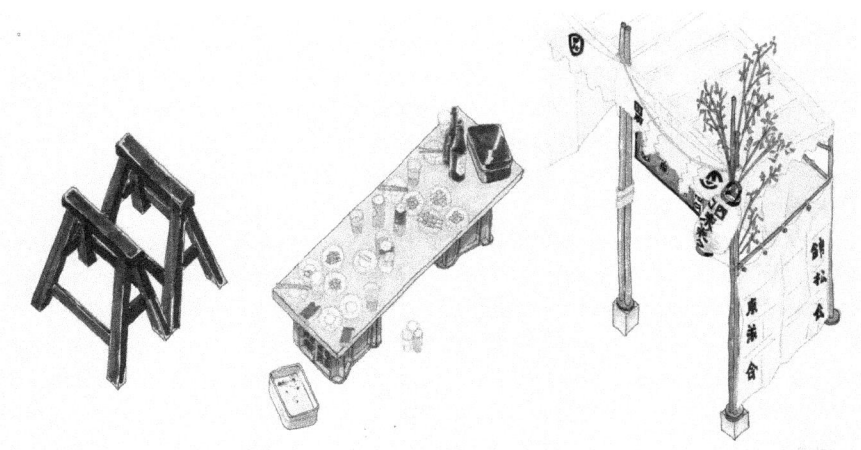

**FIGURE 7.10** *Drawings of the material culture, street decoration and appropriations found during Sanja Matsuri, including (a) Mikoshi trestles; (b) ad hoc picnic table; (c) temporary tarpaulin and scaffolding pole enclosure.*

*wasshoi wasshoi*

Or more commonly at Asakusa:

*Say ya, soi ya, sah, sorya*

These calls are used to coordinate the movement of the *Mikoshi*. At the same time, a member of the procession directs the crowd by gesturing with fans and clacking wooden blocks, using encouragement rather than direct instruction. By these means the *Mikoshi* makes its way, along with the other major shrines, to the gates of Asakusa-jinja. The shrine's movement is characteristically halting, back and forward and side to side. The shaking that results is necessary to ring the bells, which symbolize the presence of the *kami* within the shrine.

Saturday's events are much more boisterous and involve revelry on the streets of Asakusa as the *Mikoshi* representing some forty-four other districts converge on the neighbourhood. This part of the festival has a number of *Mikoshi* manned by members of Yakuza gangs, showing their characteristic tattoos flagrantly as a form of defiance against the authorities. The energetic nature of Sanja Matsuri reflects the metropolitan model of Matsuri, and this is beginning to influence the rather more sedate festivals held elsewhere in Japan (as noted by Ashenzaki, 1993:49–64). Whilst some Matsuri have been held for centuries, their form can and does change. One of the most notable recent shifts is linked to the events of the Second World War. Neighbourhood associations had been co-opted by government into the war effort for organizing and recruiting. After the war, many Matsuri had to be re-established and emerged in modified forms, particularly as their use in wartime propaganda had damaged the reputation of the associations (see Pekkanen et al., 2014:16–17).

The Sunday processions follow set paths, which are revised each year for each of the three *Ō-Mikoshi*. They include miniature pavilions for children, carts with musicians and temporary stages across the ward (Figure 7.11).

With the streets full of revellers; the movement of the three *Ō-Mikoshi* of the Asakusa-jinja is not through space, but through a medium: a medium consisting of the throng of people; the moving shrine has a ripple effect through the often tightly packed crowds as it wends its way side to side through the back streets and thoroughfares. Movement in the case of the crowded festival streets is not subject to the considerations of walking alone or in small groups discussed in Chapter 6: the density of occupation acts to change the nature of our movement altogether. It is therefore useful to borrow an alternative spatial system from James Gibson, who worked with a triad of *surface, medium and substance* (1983[1966]) in preference to the Cartesian

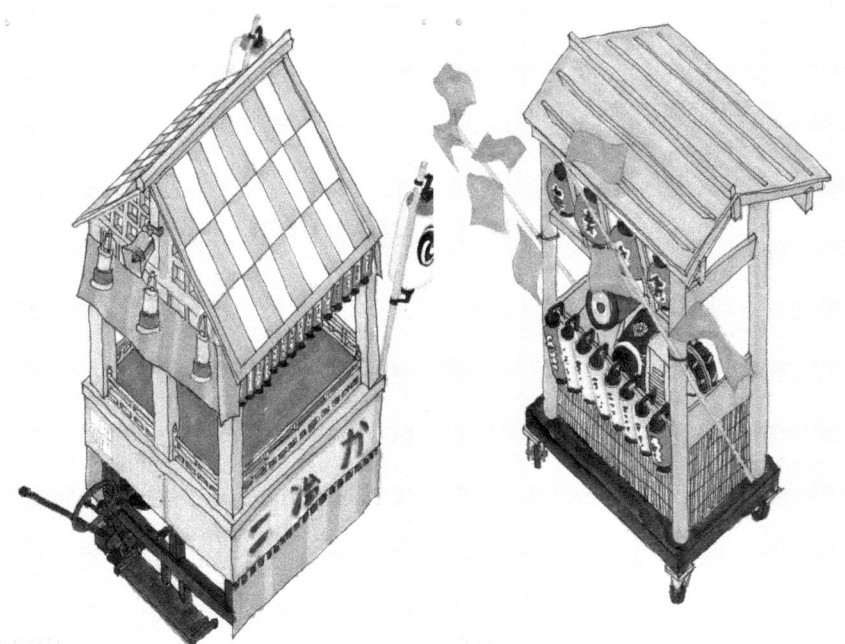

**FIGURE 7.11** *Drawings of temporary stages.*

coordinates which dominate discussions of space. Gibson's triad and later interpretations (Ingold, 2000) give us a world of atmospheres and resistance, of resistance and friction rather than abstract coordinates and forms.

This idea of the triad of medium, substance and surface is particularly useful in narrative and sensory engagements with the urban realm (Lucas, 2012), with the medium offering a less homogeneous and abstract idea than conventional undifferentiated geometrical space. Mediums have qualities of flow and resistance, even air: we do not move across a hard crust of the earth but engage with its various surfaces with varying levels of porosity.

Towards the end of the day, the sacred precinct at Asakusa-jinja and Senso-ji is closed off, using mobile fencing. This enclosure is arranged by police and festival officials, but high metal boxes are moved into place, corralling the crowds whilst the shrine continues to allow visitors. A final procession takes the main *Ō-Mikoshi* back to the shrine: members of the neighbourhood association and local dignitaries make up this procession along with priests, but it is a slow, shambling affair lacking the formality and serenity of the Friday procession. The procession is timed to coincide with sunset, and lanterns on long bamboo poles light the way. The character of the festival here is one of exhaustion: its energy is spent rather than culminating in a climactic celebration. Once the procession has passed, murmurs pass through the crowd as it is established that the Matsuri is over, and the crowds disperse through the shrine grounds towards the main street where traffic has been restored, a final indicator of the return to normality.

## Embodied urbanism

The Sanja Matsuri festival, I argue, is a form of embodied urbanism. I draw here upon the literature on how our bodies can be said to possess knowledge or muscle memory: skills that are held by the hand and eye through training, as much as they reside within the brain as memories (Sudnow, 2001[1978]; Pallasmaa, 2009; Sennett, 2008). An urbanism that is embodied is not so much a ground upon which we enact our daily lives as a condition in perpetual emergence, becoming and co-creation. This is to produce the city on a daily basis, sometimes in an energetic fashion as in the case of Sanja Matsuri, but more often in smaller ways. Urbanism and civitas are performed rather than encountered ready-made, and this performance is demonstrated as soon as we engage in an alternative activity, suspend normal rules of play and take possession of the city more fully by way of occupation. Fundamentally, human presence in space – collectively gathering in order to demonstrate a commonality, a community (Figures 7.12 and 7.13) – is a way of marking it with significance. It is to perform a collective belonging to the place, a taking possession by which the place, in turn, comes to belong to the community.

In the Sanja Matsuri, the downward gravitational forces of the *Mikoshi* are transferred through the bearers and then to the crowd with a tightly packed group of people acting like a *substance* in Gibson's spatial triad of

**FIGURE 7.12** *Watercolour studies of Sanja Matsuri participants showing* happi *coats and other uses of costume to identify affiliation.*

**FIGURE 7.13** *Author's photographs of Sanja Matsuri.*

*surface, medium and substance* – before becoming fluid again to act as a medium. This medium can be navigated through carefully, but sometimes resistance and blockage will be met whilst at other times you are drawn along a prevailing current. Gibson's triad allows us to understand how any element can recategorize itself according to its status at a given time. People can be medium when present as a large crowd, substance when supporting a heavy *Mikoshi*, and surfaces when wearing clothing decorated with symbols and colours which identify the district of the ward they belong to.

An important aspect of the carrying of a *Mikoshi* can be described by way of a structural diagram. Figure 7.14 shows how the weight of the portable

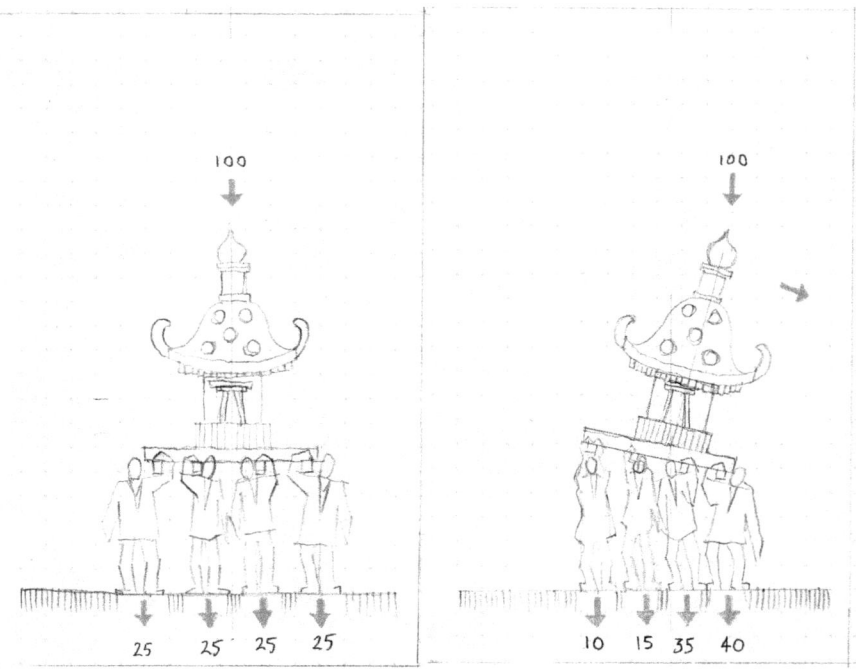

**FIGURE 7.14** *Structural diagrams of* Mikoshi *parade.*

shrine is distributed amongst the bearers. In many ways, this resembles the structural properties of a Gothic window, where the tracery splits the load of upper masonry and roof structures, dividing it as between branches of an inverted tree (Figure 7.14). In the case of the *Mikoshi*, this is a live load: a term used to discuss moving bodies, as opposed to the dead load of stone or a sudden snowfall. When the *Mikoshi* is being carried simply, the load is distributed evenly amongst the participants with each carrier taking an equal share of the load. This is not always the case, however, as part of the practice of bearing the *Mikoshi* is to jostle the divine palanquin in order to please the *kami* within. This is most often achieved by means of a bouncing gait whilst dipping the *Mikoshi* rhythmically from side to side. Pitching forward and back is not done deliberately and can cause dangerous collapses from which it is difficult to recover.

When the group of bearers (Figure 7.15) dip the *Mikoshi*, one side gains some temporary relief from the weight of the structure, whilst others bear double the usual load. This increased load is then taken, in turn, by the other set of bearers as the structure is rocked from one side to the other. This has the effect of jangling the bells attached to the *Mikoshi* ropes and of lifting the structure high above the heads of the surrounding sea of festival-goers.

**FIGURE 7.15** *Axonometric drawing of* Mikoshi *bearers.*

Sen and Silverman have suggested that there are two sides to embodiment:

On one hand, to embody something is to express, personify, and give concrete and perceptible form to a concept that may exist only as an abstraction.

On the other hand 'to embody' also suggests the art of becoming part of a body. Viewed as an act of incorporation, embodiment allows us to see the powerful ideological role played by place in the formation of human subjects. In other words, the experience of place can constitute – that is, be a substantial part of – our senses of individual and communal self-identification and can situate us within larger social contexts. (Sen and Silverman, 2014:4)

Taken in the first sense, the embodiment of Asakusa might be said to give form to the concept of the neighbourhood and its unique spirit within the larger metropolis, through the deliberate deployment of the residents' bodies both within the processions and in the large numbers who come to watch it. The festival renders the community visible.[15] But in the second sense, it can be about the construction of selfhood with reference to a larger body of people.

It is worth reinforcing one component of Sen and Silverman's argument here: the 'transient moment thus produces a new place, a new context, new act, and new meaning'. This is a powerful assertion and raises several questions of perennial architectural contention: what is the nature of *meaning* in architecture, for example, what are the means by which new places are constituted and how does this constitutive moment interact with a pre-existing context? 'Context' is by far the most suggestive term here, as it remains one of the fundamental aspects of space discussed both through the practice of architectural design *and* through discourse about architecture.

Sen and Silverman's work (2014:20) on embodiment seeks at one point to separate the term from the physical facts of the body, referring instead to what those bodies are doing, what the result of their presence and intervention is. This might be problematic, abstracting the physical facts of human bodies out of a discussion intended to rehabilitate their position in contemporary theory. This speaks to the underlying tensions in both architecture and anthropology which I intend to address here. Architecture often abstracts and eliminates the actual human body from its practices. A deeper engagement with the alternative ways in which space can be constructed is needed. For architecture to include the human, the social, the cultural, it must understand some of the ways in which spaces are produced by human bodies, both mundane and spectacular.

Embodiment can suggest a notion of the body as a stable or fixed entity. Architectural history is littered with practical examples in which the human body is used as a model, a system of proportions, a measure for the oft-cited *human scale* of buildings. *Vitruvian Man*, LeCorbusier's *Modulor* (2000), and even the *Metric Handbook* (Buxton, 2015) each perpetuates a myth of the average or standard human. This leads to a model of accommodating the body into architecture by way of efficiency and proportion rather than multiplicity and variation.

Anthropology provides evidence which contradicts this pragmatic and stable view of the body, and in doing so it problematizes the approach taken by most architects. There is a role for depictions of the human body as a set of dimensions, however: so whilst I am critical of them as our *sole* system for understanding the body in architecture, they do serve a purpose. Texts as diverse as Blackman's discussion of key concepts of *The Body* (2008); Iain Borden's account of skateboarders' unique understanding of the city (2003); Sarah Pink's discussion of the relationship between home, identity and the body (2004); and Graafland's (2005) compilation on *The Body in Architecture* all look to complicate this image of the body and to discuss the relationship between body and identity.

This is one aspect of Sanja Matsuri: an expression of identity and community, of association with a place in the world expressed through bodily interventions. Asakusa is maintained by these and other activities, and whilst it would be making too great a claim to say that the festival is alone responsible for the strength of identity in this part of Tokyo, it is certainly one very important part of the story. Architecturally, the festival gives us an alternative model of spatiality. Buildings are temporary and mobile; the role of the human body in their functioning is explicit, experiential and exhausting. Architecture's various avant-gardes have long dreamt of such fleeting and contingent architectures that would embody the collective will of the people. Such ideas have regularly led to the envisaging of highly engineered technical solutions, as in Cedric Price's *Fun Palace*[16] and similar proposals. Events such as Sanja Matsuri suggest that architects might look to extant urban conditions more carefully in order to understand the rounded nature of how practices of this kind integrate into communities and contexts.

# Notes

1. This is reinforced by positions on narrative taken by the likes of Umberto Eco (1989) and Andrey Tarkovsky (1986); see Lucas (2002:) for more on the architectural applications of narrative theory.
2. Also frequently transliterated as Noh.
3. See Bordwell (1987) for a narrative theory which, although framed around cinema, has applications elsewhere.
4. See Metz (1984).
5. See Goodman (1978) for more on this. See also Lucas (2018b) where connections are drawn between Sanja Matsuri and Goodman's (1976) work on script and score.
6. See Lucas (2002) for more on the relationship between montage theory and architecture.
7. See Goffman (1974:132–146).
8. See Barthes (1977:179–189) on the grain of the voice.
9. See Pekkanen, Tsujinaka & Yamamoto (2014:31–32).
10. See Chapter 5 for more on theories of the gift.
11. Asakusa shrine, often overlooked as the site, is dominated by the much larger Senso-ji temple.
12. The *kannushi* is followed by a rather more exotic figure: the *Tengu*. This masked figure wears elaborate robes and carries a *naginata* spear or glaive, perched on high stilt-like wooden sandals. The most striking aspect of the *Tengu* is his red mask with long nose and fierce demeanour, a capricious and martial mountain spirit who has various guises in Japanese folklore, sometimes with more crow-like features and the subject of some shamanistic elements of Shinto (see Hansen, 2008, for more details).

This representative of the spirit world walks his own route independent of the *Mikoshi* parade and is accompanied by white-robed shrine attendants carrying a drum and an offering box for small change. He is regarded with some faux trepidation by the crowd but offers a blessing to a small child on his way through, bestowing favour to the bravest children as a kind of reassurance. This personification of a spirit is called a moot entity in the literature. The collapse of spirit and mundane worlds is illustrated by this and other aspects of the festival.

**13** Binzasara, in particular, is detailed in Groemer (2010).

**14** *Kami* are nature-based spirits or minor gods in Shinto, sometimes the embodiment of important ancestors as is the case here.

**15** In a sense similar to Paul Klee's dictum (paraphrased here) that art does not render the already visible; instead it makes things visible. It is not a representation of the community spirit of Asakusa, but a revelation of it.

**16** See Hardingham (2017) and Herdt (2017) for an account of Price's work.

# 8

# Restaurants, Food Events and Sensory Architectures

## Introduction

This chapter addresses the architectures around the preparation and consumption of food. Fundamental to human life, these everyday events can often be taken for granted. Anthropological theories of food necessitate a wide range of practices to be accommodated, resulting in concepts such as *food events,* covering a range of circumstances between home-cooked meals and formal restaurants. Further anthropological approaches complicate the relationship between cooked and raw foods, problematically defining cultures according to the supposed complexity of cooked foods without accounting for foods such as sashimi where carefully prepared raw ingredients are celebrated, and spaces arranged around allowing the diner to assess the quality and freshness of those ingredients. However problematically Goody and Levi-Strauss use these distinctions, they accurately identify the factors of interest within a food culture.

A second thread to the argument of this chapter is to understand dining spaces as a form of sensory architecture. By using a methodology developed during research into the multisensory nature of urban environments, the chapter presents a series of accounts of Japanese food events from formal multi-course *kaiseki* meals through single-dish restaurants towards more informal settings of *izakaya* drinking establishments and *yatai* street food stands. Understanding architecture as multisensory allows us to move beyond the purely visual. Architecture can design the ways in which tactile and kinetic aspects of space affect us. What is the potential of determining the aural characteristics of a place beyond the acoustic control of an auditorium; or working with our thermal and chemical senses in constructing ideas comfort and a sense of place.

The architecture of food events provides a model for the multisensory understanding of other types of architecture: restaurants and kitchens are the most profoundly and directly sensory architectures, proposing the idea that we can design sensory perception through processes of analysis and recording, diagnosis and precedent, direct experimentation and iterations of design. These lessons can certainly be applicable elsewhere.

## Food events

Sensory perception and architecture is often dominated by discussions of the visual, but a growing field of research into alternative sensory modalities has extended this to the consideration of the entire perceptual field. Still neglected are taste and its associated experiences despite the prevalence of how we experience eating at home, in restaurants and in the street.

The consumption of food varies within every cuisine and is described effectively by Joy Adapon (2008) with reference to the *Art and Agency* theory of Alfred Gell (1998a). The varieties of culinary experience can be usefully mapped on to this agency diagram, moving far beyond the examples described by Adapon of Mexican culinary traditions. As such an important human activity, it is peculiar that the ways in which we eat are rarely addressed within architectural education: the fundamental everyday activities of human life are effectively erased or worse, normalized in ways which neglect to address the richness possible within this sphere. Eating has social connotations, and the spaces vary significantly within a culture never mind from one culture to another. What underlying structure can be identified to help architects to design more engaging culinary environments? What can we learn from sitting at the bench in a Japanese tempura restaurant, the carefully constructed ritual of eating in a Michelin starred upscale restaurant, taking a fresh fish from Noryangjin fish market in Seoul upstairs to a restaurant to be cooked, or the arrangement of an efficient modernist example?

This chapter addresses some of the underlying social issues around hygiene, cleanliness, function and order through the work of anthropologists including Mary Douglas, Joy Adapon, Jack Goody, Michael Ashkenazi and Jeanne Jacob each examine some of the cultural manifestations of the relationship between eating and space. This chapter uses a range of examples from Japanese restaurant culture as a starting point. As with other aspects of this book, I am drawing on my own field research, which has largely involved visiting Japan and South Korea.

Food cultures vary enormously, but represent explicitly social occasions where interaction and exchange are framed by architecture. This relationship between the built environment, cooking and eating can be extended towards the entire processes of production, the potential for urban farming and the like, but with this chapter I would like to retain the focus on the everyday: the forms of social exchange around food and drink that are all too easily taken for granted. There are implicit and explicit rules around dining, ranging from etiquette and the formalities of politeness through to processes of ordering and paying for food. This chapter overlaps with two others: *Chapter 3* on dwelling and *Chapter 5* on exchange and marketplaces. With that in mind, the focus here shall be on spaces of hospitality, dining out across a range from street food through to fine dining. Each instance shall be used to discuss a different aspect of the relationship between dining and architecture, and the social contexts generated in each instance.

The approach here is to revisit approaches from material culture studies of entanglements, co-production, status and candidacy rather than to see food and its surrounding taboos as purely symbolic. Ashkenazi and Jacob argue that cultural bans on eating certain foods tend to have their origins in very pragmatic reasons such as the value of animals being kept alive rather than slaughtered (in the case of cows in India, the production of quality fertilizer and milk outweighs the value of meat), or the economics of available prairie land explaining the US preference for beef more than its association with frontier mythologies (2013:18).

Positioning food within the broader material culture debates in anthropology is helpful, as it moves discussion of food and cuisine (not to mention their associated architectural manifestations) away from symbolism and discussion of taboo towards opportunism, economy, convenience and practicality.

One of the most important figures in elaborating the anthropology of food is Jack Goody (1982). He bridges the symbolic tradition and the material culture tradition, still focusing on class issues, but also discussing the practicalities of how food is prepared. The fundamental category of cooking can be broken into so many alternative practices, but remains at heart the process of applying heat to raw foods in order to make them more palatable. He distinguishes 'simple' and 'complex' societies which either practice *cooking* or who can be considered to have a *cuisine* in which a more complex system of rules governs the social and technical aspects of food preparation and consumption, with specialization of tasks opposed to the generalists of his simple societies. Descriptions of simple or complex cultures tend to be avoided as cultural relativism and comparison to a norm in contemporary anthropology, as the assumptions which allow us to declare on culture to be simple are largely based on romantic and well-meaning assumptions through to colonialist attitudes.

Goody's work also has a focus on class as a manifestation of the economic system and separates societies into *subsistence* cultures where one gathers food directly in order to survive and *differentiated* ones where surplus and specialism is possible, splitting out the farmers from the store owners and chefs. This supposed simplicity of survival cooking processes and the almost ritualized cuisine which offers the idea based in a historical progress narrative that rules and preferences become established and more deeply encoded over time. There are some useful aspects to Goody's categorizations, but many of his assumptions are contentious.

Early anthropologists also considered food cultures as indicative of broader societal characteristics. Starting with James Frazer's and Radcliffe-Brown's early work on taboos and Lévi-Strauss's distinction between the underlying principles of raw and cooked food, there was a focus on understanding food as symbols, demonstrative of other values held by a community. Lévi-Strauss places fire, and the transformation of raw food into cooked as central to the emergence of humanity itself. Writing in *Structural Anthropology* (1974), Lévi-Strauss develops a series of binary oppositions to describe the underlying differences between cuisines. Coining the term *gustemes* analogous to the elements of language in the semiotic theory which influenced his work, Lévi-Strauss's description involves distinctions between:

*Endogenous/Exogenous* ingredients (native or exotic)
*Central/Peripheral* components of the dish (staples versus garnishes)
*Marked/not marked* flavours (strong or bland).
(Lévi-Strauss, 1974:86–87)

Such binary oppositions have fallen out of favour in contemporary anthropology, and are now seen as rather problematically decisive. The aim of finding abstract structures and units of analysis such as Lévi-Strauss's gustemes has some currency, however, but it must be complicated by entanglements with the wider social world. Lévi-Strauss's establishment of *raw*, *cooked* and *rotten* as categories is helpful, if understood in a nuanced manner where the processes of *cultural* or *natural* transformations can be arranged diagrammatically. It forms the basis for discussing processes of drying, which might be seen as cooking through a natural process or fermentation which arrests the process from raw to rotten. Lévi-Strauss's diagrams, for all their tripartite divisions, are predicated on a binary opposition: of either natural *or* cultural transformation. This opposition becomes harder to support the more one looks, observes and participates: human life is fully part of the world, and not apart from it: describing something as belonging to culture might prevent a fuller discussion of its overall ecology.

Cuisine is not only a reflection of class divisions, but operates according to the same principles and is a part of the same overall system or economy.

Class divisions operate within surplus societies; specialization is an important factor in them. The wealthy are likely to have access to higher-quality food (and quantity) and express their wealth through the consumption of such foods: a demonstration of connoisseurship reinforcing their self-image as worthy of their greater resources (Ashkenazi & Jacob 2013:21–24).

The structure of a meal is discussed by Joy Adapon (2008) in her work which draws heavily on Alfred Gell's theory of agency. By positioning the production of food in a similar way to Gell's artworks, she establishes a series of interpretations of the meal which depend upon the degree to which the eater, the cook or other factors such as established recipes and availability of ingredients are the primary generators. This is used to great effect in describing how restaurant and home meals differ: one is not routinely presented with a menu when at home, and celebratory barbacoa feasts require everyone to be eating the same meal.

The importance of class to the meal, or 'food event' from Mary Douglas (1972), contradicts some of the assumptions made by Goody regarding categorizations of societies, and it does not follow that rules are more important to one cuisine than another: merely that those rules might be very differently framed. In *Deciphering a Meal*, Douglas develops a sophisticated letter code to describe a wide variety of social events involving food. The first distinction in this would be between meals and drinks: a system is needed which can both encapsulate these occasions and describe their differences. Douglas's essay has its limits, however, and skirts around any notions of the actual taste of the food. This is reflective of the need to abstract an event when analysing, and an absurd omission, is noted by Lalonde (1992). The phenomenology of food and food events is important, and not limited to taste: the environment where a meal is prepared and eaten is of vital importance, not least to the architectural anthropology of this fundamental human activity.

Other issues remain pertinent, particularly class and gentrification. Indeed, food and restaurants are often key drivers in the urban phenomena of economic development, driving rents upwards and pushing residents further and further from the centres of cities as they become more successful and desirable environments to live in. The processual nature of this class-based cuisine development is noted above as the maintenance of a differential: the upper classes always seeking ways to distinguish themselves from the lower through ever-more expensive ingredients and processes whilst the working class are playing catch-up. I suspect it is rather more complex than this, and that the interrelationship of culture and fashion often drives the upper classes to revisit 'lower' classes' food and bring it into their cuisine.

For our purposes, the abstraction of Lévi-Strauss is not nearly as useful as approaches which discuss food cultures as part of the world more broadly.

Cuisine is not a reflection of culture, but is deeply enmeshed with social relations, be those on environmental, economic or class basis. As such, the architecture which accompanies various forms of food event can inform us about the lifeworlds of those involved and present architects with alternatives to conventions they might have taken as a given.

Focusing on food practices where mimesis features strongly, Kristin Hunt (2018) charts some of the controversies around food and the relationship between cuisine and ingredients. Some have problematized the distance between the meal eaten and the source ingredient, connecting this to the disease narrative surrounding processed food. Hunt chooses to focus on the meal as a kind of performance, focusing on obvious manifestations of this in the realms of avant-garde cuisine; this has clear ramifications for more everyday practices. The performance might be collaborative, where preparation is collectively undertaken, perhaps under the guidance of one member of a family; or a meal might be prepared in a closed-off and secret domain of the kitchen, to be revealed to grateful guests who show their appreciation in an analogue of theatrical applause. An important aspect of Hunt's analysis is to discuss the symbolism of food, citing work by Douglas (1972) and Lévi-Strauss (1969) in this regard.

Hunt's work reconnects us with both theories of practice and performance, understanding that food is a useful prototype of a shared activity, one of participation. The dynamics of various roles in the preparation and eating of food can be extended to other realms, and the social importance of food is difficult to overstate. Architecture provides a frame for that engagement and can only do so on better terms the more closely it understands the possible natures of the interaction.

Paul Stoller argues for a recovery of the sensory in academic writing (1989:7), noting that he had 'edited' aspects of his experience in the field out from his accounts. Arguing for a sensuous anthropology, he traces some of the theorists who have abstracted us out from experience, a preference for visual underlined by Kant. Stoller argues that ocularcentrism is a distinctly Western approach and therefore a potentially colonialist approach to take when in the field, bringing a Eurocentric position when confronted with alternative ways of being in the lifeworld. Connecting this to the problematization of academic modes of writing (Clifford & Marcus, 2010), Stoller suggests that his hunch for a more sensually engaged reportage actually has much larger implications for the nature of anthropological research and dissemination. He writes grumpily of tendencies for 'sludgy' writing (1989:136) and argues passionately for anthropologies with the capability of bringing the reader into an experience.

The same could be said to hold for research and practice in architecture. Whilst there are occasional moves towards a multisensory architecture, these tend to find themselves as curiosities or special cases. Rather than celebrate the extraordinary, it is the intention of this chapter to find such sensory architectures in the most ordinary of spaces: kitchens, dining spaces, restaurants. Eating engages many of the senses at once, and the spaces are arranged around those experiences. That design is, however, often a retrofit long after the architect has fled the scene. Ad hoc and improvisatory architecture is used alongside highly specialized interior design to frame our engagement with sustenance, either to consume fuel efficiently or to elevate it to a sublime art form.

David Le Breton reinforces this position, arguing that 'the human condition is corporeal' (2017:9). Noting the multisensory nature of feasts (2017:180), his descriptive text is heavy with scents and flavours, noting the visual and aural aspects of such food events and considering the proprioceptive nature of how we eat food: the careful movements of a tea ceremony, the use of chopsticks, cutlery or one's hands. Le Breton reiterates the cultural specificity of how we eat, discussing the alternative categorizations of flavour in different cultures: Desana people of the Columbian Amazon have sweet, bitter, acid, astringent and spicy; Thai people have eight flavour categories, adding salty, bland and fatty. There are no absolute categories of flavour: each locality developing 'gustatory sensibilities that are linked in a unique away to different culinary preferences' (2017:188).

Introducing his account as a 'Proustian' anthropology, David Sutton (2001) draws a connection between culinary practices and memory. In addition to the more literal memory of a meal we have eaten (which can of course generate warm feelings of homeliness or repulsion at a flavour we found disgusting – itself an interesting category discussed in detail by Henshaw (2013)), Sutton is concerned with the wider bodily practices engendered by food. These are sedimented practices, found in gesture and posture, as well as practices we frequently engage with in order to remember: eating foods of our homelands as a way of taking ourselves back there. I can testify to this in the most ordinary ways, seeking out foods such as Lorne sausage and processed plain bread[1] from time to time as a reminder of my Scottish upbringing.

The examples which follow are each drawn from Japanese dining cultures. There are as many variations within other cuisines, but as Japan has been the site of much of my field research, these examples are most pertinent to my ongoing project. The aim is not to present these as exotic or spectacular, and many of these conventions are finding their way into restaurants in other parts of the world as Japanese food beyond sushi finds itself exported.

Subtle elements of how the space of dining is organized can have significant impacts on the socially contextualized consumption and production of that food. Some of the models exist as part of a broader ecology of work and commuting, such as the izakaya often referred to as a Japanese pub. Others, such as kaiseki, have a long history, moving from the exclusive domain of nobility to becoming the format for feasts enjoyed by a the general population.

Further examples exist within the context of events such as festivals, bringing streetscapes to life with their temporary occupation.

Each of these is a social, spatial and sensory context enmeshed in a wider cultural context. As such, the food culture of any cuisine could be depicted: the more everyday and ordinary the better.

## Sensory notations

The following accounts of Tokyo restaurants are accompanied by a form of sensory notation (Figure 8.1). These were developed as part of a project to work against the visual and geometric bias in architectural and urban design.[2] The aim of the notation is to develop a tool which accompanied descriptive text and images, noting some key elements of the sensory experience of a space. These notations could be used either to diagnose issues with a site, such as a deficit in the stimuli for one sense over others, or to aid in describing engaging multisensory environments as precedents for future design projects.

The descriptions below are intended as examples of the second model: examples which demonstrate the visual, aural, olfactory and gustatory, tactile, thermal, and kinetic qualities of each site. The categories are developed from James Gibson's work on *The Senses Considered as Perceptual Systems* where he describes sensory perception as a practice of seeking stimulation. The senses are not passive in this model, but active. This leads Gibson to question the methodologies by which environmental psychology was pursued at the time: working in neutral laboratory spaces and showing respondents pictures of things[3] in order to gauge their responses. Gibson suggests that in order to really find out, one must be truly out in the environment, however messy and time consuming that might be.

The sensory notation system consists of five main elements:

*Narrative account*: Beginning with a note of the date, time and weather conditions, these are written in a dispassionate style, flat and banal as encouraged by writers such as George Perec (1997). Whilst we aimed for a completely graphic form of representation, it was found that text-based descriptions remained useful, so long as their content was guided in some way. As the notation was designed not to give value judgements to the forms (a score of 6 could refer to an extremely pleasant smell or a disgusting and overpowering one), the text could elaborate on these features of the environment.

*Photographs*: Taken with a specific intention, photographs are a quick and easy way to record the source of a sensation. These are inserted into the

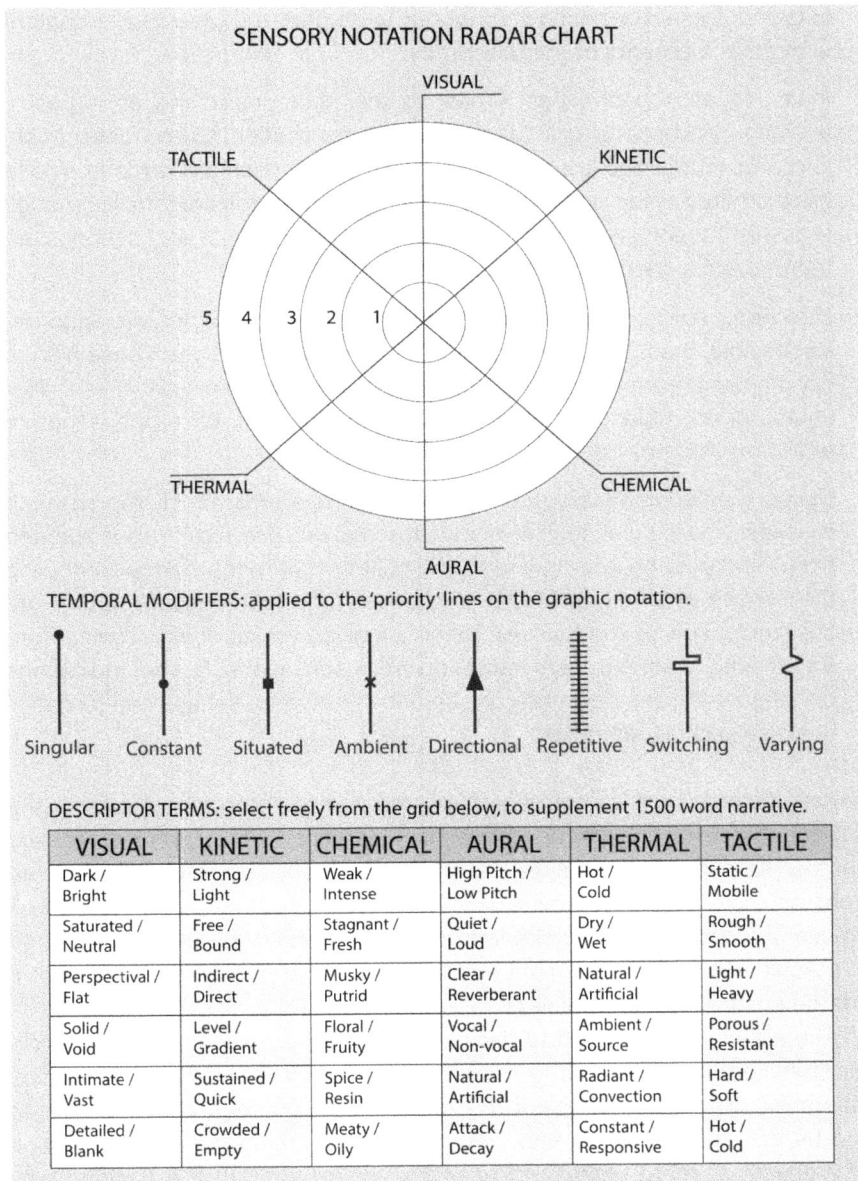

**FIGURE 8.1** *Key to sensory notation.*

text and cross-referenced throughout it, so that they worked in concert with other elements of the description.

*Plan and section drawing*: Similar to the photograph, the orthographic drawing conventions give useful spatial information to the description, showing routes and the points at which the notations are made. These were omitted when working with non-architects; maps are familiar enough to the anthropologists I have worked with in this project, but sections are rather more architecturally specific representations.

*Descriptor terms*: Chosen from a list of neutral terms as non-metaphorical as possible, these give a shorthand for the graphic notations. These help to say if a tactile sensation is rough or smooth, or a thermal quality has a clear source or is ambient. Each perceptual system has six pairs of descriptors which may or may not be used as appropriate.

*Sensory notation*: Finally, the notation itself is a radar chart diagram with six axes: visual, aural, tactile, kinetic, thermal and chemical. This is adapted from Gibson to be appropriate to the built environment, hence combining the senses of smell and taste as chemical and differentiating touch into the tactile, kinetic and thermal. These are given values of importance from 0 to 6, with lower numbers indicating weak sensations. Further indications on these notations describe corroborations between senses and temporal qualities such as repetition.

Several factors such as corroboration emerged as important issues in the design of sensorially rich environments. Elements which corroborate one another have greater presence in the mind: so a tree has visual presence from its scale and colour; aural stimulation from the rustling of leaves in a breeze; thermal qualities as shade from the sun; and is available to touch, so has tactile qualities. These might not be present in each account of a tree, but are the possibilities it represents.

The notation is designed to depict both routes and static positions, allow for multiple representations to show how a space changes over time or how different individuals understand the same space. These individual notations can be compiled either to find commonalities, a mean sensory perception of a space, or more usefully to open conversation about the outliers: why perspectives differ so much at times.

This project is an explicit cross-over between architectural and anthropological perspectives, drawing on other disciplines such as soundscape studies and environmental psychology. The method is developed in order to be loose, analogous to sketchbook practices rather than loading the activity with technologies and mediation. This means that the outcomes are subjective, but no less useful for that.

## Izakaya

The *izakaya* is most often translated as a kind of Japanese version of the pub (Figure 8.2), but this is to miss many of the unique features of these small alleyway establishments. The izakaya does feature drinking as a primary activity, but also offers a range of food, generally small portions, but often of reasonably good quality and adventurous fare by Western standards.

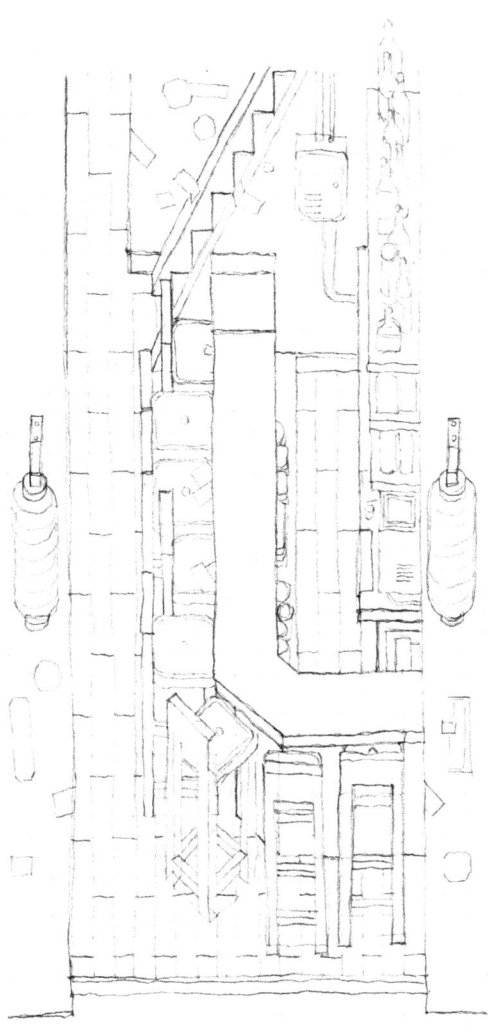

**FIGURE 8.2** *Oblique drawing of izakaya.*

Tokyo boasts alleyways near to large railway stations, and this location reveals one of the main features of the typology: that they rely in part upon the long work hours which are part of Japanese urban life. These *yokochō* are described in detail by Heide Imai (2017: Loc 932) as alleyways adjacent to a main street, and had their origins in post–Second World War black markets. The izakaya is a stopping-off point between the office and the railway station before the long commute home: it is often too late to eat by the time workers get home, so this interstitial space has developed to allow unwinding with colleagues over a beer to be accompanied by some food. These bars tend to be small in scale, and clustered tightly together, in close proximity to one another meaning that they are both in competition with one another and also cooperative relationships. They are accompanied in the yokochō by *yatai* and *tachinomi*: food stalls and even smaller standing room only bars. Some of these clusters retain their slightly edgy and illicit origins, such as the Golden Gai (Figure 8.3) in Shinjuku, Tokyo, but a more recent development has been redevelopment of the alleyways as a kind of gastronomic or touristic destination, with cleaner and brighter gentrified yokochō such as those at Ebisu making for a safer, more consumer-friendly feeling option.

**FIGURE 8.3** *Author's photograph of Golden Gai in Shinjuku.*

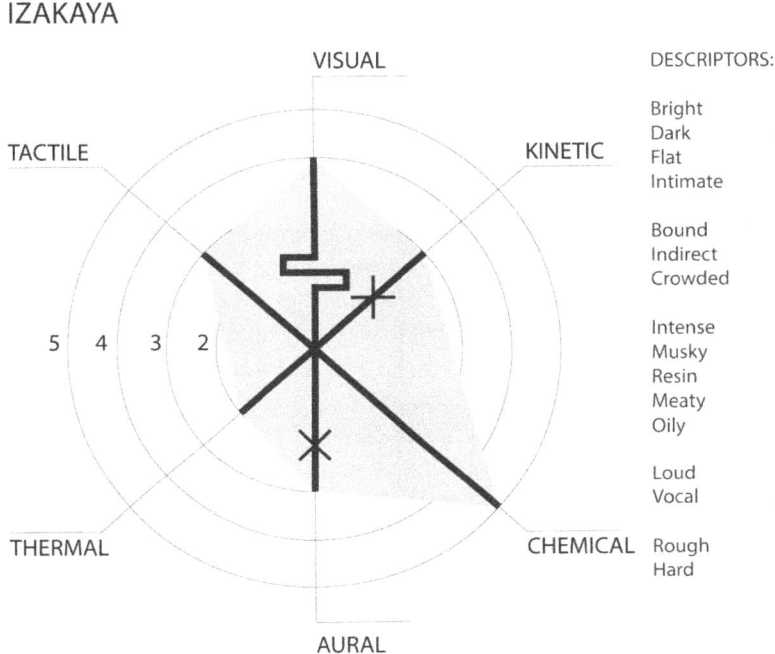

**FIGURE 8.4** *Sensory notation of izakaya in Shinjuku's Omoide yokochō.*

The tightness of space makes for a very intimate experience, and the izakaya becomes something of a social condenser, where individuals from a range of backgrounds come into fairly direct, even bodily, contact with one another (Figure 8.4).

The format is relatively simple. Each bar is one or two storeys tall, packed into an alleyway with similar establishments. Some have rooms for bench-like tables, but the majority of the seating is at bar stools facing into the bar area where food is also prepared. A space near the alleyway is often reserved for the cooking of some of the most aromatic foods, so as to entice passing trade. Stools are tightly arranged, ensuring that negotiation is required in order to sit down. Everything has its place: baskets are provided for bags, coat hooks arranged on the wall behind.

Upon taking a seat, a small appetizer is placed down, representing that you have already agreed to drink here; this is not free, but rather included in the cover charge (usually a few hundred yen). This is often a modest plate of pickles or snacks, but most importantly forms a contract with the vendor. Often, a menu is not forthcoming: long vertical signs in timber or paper sometimes adorn the walls with prices written in Japanese numerals (an increasingly uncommon practice): it is easy enough to order with the assistance of the owner or by pointing to what other guests are eating.

There is a general air of conviviality to the establishment, people are interested in strangers and want to hear their story; see their reaction to unfamiliar (but much loved) foods and so on: the izakaya is a place for exchange. One feature of the izakaya, which is most like the pub typology, is the concept of the regular patron. It is common to have a favourite establishment, to be disappointed when it is too busy to get in, or heartening when the owner goes to special efforts to rearrange patrons and seating in order to accommodate you: all in the name of being a regular. Of course, this status can become rather toxic, becoming exclusionary to new patrons even when it's a slow night, so much so that establishments can give off a decidedly frosty impression to the unwary who try to get served.

The compression of space in the izakaya is one of the main features of its typology, both spatially and socially: one cannot help but come into contact with others when negotiating something as simple as finding a seat, the series of polite apologies that come with inevitable brushing against and bumping in to other patrons serving as a kind of introduction.

In many ways, conventional design thinking would declare the izakaya a failure, an unintended or accidental form: as something which should not work. Yet, these establishments have an important role in the social life of large Japanese cities.

## Kaiseki

*Kaiseki*[a] is one of the more formal cuisines in the Japanese repertoire and has its origins in court traditions. Kaiseki meals consist of a large number of small plates, often in sequence rather than presented simultaneously (Figure 8.5). As such, kaiseki is a deeply aestheticized form of dining, where unusual and rare dishes are offered up as part of the experience, which is arranged with a degree of theatricality.

As we shall see later, this flourish of drama can take different forms, and the on-stage/off-stage nature of preparations can tell us a great deal about the intentions for the meal. In kaiseki, the focus is entirely upon the quality of the food, and our appreciation of it.

> The taste of the apple... lies in the contact of the fruit with the palate, not in the fruit itself; in a similar way... poetry lies in the meeting of poem and reader, not in the lines of symbols printed on the pages of a book. What is essential is the aesthetic act, the thrill, the almost physical emotion that comes with each reading. Borges, J. L. Foreword to Obra Poética (cited in Pallasmaa, 1996: 14)

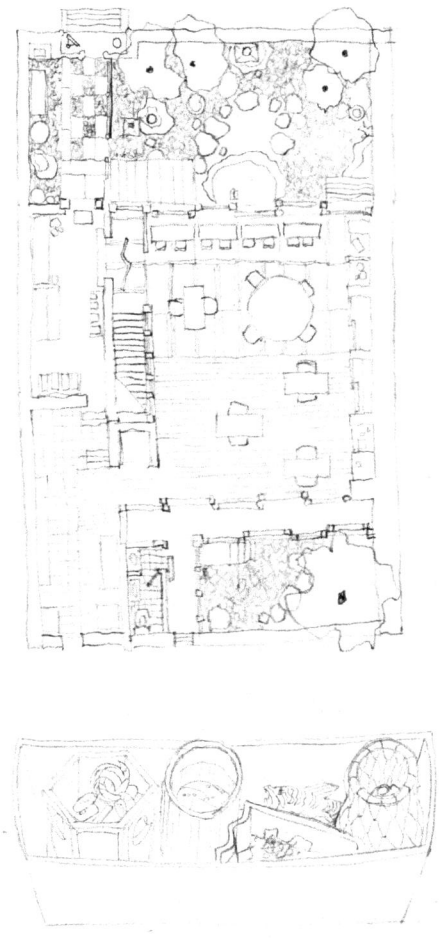

**FIGURE 8.5** *Sketch plan of kaiseki restaurant and typical arrangement of small dishes.*

Spatially, kaiseki meals can be consumed in a variety of establishments ranging from conventional Western-style dining rooms to austere counter arrangements or the simple tatami flooring of a traditional inn. Courses are brought to the table, cleared away and replaced by the next course. The crockery is selected specifically for the morsel of food in question each time: tiny dishes of roughly hewn folk pottery followed by the most highly decorated satsuma-ware are presented with precision and care. Often, a selection of sake cups will be presented to the diner for their choice: adding a note of personality and connoisseurship to the meal.

Kaiseki meals take great efforts to sequence elements of the experience, flavours are not to overlap: but to be experienced fully in themselves. The messiness of the izakaya is a significant contrast here, where a selection of plates accumulates over the course of the evening, to be dipped into and shared across a group of friends or colleagues. The kaiseki meal is a course: an undeviating orchestration of tastes which occasionally comes with warnings for diners who have intolerances to certain foods: that if you are intolerant to a food, then this restaurant may not accommodate your needs and you should look elsewhere.

Key to the aura around kaiseki dining is the manner in which foods are prepared away from the diners: there is no hint about the preparation of the meal, no sense of where the kitchen is, who works there or how large it is. There is a sleight of hand at work, in a sense: the magic trick in three parts where the diner is expected to dwell in the moment of the exciting and unusual textures and flavours without any exposure to the skill and effort that went into its production.

Aura is a concept which was discussed at length in the correspondence between Theodore Adorno and Walter Benjamin – their concern with the extent to which the apparatus around an aesthetic expression can eclipse the expression itself. Adorno was suspicious of such processes, seeing in them an attempt to smuggle conservative political positions into the work, encoded through the act of producing an aura which sets it apart as something special. This can certainly be argued in the case of kaiseki, which is an expression of a particularly traditionalist view of Japanese culture, with its origins in the life of nobility; it is a form of consumption still out of the reach of many due to the sheer expense of producing food with this level of care and detail: it is not democratic in the way that anyone can and does go to an izakaya.

That said, there is a place for this kind of virtuosity, and the austere setting plays a part in ensuring the carefully prepared food is accorded high enough status to be fully appreciated and not wolfed down hungrily with an Asahi beer. Kaiseki meals are arranged as celebrations, as aesthetic experiences akin to visiting a gallery and buying artwork, as recitals of classical music (and all the reverence for setting and canon which goes with it), or as ways to display wealth to business partners: all of which is produced by a machinery designed to place the diner in the correct frame of mind to be able to appreciate the tiniest amount of the very best wagyu beef or the rarest sea urchin (Figure 8.6).

Spatially, the settings vary, but have a logic of hidden and occluded activities: to show too much might shatter the illusion and break the concentration of the diners, whose appreciations and gasps of delight at the often astonishingly beautiful food are met with satisfied bows and nods from the serving staff. This sharing of reactions is part of the theatricality of dining.

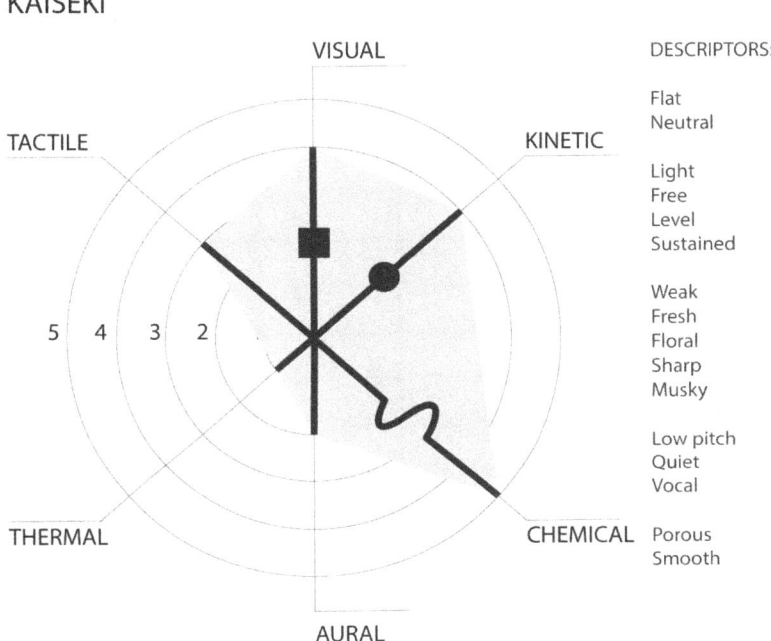

**FIGURE 8.6** *Sensory notation of kaiseki-style restaurant.*

## Tempura counter

Whilst the formal space occupied by different types of restaurant does not differ radically, the nature of the performances around that food can vary enormously. One such example is the counter experience of either a sushi or tempura restaurant (Figure 8.7). These differ from the katsu restaurant in the next section in some significant ways: largely expressed socially rather than spatially.

Whilst arranged similarly to some of the kaiseki establishments above, and often mixed with conventional tables where space allows it, specialist sushi and tempura restaurants offer diners the opportunity to sit at a counter facing the chefs who are preparing the food. This, along with the rather more singular nature of the food preparation style, makes for a significantly different experience to the kaiseki meal where food appears as if by magic.[5] The chef is given a great deal of prominence and agency by this arrangement: present physically, the chef welcomes you personally and looks after the guests directly with minimal intervention from other waiting staff.

**FIGURE 8.7** *Drawing of tempura counter.*

The menu is often a course or set menu, but with a great deal of variation built into it: it may include specifics such as a tempura tiger prawn, or be as vague as 'seasonal white fish'. The various grades of the menu include ever-more exotic items, but again, these often leave room for interpretation. This gives the chef the opportunity to assess the needs of the guests directly, to respond to the dishes they enjoyed, either by giving them more of that kind of food or by seeing how daring and adventurous they might become.

The personality of the counterman (as the chef is named in Ashkenazi & Jacob, 2013:90) is implicated into the whole meal in a direct manner, and the interaction between diner and cook is intertwined with the process of dining. The space is arranged with some subtle differences from the counter of the kaiseki or the izakaya bar, and almost sets the chef on a stage as the central attraction – the food perhaps even secondary to the display of virtuosity by a skilled sushi chef, whose mannered hand movements are accompanied by demonstrative selection of seafood and precisely choreographed knife movements honed over the course of a long and unforgiving apprenticeship.

The character played by the counterman is often authoritarian on the surface, but with a nod and a wink to the guests who are made to think that they are receiving special attention because the chef likes them: it is a performance, a role and an acceptedly artificial part of the experience to be entertained by these gruff craftsmen in a direct way.

The material culture of the tempura restaurant has a number of features. Implicit in the distance between cook and diner is the idea that it indicates freshness and speed, making tempura and counter dining a distinctly temporal affair:

> Properly speaking, every tempura meal should be, as one cook interviewed implied, a 'feast'. Most tempura dishes are a series of small servings served directly by the cook to the diner's plate as soon as they are lifted out of the oil. Sizes are small, which means that a large number of servings are necessary, which, in turn, means that even more than sushi, good quality tempura is labour-intensive, because meticulous attention is required to ensure that each item of food reaches the diner still piping hot. (Ashkenazi & Jacob, 2013:90)

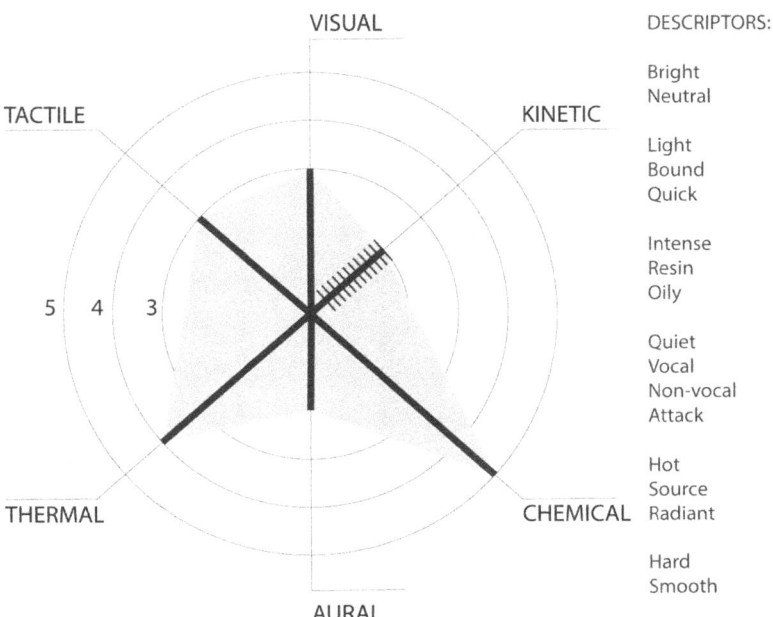

**FIGURE 8.8** *Sensory notation of tempura restaurant.*

Ashkenazi and Jacob go on to discuss the importance of this relationship between the diner and counterman to the connoisseur of such restaurants (2013:91), that it is in many ways more important than the qualities of the food: the rapport and social engagement is characterized as a form of attention and social reinforcement (Figure 8.8). The entire apparatus of the cuisine and the restaurant co-produce one another to engender this relationship: such that even for a lone diner, the experience constitutes a social interaction (Figure 8.9).

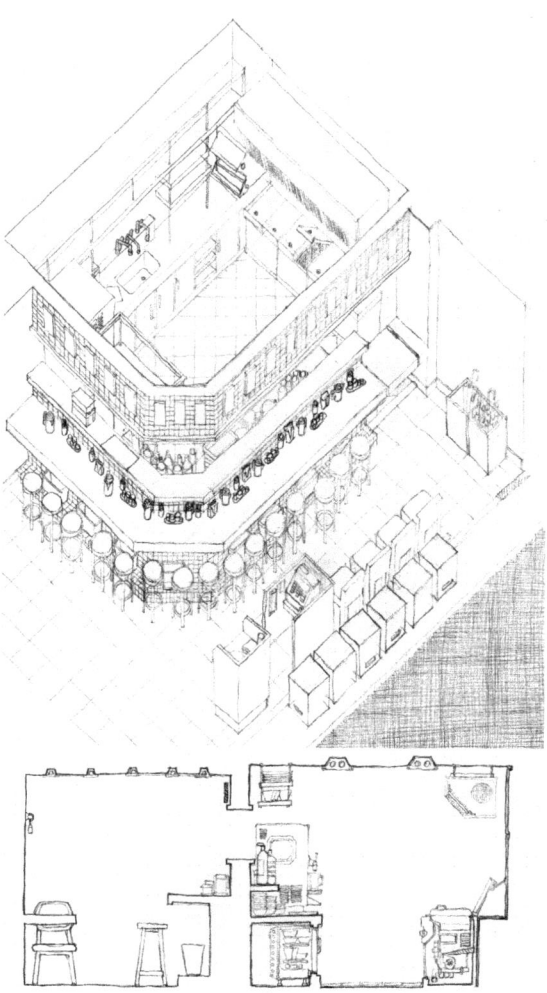

**FIGURE 8.9** *Drawing of gyoza restaurant showing similar counter arrangement to the tempura restaurant.*

# Single-dish restaurants

Specialization in one kind of food is a common strategy for Japanese restaurants: there is an argument that to get the best of anything, then you should go to the specialist who makes this singular dish and nothing else. Here, the counter seats exist again, perhaps more as a window into the hubbub of the kitchen than a celebration of high levels of craft and care.

The katsu restaurant used as an example here does one thing and one thing only: beef cutlets deep fried in panko breadcrumbs. Small variations on the menu indicate the portion size, and which side dishes are desired: but the focus is on one dish. This is informal dining, quick and paid up front. The diner gets to choose several things: provided with a small cooking stone (Figure 8.10), you place the slices of cutlet onto it in order to get it to the degree of cooking desired: the kitchen deep fries it swiftly, crisping the

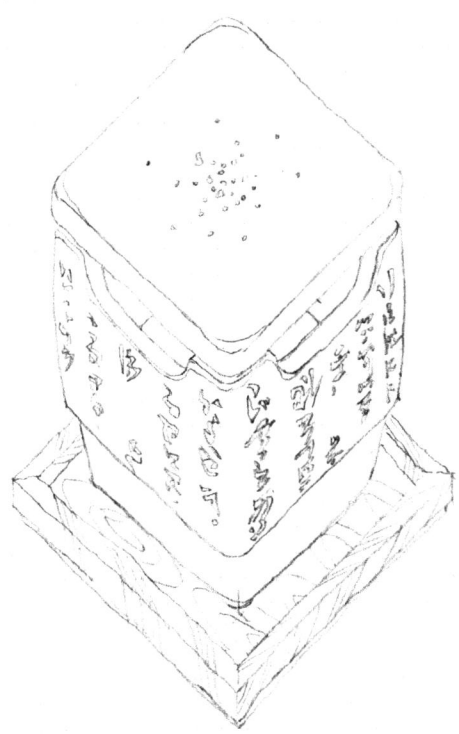

**FIGURE 8.10** *Drawing of ceramic burner from katsu restaurant.*

exterior, but leaving it to the patron to decide if they want it rare or relatively well done.

A selection of sauces is provided, from a thick fruity dark brown katsu sauce to a paler ginger-based sauce for the shredded cabbage served on the side. The meal is accompanied by miso soup, rice, pickles and tea, with added grated yam for those who wish it (Figure 8.11).

This form of dining is more anonymous (Figure 8.12) than any of the prior examples; the choices about what to eat are limited in terms of the menu, but open to some of the agency of the diner in how they choose to finish the cooking of their food. The cook is not present, and hosting staff have a minimal presence (Figure 8.13), placing it further down the scale of interaction than the austere kaiseki experience whilst being in a similar cost bracket to the izakaya. The levels of social interaction in the meal are not a function of cost or exclusivity, but are a variable which contributes to the diversity of dining experiences within even a single food culture.

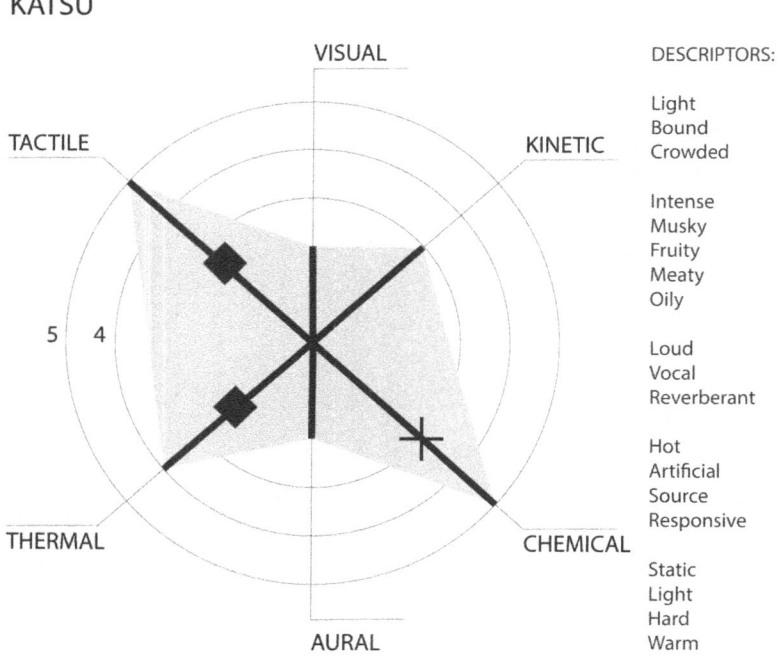

**FIGURE 8.11** *Sensory notation of gyukatsu restaurant.*

**RESTAURANTS, FOOD EVENTS AND SENSORY ARCHITECTURES** 207

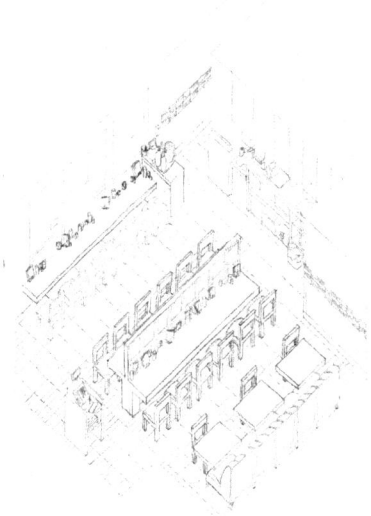

**FIGURE 8.12** *Drawing of metro station ramen restaurant.*

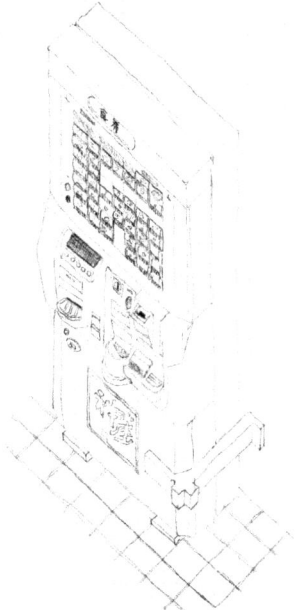

**FIGURE 8.13** *Drawing of vending machine. Diners select their meal from the options on the buttons and pay outside the restaurant, handing over a ticket when seated.*

## Cooking at the table

The theme of cooking one's own meal in the restaurant, so flippantly regarded by Bill Murray's character in *Lost in Translation*,[6] is taken even further by a number of other settings. Various forms of grill and barbecue restaurants along with hotpots and hot plate cooking place the diner at the centre of the meal.

Here, the restaurant's role is preparation, and providing of the setting, necessary infrastructure for the preparation of the food. This speaks to one of the roles of restaurants as a socializing space within Japanese culture. As noted by Inge Daniels (2010), the Japanese home is not a place where socializing and entertaining would routinely take place, for both social and practical reasons: often city dwellers live in cramped apartments not designed for hosting guests, and these homes can sometimes be over an hour's commute from the city, making it much more convenient to celebrate in a common space such as a restaurant.

More important again is the role of material culture in this: the development of high-quality metal blades in Japanese culture means that chef's knives are sharp and accurate instruments (Ashkenazi & Jacob, 2013:86). The degree of detail in the cutting of ingredients, from the care taken to prepare meat and vegetables for hot pot dishes allows for a cuisine to develop whereby fresh and continuous cooking is necessary. As such, the feeding of the light pot of stock with vegetables and meat needs to be done by the diners rather than prepared completely within the kitchen (Figure 8.14). The role of the kitchen is then to prepare ingredients rather than cook the dish.

The space of the restaurant, then, is a primary social space, where life events such as birthdays or engagements might be celebrated, and where workmates are encouraged to bond outside of their paid hours. This makes it less jarring that one might actually prepare the food oneself: the restaurant in this case is much more the establishment than the chef or the food: the quality of the food is entirely down to the preferences and skill of the patron.

These cook-and-feed-yourself modes of eating are even graphically different. In a formal dining situation, the diners will be arranged in the shape of an open rectangle, seated by rank, with the most important person at the outside of the head, lesser luminaries trailing around the outside, and the lowest social standings sitting inside the square, if necessary. That is of course impossible in self-cook forms of dining. In most cases, the diners have to sit at a round table, where a proper hierarchy is hard to establish. For a society which prides itself on its hierarchic nature, the ability to relax

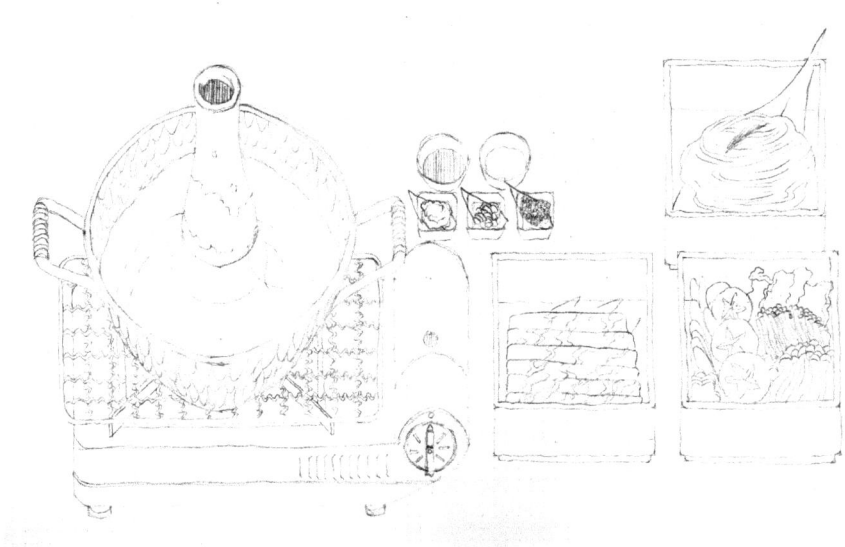

**FIGURE 8.14** *Drawing of shabu shabu table.*

stiff social rules in socially sanctioned ways is perhaps a necessity: the flip side of hierarchy and order. (Ashkenazi & Jacob, 2013:88)

Such restaurants are equipped with specialized tables which have integrated hot plates, grills or other forms of heating element (Figure 8.15). The staff remain on hand to operate these tables, and to offer instruction where needed on the cooking of the ingredients brought to the table. In a sense, it is this table: designed to cook in a specific way, which has the greatest degree of agency in the meal. It determines the interactions between diners, who must coordinate their actions with one another so as to give space to each others' food, not monopolising on the hottest parts of the grill or accidentally stealing each others' food.

Such meals are also an opportunity for diners to demonstrate their command of the cooking technologies, to be able to prepare an okonomiyaki pancake from the provided raw ingredients, condiments and sauces: it is a skill which leaves very little room for error: timing and skilled practice become a part of the process of dining in much the same way as a dinner party hosted in the home provides the host with an opportunity to demonstrate their sophistication and good taste (Figure 8.16). Discernment, skill and taste have a class element to them in this context:

# ANTHROPOLOGY FOR ARCHITECTS

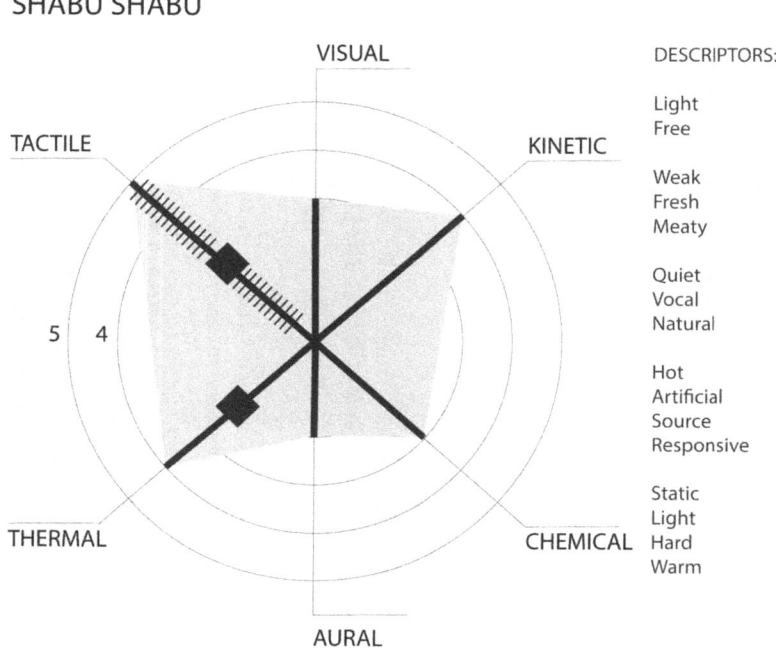

**FIGURE 8.15** *Sensory notation of shabu shabu restaurant.*

> Now, in practice, the taste of monjya-yaki is a meagre version of okonomiyaki, a food that is usually associated with student life, and hardly haute-cuisine. The association is made more powerful simply by the fact that okonomiyaki places may also serve monjya-yaki, partly to indicate their roots in Tokyo (lower class) shitamachi culture … by the gradual addition of new, enriching elements, what has been the food of the poor becomes a gourmet item for the rich, or more precisely, the novelty-chasing rich. Unlike Mennel's model, what has happened in Japan is that the entire nation has become rich: the enrichment and elitisation of the food is not a transfer between classes but a transfer between generations. (Ashkenazi & Jacob, 2013:95)

Ashkenazi and Jacob discuss this in terms of generational shift due to the demographics of Japan (the narrative being that peasant foods become elevated and gentrified by other cultures with a clearer contemporary class division), but there is also an aspect of affectation, 'playing at', or reminiscing over more austere times has a role in this: adoptions and appropriation of peasant life have a long history in Japanese architecture and culture, for

# RESTAURANTS, FOOD EVENTS AND SENSORY ARCHITECTURES 211

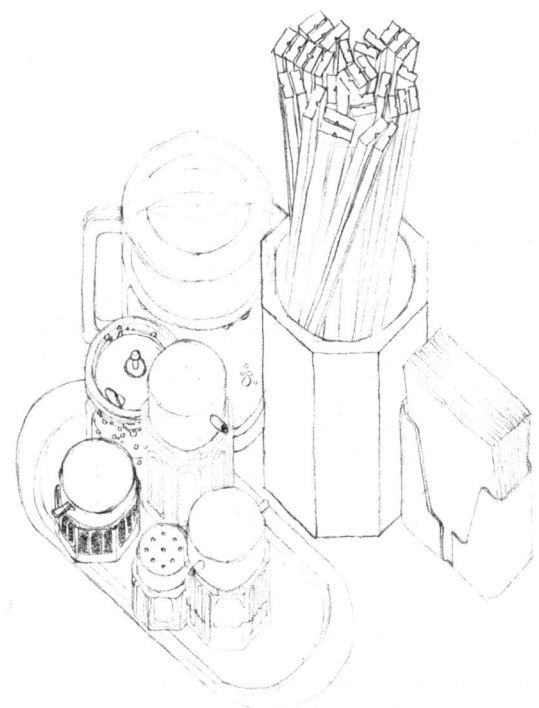

**FIGURE 8.16** *Drawing of condiments provided to allow diners to adapt a dish to their tastes.*

example, the rural style of elements at Katsura Rikyu, an Imperial Palace in Kyoto, or the celebration of *mingei* pottery.

The cooking technology is fairly singular in each case, with some speciality dishes being prepared in a kitchen; the food is otherwise brought to the table as prepared ingredients rather than a finished meal. The role of the restaurant then becomes one of mediating between the diner and this technology more than the provision of the meal directly.

## Yatai street food stalls

Festivals in Japan are often associated with temples and shrines. During the festive periods, these precincts – often shared by Buddhist and Shinto buildings – are occupied by a range of street food stalls. Rather than being local businesses, the owners of these stalls are often peripatetic, moving from festival to festival according to a regular timetable (Figure 8.17).

**FIGURE 8.17** *Author's photograph down Nakamise Dori towards Senso-ji.*

The spatiality of these stalls is particularly interesting, as several distinct areas are given over to them in the grounds of Senso-ji (Buddhist temple) and Asakusa-jinja (Shinto shrine) in the Asakusa part of Tokyo, one of the biggest pilgrimage sites in the country for the popular temple (Figure 8.18). The sensory experience of the approach to the complex is often festive in nature, regardless of the point in the calendar.[7]

*Yatai* is a term covering a wide variety of shop stands, be they wheeled and mobile timber versions, or the temporary tarpaulin and steel framework structures which cluster at the temple precinct in May. Each pitch is around 2.5 by 1.5 metres, often with custom printed tarpaulin advertising the food on offer, be it takoyaki octopus balls, spiralized potato, moniya-yaki pancakes or kara-age fried chicken (Figure 8.19).

The atmosphere generated by these stalls is a significant shift for the normally quieter areas to the sides of the religious buildings and promenade with tourist and religious goods on sale, bringing gaudy bright colour, packed crowds, flashes of flame and heat, and scents from boiling oil to bursts of steamed potato, all with vendors calling out for the attention of potential customers.

# RESTAURANTS, FOOD EVENTS AND SENSORY ARCHITECTURES 213

**FIGURE 8.18** *Photograph of street food stalls at Senso-ji and Asakusa-jinja during the Sanja Matsuri festivities.*

**FIGURE 8.19** *Watercolours of yatai stalls from Sanja Matsuri.*

The yatai have an urban character to them and, when mobilized en masse, have a real presence within the city. This activation of urban space with temporary architecture is a feature of Japanese cities, which lack meaningful urban space, sometimes meaning that the clusters of stalls take over the pavement and street for short periods of time (Figure 8.20). This controlled occupation of space operates as a release valve for the city during festive periods: where energy is released, and social bonds are reinstated for the coming year or two.

The transformation of the sacred precinct into a vast food market during the festival[8] brings people to the space in large numbers; once there, they linger for longer and make more of their time there: rather than the relatively swift ablutions and prayers made at Senso-ji by most visitors outside of these times. The food stalls have a temporal and spatial impact, slowing the place down significantly and encouraging visitors to linger with the sharp contrast of gaudy graphics and typography against the powerful architecture of the temple and modest austerity of the shrine.

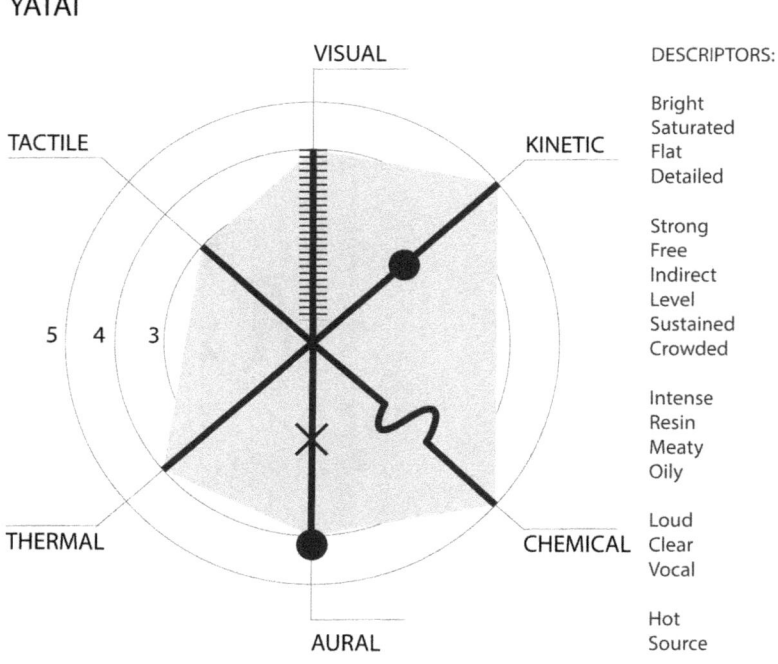

**FIGURE 8.20** *Sensory Notation of yatai stalls on the Senso-ji precinct.*

## Notes

1. Hardly fine dining, the Lorne sausage (aka square sausage) is most often eaten as a breakfast staple and resembles a square hamburger to the untrained eye. It consists of fatty minced pork or beef mixed with rusk and seasoned with pepper. It forms part of a cooked breakfast alongside bacon and black pudding, or is served in a roll – preferably a 'well fired' morning roll, scorched on top, but white and fluffy on the interior. In the absence of such rolls, a form of stodgy processed bread common in Scotland is a good substitute.
2. See Lucas (2009a, 2009b) and Lucas & Romice (2008).
3. This method argues that the responses are immediate and evolutionary in nature; the gathering of data in this way is relatively efficient and allows for large datasets to confirm findings.
4. Ashkenaizi & Jacob (2013:42) note that *kaiseki ryōri* can refer to a number of forms of food: the meal accompanying a tea ceremony and a banquet for a group of people who share a hobby or activity can both be referred to as *kaiseki ryōtei*. The form referred to here is a multi-course meal normally served in a restaurant or *ryōkan* traditional inn.
5. Indeed, some novelty restaurants really play this up with a ninja-themed deliver using darkness, secret panels and smoke bombs.
6. Coppola, Sophia. (Dir.). 2003. *Lost in Translation*. Japan/USA: Focus Features.
7. See Lucas (2009a) for a sensory notation of sacred spaces in Tokyo comparing the spatially similar Meiji-jingu and Senso-ji, noting that the experience of the space is different due to the wider sensory design of the spaces rather than formal factors.
8. For more on the Sanja Matsuri festival, see Chapter 7 and Lucas (2018b).

# 9

# Conclusion: Towards an Anthropological Architecture

## Introduction

This chapter brings the findings of the book together as a pair of manifestoes: for an anthropological architecture and an architectural anthropology. This represents more than a play on words, but suggests that the transfer of knowledge between disciplines needs to occur in both directions. Architecture is a body of knowledge about how we build and dwell, about geometry and design, and many more aspects of how we understand the environment by manipulating it.

Building typologies are presented as ways of understanding the key theories presented from anthropology, a selection which is far from exhaustive: each chapter represents an exemplar of an approach to architectural anthropology rather than a fully resolved synthesis. Theories of practice are present throughout our engagements with the built environment and not restricted to studio practices of drawing and making; the co-production of identity is most obviously bound up in domestic space, but is present elsewhere. Similarly, the discussion of collection, whilst focused on the example of museum space, can be extended into other realms such as the trans-national networks of modernist architecture, the transmission of classical architecture as a code across a diverse range of localities, or even the notion of architecture codified as a profession. Each example could be matched up with other theories, offering an alternative understanding of that space or phenomenon in each instance.

As such, the book is constructed as a set of initial experiments, lines of enquiry to be followed and questions to be asked. One way forward is suggested: not an *architectural anthropology*, but a *graphic* one. Architecture, like many other disciplines, has already made successful use of ethnographic research in order to find out more about the realities of design, the politics of commissioning and the ecologies of material. As a method, graphic anthropology suggests a way for anthropologists and architects to understand through inscriptive practices. By sketching, drawing, notating, draughting, diagramming and mapping, we perform analysis of our environments. Each inscription has an implicit or embedded theory that allows a tightly edited understanding to emerge, where orthographic drawings allow for interpretations including the precise dimensioning of space, proportion and geometry, including the relationship to the human body, light and air, atmosphere and acoustics: all within an efficient and commonly understood code. The use of notations such as Laban allows for details of human kineticism to be deconstructed in order for the action to be re-enacted with precision. Sketching and fine-art drawing traditions are the traces of movements, with intentionality and gesture generating an enduring mark into a surface. Each of these conventions has rules determining their making and interpretation: graphic anthropology argues that, in learning and using multiple forms of inscriptive practice (and we can include the various forms: academic, fictional and biographical writing here), we can widen our interpretative faculties significantly.

# A manifesto

Architecture has, of course, always been anthropological, and anthropology always architectural. The aim of this book has made many of the intersections more apparent and examined the implications of thinking in this way. It leads us to re-categorize ephemeral structures and socially constructed space as every bit as sophisticated and important to the discipline of architecture as the great edifices of the established canon. Anthropological enquiry has brought great insights to many aspects of life which we take for granted: the manner in which dwelling is related to selfhood through a process of co-construction; the sensory engagements we have with everyday foodstuffs; the social nature of walking allowing us to rewrite the environment through bodily engagements with it.

There are significant further possibilities in this relationship. Whilst anthropologists might be able to speak in the abstract about the agency of a building, architecture expresses this in material and formal detail, understanding the roles of each threshold, volume, and articulation of a surface and the effect this can have on people. By making anthropological architecture and architectural anthropology more apparent, we are committing to a fertile cross-disciplinary field where methodologies and theories are not only shared, but new ones develop.

The recent development of design anthropology[1] as a distinctive sub-discipline has some lessons for collaborations between architecture and anthropology. Many of the issues raised are of interest to architecture, most notably the opportunity to integrate anthropological theory and methodology into the design process. A distinction must be drawn between the needs of a design anthropologist and those of an architectural anthropologist. This distinction is more than merely one of scale, however: most notably in the use of prototypes within design anthropology. This is inappropriate for architecture, where the map would become the territory to paraphrase (Borges, 2000:181). Constructing prototypes of architecture is simply to make architecture. I would therefore suggest that sharing practices of close observation and theory making go side by side with drawing, model-making, notation and diagramming.

There are a growing number of studies in the mode of an 'anthropology of architecture'[2] or an 'ethnography of architects'[3], but this book asks what it means to produce anthropology by way of architecture[4]? It is relatively easy to see what architects can learn from anthropology, but a greater challenge to ask anthropologists to learn from architects and designers. Again, returning to the value of our own discipline is important, restating the architectural sensibility towards space and place, the understanding of precedent and possibilities of an intervention. Defining this as a movement towards rather than a definition of an architectural anthropology is important. Anthropology is a discipline which concerns itself with matters in the making rather than as finalized and static forms: anthropology's relationship with architecture is one of continual becoming, an immanent relationship which must perpetually be critiqued and refined.

## Knowledge production

Throughout the preceding chapters, this book has explored the architectural uses of a wide range of architectural theories. By applying these to real world examples and giving alternative discussions of the underlying meaning of each instance, anthropological ideas and theories have been brought into direct contact with architecture and the built environment. These demonstrations are not the limits of that engagement, but rather serve as starting points for further exploration.

Key to this is the idea of knowledge production itself. Knowledge is actively made through the application of skilled practice to a context in the world. This might appear to be stating the obvious, but this concept has fundamental implications for how we consider our own practices. To understand knowledge production in this way opens us to questions about what our current *habitus* might mean: what knowledge are we closed off from by ignoring certain practices? How might adopting alternative practices bring fresh understandings to the design process?

Contemporary anthropology has a focus on emergent conditions, overturning presumptions that even practices such as rituals are fixed and unmoving. In the case of architecture, where a structure might have lasted for hundreds of years, its apparent permanence is only ever contingent. Buildings are understood differently by each generation who is custodian over it: uses adapt over time, weathering takes a toll, and maintenance attempts to arrest or repair wear and tear. An architectural anthropology is therefore temporal in nature, mindful of the passage of time, both in the short and medium terms and over a much longer duration. This has implications for how we understand architecture which exists, critiquing the postwar avant-garde and their disposable architecture modelled after consumer goods and vehicles; it has implications for the way in which grand old structures can behave in their environment symbolically representing a toxic social context or preventing a community from meeting their current needs in the name of conservation. The attachment of identity to the most unlikely pieces of architecture can also be revealed by this attitude towards time: a building's importance might come from factors other than its ability to represent a type, or as an aesthetically pleasing and prominent historical example.

Understanding the world through all of our senses overturns a persistent visual and geometric bias in architecture and other associated disciplines. Applying lessons from emerging discussions in sensory ethnography might encourage architects to have a deeper sensitivity to the full materiality of their proposals. The very best architects have, of course, been able to do this: but it has remained something of a mystery to mainstream architecture. Methods for the design of buildings which respond to the full aural environment (not only the formal acoustics of the concert hall and auditorium), the chemical senses of taste and scent are only rarely considered. Our notion of the senses might well be expanded from the conventional five senses to divide the tactile sense into thermal, kinetic and haptic senses: what are the implications for design, and how might such approaches provide an architecture more friendly to those with impairment to one or more senses?

Movement is a particular case in point and can be seen as an example of sensory engagements. Architecture is activated by our movements around and within it, the daily routines of sleeping, cooking, eating, relaxing and

## CONCLUSION: TOWARDS AN ANTHROPOLOGICAL ARCHITECTURE 221

cleaning all involve our bodily engagement with a building. Conceptualized here as walking (which admittedly excludes those with mobility issues) on account of the wide literature available on this, the kinaesthetic sense involves many of the senses simultaneously. The tactile sense of the feet is verified by the visual sensation of our eyes as they scan the environment and focus on pertinent details; auditory cues are subtle, but give an impression of volume and the hardness of materials. The senses verify and corroborate one another, giving a rounded impression of the space as we explore it. Our understanding of the senses is trained and encultured, perception can be trained and, as we shall see later, the role of attention is paramount.

How we make ourselves at home is a key point of contact between anthropologists and architects. This is a central concern for both disciplines, and the question of what it means to dwell implies that this fundamental association of people with places can be understood across cultures in different ways, but that it is an element of all cultures. Making camp along a nomadic herding route might fall at one extreme of this, but it is one manifestation of a wider concern, and has much in common with the Western home-owner who makes selections from a plethora of consumer goods to express their sense of self and how they wish to live their life. Being at home is an important category of our spatial experience and is one of the most challenging and celebrated briefs to be given as an architect: the design of a house.

The home is, of course, a site where all manner of things are arranged and collected; some materials flow through the home over a relatively short period and others stay for some time, representing relationships with other people or serve as indicators of our identity and personality. Throughout the book, ideas from material culture studies have returned in order to explore how objects can be social: not merely reflections of socio-cultural phenomena. This approach attaches even more importance to the architecture we inhabit, pass through and occupy: that it can be intertwined so closely with our own evolving biographies and mean entirely different things to different people. The frames within which we understand these engagements are important: a large masonry banking hall is experienced differently by the customer and the teller, the manager and the cleaners, the security guards and the architects, the conservationists and the developers who might be looking to convert it for to a more profitable contemporary function.

One important element of material culture is to find interest in the everyday and ordinary stuff of life. Indeed, much of the terminology struggles to find ordinary words and invest them with deeper theoretical meanings, hence Daniel Miller's position towards *stuff*, and others in the field struggling with *things* in order to avoid the rather toxic terminology around *objects* which suggests objectification amongst other things. We might see material culture as reflecting several layers of each thing: the bare facts of an item, its size and shape, the methods of making and the materials used; the ways in which the thing is perceived, perhaps by different individuals; the cultural codes surrounding the item, what it represents in terms of class, power relations, historical associations and aspirations; and finally, where does anthropology's position of *methodological philistinism* leave us with regard to the aesthetic qualities and beauty of the thing, the virtuosity and care with which it has been made, the level of skill required to make it. Seeing our homes and buildings in this way reinforces the place that they have in our own biographies, respecting the investment of the most innocuous items with aspects of our personal history and identity.

Particularly valuable items often find their way into collections, and this impulse to gather and display finds expression most clearly in museums. There are ways in which this strategy of deliberate display transforms the thing into an object primarily by depriving it of context (or placing it into a new context which makes it one of many similar objects). The logic of collecting and display finds an urban expression through various forms of conservation, arresting the structure at an often arbitrary point in its history and disallowing any further passage of time. Understanding this process, and what people might make of the display itself, is important, both as an attempt to preserve a unique identity for each place at the same time as denying future developments and modifications. Cities might commission international architects with a similar intention to the curator or art collector: the status attached to having a Gehry, Libeskind or Hadid building reflecting the ambitions of the city itself. A deeper understanding of these processes and the architect's part in them allows them more opportunities to knowingly navigate their politics in order to propose a more appropriate and less spectacular building.

The above is political; an expression of power relations through architecture can be discussed anthropologically. Where buildings are preserved and retained in order to indicate a continuity of inhabitation, it is often an official version of that history which is promoted: a meaningful expression of the current power structures by mobilizing the past. Similarly, the relationship new architecture has with these old buildings is instructive of the efforts power structures will go to in order to communicate and consolidate their position.

The strategy of abstracting units of analysis from complex social phenomena might seem counter-productive in this wider discussion of the complexity of human life and how it needs to be considered more holistically, but there are instances where such a narrow focus is helpful. By considering abstraction as a kind of editing process, it is possible to see how *food events* or *gustemes* can allow us to interrogate cuisine and cooking in greater detail. Clearing out distractions from the account allows detail to emerge, and additional complexities can be reinstated later, showing how that event or phenomenon is placed within the wider world. The variation possible within the most basic

## CONCLUSION: TOWARDS AN ANTHROPOLOGICAL ARCHITECTURE 223

activities – how we feed ourselves – is instructive in highlighting how every part of our lives is culturally and socially informed, specific to a given context. These arrangements of life events offer potential patterns for future design: by examining places visited and interrogating the experiences we have there, the architect's sketchbook becomes a rich store-house of ideas for further development in the studio.[5]

Further processes of how we arrange exchanges of goods and services can be found across cultures as gift or monetary economies. The flow of goods is reflected in the architecture which supports and surrounds it; the mutual co-production of the exchange process and its architecture is part of a wider trend where the programme reflects and informs the underlying process. New forms of exchange emerge as new architecture supports it; continual reinvention of informal architecture is responsive to the constraints vendors are working within.

Some instances of anthropological theory have clear analogues with architectural thinking. The discussion of liminal space, for example, echoes the threshold within architecture. The focus is on changes of state to do with performance and ritual, but there is a close kinship with thresholds, where spatial states are mediated and altered, the act of passing through celebrated and marked by some of the most significant elements of the architecture. Similarly, frames and keying have a spatial quality, allowing us to consider the manner in which we require a frame of reference or datum to understand what we are part of, what is happening around us.

> In sum, as natural persons we are supposed to be epidermal bounded containers. Inside there are information and affect states. This content is directly indexed through open expression and the involuntary cues always consequent upon suppression. Yet when the individual engages in bluff games such as poker, one finds that he either blocks off almost all expression or attempts the most flagrant, expressively ratified deceptions – the kind which would give him a very bad reputation were he to attempt unsuccessfully such a display in his actual, literal activity.
> (Goffman, 1974:572)

In an architectural sense, the reverence of visiting a cathedral might be deeply inappropriate in the boisterousness of a marketplace, and vice versa: the hustle and bustle, exchange and negotiation of a market are not appropriate elsewhere. The disturbance caused to worshippers when some visitors treat the cathedral like any other kind of tourist site is notable. Goffman's frames recall Tschumi's[6] cross-programming experimentation: the suggestion that one cannot truly experience a building 'until one has committed a murder' there – as an extreme and absurd version of this idea. This ties us back to the idea of the programme of the building as a key element of architecture, not an external driver like a brief.

> Thus, auctioneering and stewarding provide more than roles; they provide particular ways of keying literal events. In sum, whenever we are issued a uniform, we are likely to be issued a skin. It is in the nature of a frame that it establishes the line for its own reframing. (Goffman, 1974:575)

Thus, an important part of our experience of any space is as social as it is material. Our expectations and actions are determined by the frame we are either given or choose to occupy.

## Establishing a graphic anthropology

The preceding chapters build a case for an approach to architecture which I have been working on for some time: graphic anthropology. The aim here is to blend the approaches of architecture and anthropology into a set of approaches which work with existing methods and approaches, but expands these through a strategy of multiple representations. Graphic anthropology does not rely on the invention of new inscriptive practices, but instead on a deeper understanding of their affordances, and the benefits of working with multiple forms of graphic representation simultaneously in order to produce a rounded account.

Each form of graphic representation carries a set of operating assumptions and priorities. Most often, when anthropologists discuss drawing as a method, they are suggesting quick sketches: maps of a settlement, brief in situ sketches of people and objects. More fully rounded forms of investigation use sequential or comic art as a way of integrating narrative into representational forms. These are valuable contributions, but I am suggesting that in working across the disciplines of architecture and anthropology, both disciplines have a great deal to learn from one another.

With regard to conventional orthographic representation, the architectural plan allows us to give precise detail of the spatial relationships between elements of a design – the alignments of structural and programmatic elements – and presents the capable reader of the drawing with a matrix of all the movements possible and encouraged by that space. The cross-section drawing focuses instead on volumetric data, with more detailed depictions of potential inhabitation the pay-off is that it is less complete, presenting an example of how the building can be occupied. Elevations, with their flattening effect, give us a way of presenting the context of the structure, its composition and rhythm: ideally suited to

## CONCLUSION: TOWARDS AN ANTHROPOLOGICAL ARCHITECTURE

describing how a building works harmoniously or discordantly within an existing urban context.

Parallel projections such as isometric and axonometric drawings[7] synthesize more of this information, standing in for the maquette in some ways and showing the overall geometry with greater fidelity. Perspective is often seen as a presentational drawing, an attempt to demonstrate how the building might be seen from one unique viewpoint, but it also presents us with a geometry, looking at the building experientially and sequentially.

Each of these forms is replicated in various forms of computer-aided and digitally based drawing, often generated by the computer from a three-dimensional (3D) model constructed by the draughtsperson. The conventions of drawing remain relevant, however: each of the above variations in drawing conveys alternative aspects of a building, effectively editing the available data into a coherent and comprehensible form.

We are reminded of Borges's parable on the representation that is *too detailed*:

> In that Empire, the Art of Cartography attained such Perfection that the map of a single Province occupied the entirety of a City, and the map of the Empire, the entirety of a Province. In time, those Unconscionable Maps no longer satisfied, and the Cartographers Guilds struck a Map of the Empire whose size was that of the Empire, and which coincided point for point with it. (Borges, 2000:181)

The forms of graphic representation available do not stop there, however. In my work, I have investigated cartographic methods, including those developed by Kevin Lynch, or the mental mapping of Gould and White, as well as further discussions of radical cartography and the full gamut of mapping methods.[8] Other processes such as the *serial vision* of Gordon Cullen (1961), environmental notations by Philip Thiel (1996) and Lawrence Halprin (1982); austere editing of the city by Mario Gandelsonas (1987, 1995, 1998); and the diagramming techniques of Patrick Geddes (Welter, 2003), Alfred Gell (1998a, 1999) are potential models for graphic anthropology. The aim is to open graphic representations up in order to see how they can give a more complete and holistic impression when taken together.

Where methods are insufficient or absent, we might consider developing new forms of inscriptive practice in order to enhance our understanding. Whilst it is easy to be critical of the history of such alternative practices and their relative failures and successes (Thiel's *envirotecture*, for example, is so idiosyncratic as to be unusable as much other than a teaching tool[9]), many have proven to be successful and influential tools, such as Hillier and Hanson's Space Syntax theory and practice (2008). In this vein, *Sensory Notation*[10](Figure 9.1) is one such tool which did not implicate itself into the

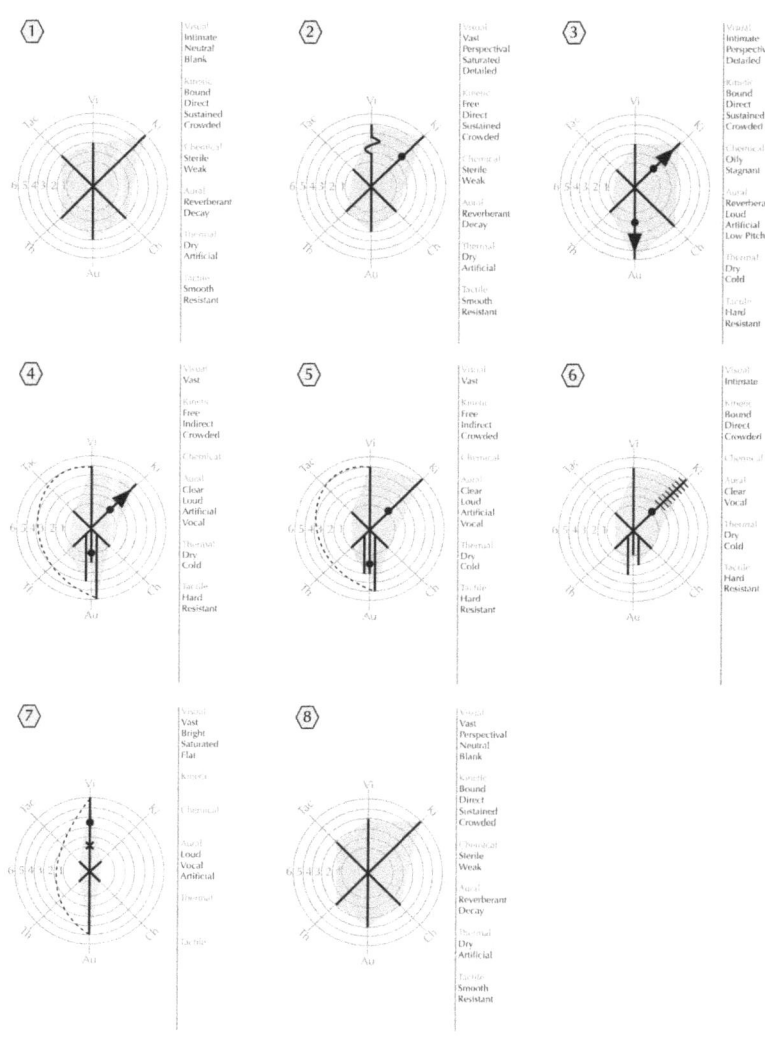

**FIGURE 9.1** *Examples of sensory notation.*

design process directly, but which can be used both as a teaching tool and as an analytical process, revealing much about the multisensory nature of an environment through focused attention and *organized perception* with a sound theoretical basis.

Furthermore, possibly esoteric forms of representation come in the form of dance and movement notations. The use of such notations to give detailed descriptions is, despite the discomfort and controversy within their home disciplines, very powerful indeed. My PhD thesis[11] gives detail of how such inscriptive practices might be used in order to describe a range of different movements as framed by the built environment. These depictions then open the phenomena up to analysis and further translation. Graphic representations open opportunities creatively and analytically, and present us with alternative ways of producing knowledge.

By engaging in the work to produce a Laban movement notation of a Sumo bout (Figures 9.2 and 9.3), details are revealed about the roles of various participants beyond the most obvious of the two fighters; the referees, callers, sweepers and judges all have a part to play and a position around the ring. The sequencing of a bout is understood, with the staggered activity of these actors ahead of and during each short bout. The spatiality of the event is described differently by a plan or series of photographs, and such a notation allows the inscription to describe details such as posture, balance of weight, application of force and the grips of the hands. By drawing a detailed notation, one steps out of familiar modes of spectatorship and pays attention much more closely.

This has been used by anthropologists effectively to describe situations such as Brenda Farnell's (1995) work with the unique sign language of Plains Indians. I have used these methods to describe a range of situations, including my navigation of the Tokyo Metro, a scene from Kurosawa's *Seven Samurai*, the rocking movement of a *Daruma* doll and the carrying of *Mikoshi* portable shrines during a festival.[12]

Architects are no strangers to the production and reading of information across sets of drawing. The aim here is to expand these representations (acknowledging that many architects already produce their own innovative forms of drawing, diagramming and notation) and to use them in the production of architectural theory, architectural design, and anthropological fieldwork and texts.

Attention is a theme we return to in this discussion of methods, practices and skills. The training of attention is sharpened in different ways by different academic disciplines. Architects are trained to pay attention to certain things about their environment in a manner that might baffle the anthropologist. The anthropologist will be paying attention in an entirely different way, focusing on other elements and processes. In my discussions with others around

228　　　　　　　　**ANTHROPOLOGY FOR ARCHITECTS**

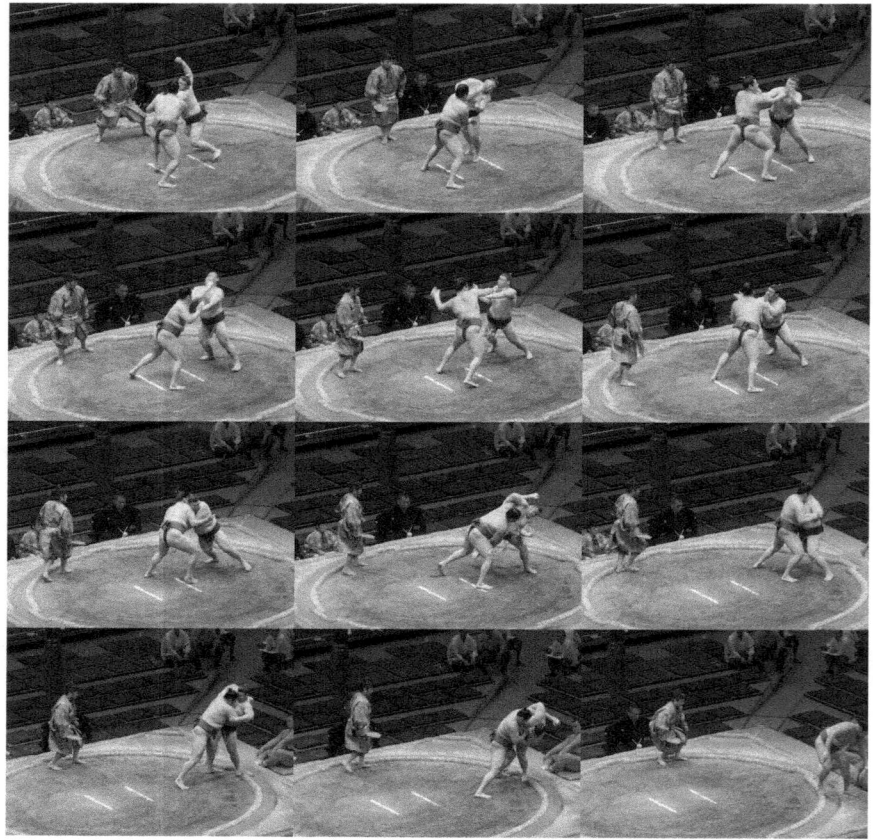

**FIGURE 9.2** *Sequential photographs of junior Maezumo Sumo bout.*

anthropology's intersections with other disciplines such as educational theory, fine art and design, attention has become common ground.

Training our attention[13] in three realms is important to a future discipline lying between architecture and anthropology.

> *Introverted attention.* Looking inwards is frowned upon a little within anthropology, given that the focus is often on the lives of others. There is always a tension, however, with both the presence of the observing anthropologist and understanding activities which are fundamentally introverted in nature. The self-knowledge of a dance practitioner, the meditations found in a range of religious and secular practice, and some processes of gestural drawing – each requires a way of understanding oneself as a part of the wider picture. In architecture, an understanding of our own creative process offers potential for development in the discipline,

# CONCLUSION: TOWARDS AN ANTHROPOLOGICAL ARCHITECTURE

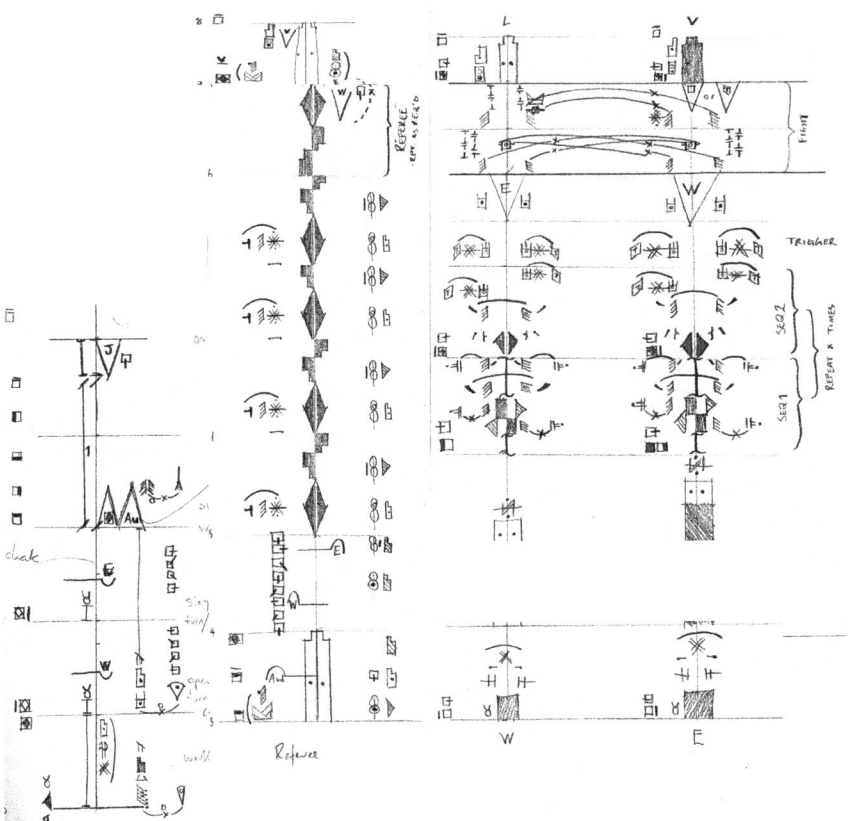

**FIGURE 9.3** *Laban notation of Sumo bout.*

really questioning the manner in which we know the world and how our practices channel this in particular directions. What do we gain and what do we miss?

*Extravert attention.* An outward attention encompasses a wide range of activities, not only those which are observational such as drawing, photography and filmmaking; but also to consider those practices which work directly with materials. Craft practices of making focus their attention on materials, on the interactions these have with one another and on the forces which can be applied to transform them from one state to another. Architecture has a long history of developing attitudes towards materials, contexts, climates and the environment. An architectural anthropology of extraverted attention looks towards material culture studies and how the biographies of things intertwine with our own lifeworlds.

*Social attention.* Anthropology has been at the forefront of developing socially based theories; working within a social context is rarely a completely isolating activity – meaning that the intentions, thoughts and actions of others have an impact on everyday life. Appreciating the fuller group of people involved is important here; the wide range of experts who contribute to the commissioning and construction of architecture goes far beyond the designer alone – a kind of performance orchestrating the activities of professionals and individuals with overlapping interests and requirements.

The above suggests some of the ways in which practices of continual learning about the world can inform us as theoreticians and practitioners. By ceasing to restrict ourselves to textual communication, particularly in the analytical and theoretical fora, we can encourage the co-production of environments where each of us can learn about the wider environment and communicate that understanding with one another. Engaging in the same *introverted* activity allows a shared experience to form the basis of communication about both the similarities and the differences in how we perceived our own bodies during that event. Similarly, in working within a material or geographic context together, we can respond to each others' actions with immediacy and through physical engagement rather than filtering by verbal communication. Finally, full co-creation within a social context opens up viable new forms of practice which offer opportunities for a range of different expertise and knowledge appropriate to each part of an activity. The interaction between these actors moves beyond the mobilization of skills and interests and becomes fully social, with all the benefits and problems that might entail.

In this way cross-disciplinary understandings between architects and anthropologists can flourish beyond the (valuable) work on anthropologies *of* architectural practice and anthropologies *of* skilled practices such as drawing. The aim is to work with anthropology *by way of* architectural skills and practices, and an architecture with the observational and theoretical rigour of anthropology, sweeping assumptions aside and working more holistically to better serve the needs of clients, users and the wider environment we are building in.

# Notes

1. See Gunn & Donovan (2013); Gunn, Smith & Otto (2013); Smith, Vangkilde, et al. (2016).
2. Such as Buchli (2013) and Marchand (2009).

## CONCLUSION: TOWARDS AN ANTHROPOLOGICAL ARCHITECTURE

3   Such as Yaneva (2009) and Houdart & Chihiro (2009); see also Kaijima, Stalder & Iseki (2018).
4   See Ingold (2013) for more on this distinction.
5   See Lucas (2014). for more on the role of the sketchbook.
6   See Tschumi (1996) for more on this.
7   Discussed much more fully in Lucas (2019a).
8   Such as Lynch (1960) and Gould & White (1986).
9   As discussed by Cureton (2016:80–88).
10  See Lucas & Romice (2008) and Lucas (2009a, 2009b) for more details on this project.
11  This notation is fully detailed up as part of Lucas (2006).
12  See Lucas (2008a) for the Tokyo Metro project and Lucas (2009c) for the Daruma notations. The notations of Sanja Matsuri (discussed in Chapter 7 of this volume) can be found in Lucas (2018b).
13  This discussion of attention is indebted to the *Knowing from the Inside* European Research Council research group, with this epistemology of attention forming the basis of discussions about a new curriculum exploring the themes of how we can come to know the world and communicate our knowledge of it. https://knowingfromtheinside.org https://www.abdn.ac.uk/research/kfi/.

# References

Adapon, Joy. 2008. *Culinary Art and Anthropology*. Oxford: Berg.
Adorno, Theodore. 2004 [1970]. *Aesthetic Theory*. London: Continuum.
Appadurai, Arjun (Ed.). 1986. *The Social Life of Things*. Cambridge: Cambridge University Press.
Arnheim, Rudolf. 1969. *Visual Thinking*. Berkeley: University of California Press.
Ashkenazi, Michael. 1993. *Matsuri: Festivals of a Japanese Town*. Honolulu: University of Hawaii Press.
Ashkenazi, M. & Jacob, J. 2013. *The Essence of Japanese Cuisine: An Essay on Food and Culture*. London: Routledge.
Augoyard, Jean-François. 2007. *Step by Step: Everyday Walks in a French Urban Housing Project*. Minneapolis: University of Minnesota Press.
Augoyard, Jean-François & Torgue, Henri. 2006. *Sonic Experience: A Guide to Everyday Sounds*. Montreal: McGill University Press.
Bachelard, Gaston. 1992 [1958]. *The Poetics of Space*. Boston, MA: Beacon Press.
Banham, Reyner. 1969. *The Architecture of the Well Tempered Environment*. Oxford: The Architectural Press.
Barthes, Roland. 1977. *Image, Music, Text*. London: Fontana Press.
Bateson, Gregory. 1972. *Steps to an Ecology of Mind: Collected Essays in Anthropology, Psychiatry, Evolution and Epistemology*. Chicago: University of Chicago Press.
Baudelaire, Charles. 2006 [1863]. *The Painter of Modern Life and Other Essays*. London: Phaidon.
Baudrillard, Jean. 1994. 'The System of Collecting' in Elsner, John & Cardinal, Roger (Eds). *Cultures of Collecting*, pp. 7–24. London: Reaktion Books.
Beaumont, Matthew. 2015. *Nightwalking: A Nocturnal History of London from Chaucer to Dickens*. London: Verso.
Belardi, Paolo. 2014. *Why Architects Still Draw*. Cambridge, MA: MIT Press.
Bestor, Theodore. 1990. *Neighbourhood Tokyo*. Stanford, CA: Stanford University Press.
Bestor, Theodore. 1999. 'Wholesale Sushi: Culture and Commodity in Tokyo's Tsukiji Market' in Low, S. (Ed.). *Theorizing the City: The New Urban Ethnography Reader*, pp. 201–241. New Brunswick: Rutgers University Press.
Bestor, Theodore. 2004. *Tsukiji: The Fish Market at the Centre of the World*. Berkeley, CA: University of California Press.
Blackman, Lisa. 2008. *The Body*. Oxford: Berg.
Borden, Iain. 2003. *Skateboarding, Space and the City: Architecture and the Body*. Oxford: Berg.
Bordwell, David. 1987. *Narration in the Fiction Film*. London: Routledge.

Borges, Jorge Luis. 2000. 'On Exactitude in Science' in *The Aleph*, p. 181. London: Penguin.
Bourdieu, Pierre. 1990. 'Appendix: The Kabyle House or the World Reversed' in *The Logic of Practice*, pp. 271–283. Cambridge: Polity Press.
Brunskill, R. W. 2000. *Vernacular Architecture: An Illustrated Handbook*. London: Faber & Faber.
Buchli, Victor. 2000. *An Archaeology of Socialism*. Oxford: Berg.
Buchli, Victor. 2002. 'Khrushchev, Modernism and the Fight Against *Petit-Bourgeois* Consciousness in the Soviet Home' in Buchli, V. (Ed.). *The Material Culture Reader*, pp. 207–236. Oxford: Berg.
Buchli, Victor. 2013. *The Anthropology of Architecture*. London: Bloomsbury.
Buxton, Pamela (Ed.). 2015. *Metric Handbook: Planning and Design Data*, Fifth Edition. London: Routledge.
Cairns, S. & Jacobs, J. M. 2014. *Buildings Must Die: A Perverse View of Architecture*. Cambridge, MA: MIT Press.
Cali, Joseph & Dougill, John. 2013. *Shinto Shrines: A Guide to the Sacred Sites of Japan's Ancient Religion*. Honolulu: University of Hawaii Press.
Calvino, Italo. 1974. *Invisible Cities*. W. Weaver (Trans.). Orlando: Harcourt Brace & Company.
Careri, F. 2002. *Walkscapes: Walking as an Aesthetic Practice*. Barcelona: Gustavo Gili.
Causey, Andrew. 2017. *Drawn to See: Drawing as an Ethnographic Method*. Toronto: University of Toronto Press.
Cho, Byoungso. 2018. 'Imperfection and Emptiness' in *Architectural Review*, Vol. 1448, February 2018, pp. 44–50.
Classen, Constance & Howes, David. 2006. 'The Museum as Sensescape: Western Sensibilities and Indigenous Artifacts' in Edwards, Elizabeth, Gosden, Chris & Phillips, Ruth B. (Eds.). *Sensible Objects: Colonialism, Museums and Modern Culture*, pp. 199–222. Oxford: Berg.
Clifford, James & Marcus, George (Eds.). 2010. *Writing Culture: The Poetics and Politics of Anthropology*. Berkeley, CA: University of California Press.
Cook, Peter & Webb, Michael. 1999. *Archigram*. Princeton Architectural Press.
Cullen, Gordon. 1961. *The Concise Townscape*. The Architectural Press.
Cureton, Paul. 2016. *Strategies for Landscape Representation: Digital and Analogue Techniques*, pp. 80–88. London: Routledge.
Daniels, Inge (Author) & Andrews, Susan (Photographer). 2010. *The Japanese Home: Material Culture in the Modern Home*. Oxford: Berg.
De Certeau, Michel. 1984. *The Practice of Everyday Life*. Berkeley & Los Angeles: University of California Press.
Debord, Guy. 1994. *The Society of the Spectacle*. D. Nicholson Smith (Trans.). New York: Zone Books.
Deliss, Clémentine (Ed.). 2012. *Object Atlas: Fieldwork in the Museum*. Frankfurt: Kerber.
Donahue, Sean. 2014. 'Unmapping' in Yelavich, Susan & Adams, Barbara (Eds.). *Design as Future Making*, pp. 36–46. London: Bloomsbury.
Douglas, Mary. 1972. 'Deciphering a Meal' in *Daedalus*, Vol. 101, Issue 1, Myth, Symbol, and Culture (Winter 1972), MIT Press on behalf of American Academy of Arts & Sciences, pp. 61–81.

Douglas, Mary. 1991. 'The Idea of Home: A Kind of Space' in *Social Research*, Vol. 58, Issue 1, Spring 1991, pp. 287–307.
Douglas, Mary. 2002. *Purity and Danger*. London: Routledge.
D'Souza, Aruna & McDonough, Tom (Eds.). 2008. *Gender, Public Space and Visual Culture in Nineteenth Century Paris*. Manchester: Manchester University Press.
Dunn, Nick. 2016. *Dark Matters: A Manifesto for the Nocturnal City*. Winchester: Zero Books.
Eco, Umberto. 1989. *The Open Work*. Cambridge, MA: Harvard University Press.
Elkin, Lauren. 2017. *Flâneuse: Women Walk the City in Paris, New York, Tokyo, Venice and London*. London: Vintage.
Elliot, Denielle & Culhane, Dara (Eds.). 2017. *A Different Kind of Ethnography: Imaginative Practices and Creative Methodologies*. Toronto: University of Toronto Press.
Farnell, Brenda. 1995. *Do You See What I Mean: Plains Indian Sign Talk and the Embodiment of Action*. Lincoln, NE: University of Nebraska Press.
Forty, Adrian. 2004. *Words and Buildings: A Vocabulary of Modern Architecture*. London: Thames & Hudson.
Forty, Adrian & Küchler, Suzanne (Eds.). 1999. *The Art of Forgetting*. Oxford: Berg.
Foucault, Michel. 1986. 'Of Other Spaces'. Jay Miskowiec (Trans). In *Diacritics*, Vol. 16, Issue 1, Spring 1986, pp. 22–27.
Frazer, James G. 1994 [1890]. *The Golden Bough*. Oxford: Oxford University Press.
Gandelsonas, Mario. 1987. 'The Order of the American City: Analytic Drawings of Boston' in *Assemblage*, Vol. 3, July 1987, pp. 63–71. Cambridge, MA: MIT Press.
Gandelsonas, Mario. 1995. 'The Master Plan as a Political Site' in *Assemblage*, Vol. 27, August 1995, pp. 19–24. Cambridge, MA: MIT Press.
Gandelsonas, Mario. 1998. 'The City as Object of Architecture' in *Assemblage*, Vol. 37, December 1998, pp. 128–144. Cambridge, MA: MIT.
Geismar, Haidy. 2009. 'The Photograph and the Malanggan: Rethinking Images on Malakula, Vanatu' in *Australian Journal of Anthropology*, Vol. 20, pp. 48–73.
Gell, Alfred. 1992. *The Anthropology of Time: Cultural Constructions of Temporal Maps and Images*. Oxford: Berg.
Gell, Alfred. 1998a. *Art and Agency*. Oxford: Oxford University Press.
Gell, Alfred. 1998b. 'The Maori Meeting House' in *Art and Agency*, pp. 251–258. Oxford: Clarendon Press.
Gell, Alfred. 1999. 'The Technology of Enchantment and the Enchantment of Technology' in *The Art of Anthropology: Essays and Diagrams*, pp. 159–186. London: Athlone Press.
Gibson, James J. 1983 [1966]. *Senses Considered as Perceptual Systems*. Westport, CT: Greenwood Press.
Gibson, James J. 1986. *The Ecological Approach to Visual Perception*. New York, NY: Psychology Press.
Glassie, Henry. 2000. *Vernacular Architecture*. Bloomington, IN: University of Indiana Press.
Goffman, Erving. 1974. *Frame Analysis: An Essay on the Organisation of Experience*. Boston: Northeastern University Press.

Goodman, Nelson. 1976. *Languages of Art*. Indianapolis & Cambridge: Hackett Publishing.
Goodman, Nelson. 1978. *Ways of Worldmaking*. Indianapolis & Cambridge: Hackett Publishing.
Goodwin, James. 1993. *Akira Kurosawa and Intertextual Cinema*. The Johns Hopkins University Press.
Goody, Jack. 1982. *Cooking, Cuisine and Class: A Study in Comparative Sociology*. Cambridge: Cambridge University Press.
Gould, Peter & White, Rodney. 1986. *Mental Maps*. London: Routledge.
Graafland, Arie (Ed.). 2005. *The Body in Architecture*. Rotterdam: 010 Publishers.
Greenblatt, Stephen. 1991. 'Resonance and Wonder' in Karp, I. & Lavine, S. D. (Eds.). *Exhibiting Culture*, pp. 42–56. Washington: Smithsonian Institution Press.
Grimshaw, Anna. 2001. *The Ethnographer's Eye: Ways of Seeing in Anthropology*. Cambridge: Cambridge University Press.
Grimshaw, Anna & Ravetz, Amanda (Eds.). 2005. *Visualizing Anthropology*. Bristol: Intellect.
Groemer, G. 2010. 'Sacred Dance at Sensoji: the Development of a Tradition' in *Asian Ethnology*, Vol. 69, Issue 2, pp. 265–292. Nanzan University.
Gropius, Walter, Tange, Kenzo & Ishimoto, Yasuhiro. 1960. *Katsura: Tradition and Creation in Japanese Architecture*. New Haven: Yale University Press.
Gros, Frédéric. 2015. *A Philosophy of Walking*. London: Verso Books.
Gunn, Wendy. 2008. 'Learning to Ask Naïve Questions with IT Product Design Students' in *Arts and Humanities in Higher Education*, Vol. 7, Issue 3, pp. 323–336.
Gunn, Wendy (Ed.). 2009. *Fieldnotes and Sketchbooks: Challenging the Boundaries between Descriptions and Processes of Describing*. Peter Lang Publishers.
Gunn, Wendy & Donovan, Jared (Eds.). 2013. *Design and Anthropology*. Farnham: Ashgate.
Gunn, Wendy & Løgstrup, Louise. 2014. 'Participant Observation, Anthropology Methodology and Design Anthropology Research Inquiry' in *Arts and Humanities in Higher Education*, Vol. 13, Issue 4, pp. 428–442.
Gunn, Wendy, Smith, Rachel C. & Otto, Ton (Eds.). 2013. *Design Anthropology: Theory and Practice*. London: Bloomsbury.
Halprin, Lawrence. 1982. *The R.S.V.P. Cycles: Creative Process in the Human Environment*. George Braziler Inc.
Hann, Chris & Hart, Keith. 2011. *Economic Anthropology*. London: Polity.
Hansen, Wilburn. 2008. *When Tengu Talk: Hirata Atsutane's Ethnography of the Other World*. Honolulu: University of Hawaii Press.
Hardingham, Samantha (Ed.). 2017. *Cedric Price Works 1952–2003: A Forward Minded Retrospective*. London & Montreal: Architectural Association & Canadian Centre for Architecture.
Harkness, Rachel. 2011. 'Earthships: The Homes That Trash Built' in *Anthropology Now*, Vol. 3, Issue 1, April 2011, pp. 54–65.
Helliwell, J. F. & Putnam, R. D. 1995. 'Economic Growth and Social Capital in Italy' in *Eastern Economic Journal*, Vol. 21, Issue 3, pp. 295–307.
Henare, Amira, Holbraad, Martin & Wastell, Sari (Eds.). 2007. *Thinking through Things: Theorising Artefacts Ethnographically*. London: Routledge.

Hendry, Joy. 1987. *Understanding Japanese Society*. London: Routledge.
Hendry, Joy. 1993. *Wrapping Culture: Politeness, Presentation and Power in Japan and Other Societies*. Oxford: Clarendon Press.
Hendry, Joy. 2000. *The Orient Strikes Back: A Global View of Cultural Display*. Oxford: Berg.
Henshaw, Victoria. 2013. *Urban Smellscapes: Understanding and Designing City Smell Environments*. London: Routledge.
Herdt, Tanja. 2017. *The City and the Architecture of Change: The Work and Radical Visions of Cedric Price*. Zurich: Park Books.
Heschong, Lisa. 1979. *Thermal Delight in Architecture*. Cambridge, MA: MIT Press.
Higgin, Marc. 2016. 'What Do We Do When We Draw?' in *Tracey Journal: Drawing and Visualisation Research*, July 2016: Presence.
Hillier, Bill & Hanson, Julienne. 2008 [1984]. *The Social Logic of Space*. Cambridge: Cambridge University Press.
Hoskins, J. 2006. 'Agency, Biography and Objects' in Tilley, C., Keane, W., Küchler, S., Rowlands, M. & Spyer, P. (Eds.). *Handbook of Material Culture*, pp. 74–84. London: Sage.
Houdart, Sophie & Minato, Chihiro. 2009. *Kuma Kengo: An Unconventional Monograph*. Paris: Editions Donner Lieu.
Hunt, Kristin. 2018. *Alimentary Performances: Mimesis, Theatricality, and Cuisine*. London: Routledge.
Hwangbo, Alfred. 2010. 'Beyond the Nostalgic Conservation of the Past: The Urban Courtyard House in Korea (1920–60)' in Rabbat, N. O. (Ed.). *The Courtyard House*. Farnham: Ashgate.
Hwangbo, Alfred & Jarzombek, Mark. 2011. 'Global in a Not-So-Global World' in *Journal of Architectural Education, Special Issue: Beyond Precedent*, Vol. 64, Issue 2, March 2011, pp. 59–66. New York: Wiley Periodicals.
Ikuya, Takamori. 2001. *Family Crests of Japan*. Tokyo: Tuttle & ICG muse, Inc.
Imai, Heide. 2017. *Tokyo Roji: The Diversity and Versatility of Alleys in a City in Transition*. London: Routledge [kindle edition].
Ingold, Tim. 2000. 'Building Dwelling Living' in *The Perception of the Environment*, pp. 172–188. London: Routledge.
Ingold, Tim. 2011. *Being Alive: Essays on Movement, Knowledge and Description*. London: Routledge.
Ingold, Tim. 2013. *Making: Anthropology, Archaeology, Art and Architecture*. London: Routledge.
Ingold, Tim. 2014. 'That's Enough about Ethnography!' in *HAU: Journal of Ethnographic Theory*, Vol. 7, Issue 1, pp. 383–395.
Ingold, Tim (Ed.). 2016. *Redrawing Anthropology: Materials, Movements, Lines*. London: Routledge.
Ingold, Tim. 2017. 'Anthropology Contra Ethnography' in *HAU: Journal of Ethnographic Theory*, Vol. 7, Issue 1, pp. 21–26.
Ingold, Tim with Ray Lucas. 2007. 'The 4 A's (Anthropology, Archaeology, Art and Architecture): Reflections on a Teaching and Learning Experience' in Harris, M. (Ed.). *Ways of Knowing: New Approaches in the Anthropology of Knowledge and Learning*, pp. 287–305. Oxford: Berhgahn Books.
Ingold, Tim & Lee Vergunst, Jo (Eds.). 2008. *Ways of Walking*, pp. 169–184. Aldershot, Hampshire: Ashgate.

Ishimoto, Yasuhiro. 2010. *Katsura: Picturing Modernism in Japanese Architecture*. New Haven: Yale University Press.

Isozaki, Arata. 1986. 'Floors and Internal Spaces in Japanese Vernacular Architecture: Phenomenology of Floors' in *Res: Anthropology and Aesthetics*, Issue 11, Spring 1986, pp. 54–77. Cambridge, MA: Peabody Museum of Archaeology and Ethnology.

Isozaki, Arata. 2006. *Japan-ness in Architecture*. Cambridge, MA: MIT press.

Jackson, Michael. 2013. *Lifeworlds: Essays in Existential Anthropology*. Chicago: University of Aberdeen Press.

Jinnai, Hidenobu. 1995. *Tokyo: A Spatial Anthropology*. University of California Press.

Kaijima, Momoyo, Laurent, Stalder & Iseki, Yu (Eds). 2018. *Architectural Ethnography: Japanese Pavilion Venice Beinnale*. Tokyo: TOTO.

Kim, Dan Bi & Lee, Jae Soek (Eds.). 2016. *Hanok, Korean Traditional Architecture: 2011–2016 National Hanok Competition*. Seoul: Architecture & Urban Research Institute & Kim Dae Ik.

Kinchin, Juliet with O'Connor, Aidan. 2011. *Counter Space: Design and the Modern Kitchen*. New York: Museum of Modern Art.

Koolhaas, Rem. 1994. *Delirious New York: A Retroactive Manifesto for Manhattan*. New York: Rizzoli.

Küchler, Suzanne. 2002. *Malanggan: Art, Memory and Sacrifice*. Oxford: Berg.

Kuma, Kengo. 2010. *Anti-Object*. London: the Architectural Association.

Lalonde, M. P. 1992. 'Deciphering a Meal Again, or the Anthropology of Taste' in *Social Science Information*, Vol. 31, Issue 1, pp. 69–86.

Le Breton, David. 2017. *Sensing the World: An Anthropology of the Senses*. London: Bloomsbury.

Le Corbusier. 1989 [1923]. *Towards a New Architecture*. Oxford: The Architectural Press.

Le Corbusier. 2000. *The Modulor and Modulor 2*. Paris: Fondation Le Corbusier.

Lefebvre, Henri. 2004. *Rhythmanalysis*. New York: Athlone Press.

Lefebvre, Henri. 2014. *Critique of Everyday Life*. London: Verso.

Lévi-Strauss, Claude. 1969. *The Raw and the Cooked*. Chicago: University of Chicago Press.

Lévi-Strauss, Claude. 1974. *Structural* Anthropology. Oxford: Basic Books.

Lucas, Ray. 2002. *Filmic Architecture: An Exploration of Film Language as a Method for Architectural Criticism and Design*. Unpublished MPhil thesis. Glasgow: University of Strathclyde.

Lucas, Ray. 2006. *Towards a Theory of Notation as a Thinking Tool*. Unpublished PhD thesis. Aberdeen: University of Aberdeen.

Lucas, Ray. 2008a. 'Taking a Line for a Walk: Flânerie, Drifts, and the Artistic Potential of Urban Wandering' in Ingold, Tim & Lee Vergunst, Jo (Eds.). *Ways of Walking: Ethnography and Practice on Foot*, pp. 169–184. Farnham: Ashgate.

Lucas, Ray. 2008b. 'Getting Lost in Tokyo' in *Footprint*, Delft School of Design Journal, Issue 2. https://journals.open.tudelft.nl/index.php/footprint/issue/view/372. Accessed January 2019.

Lucas, Ray. 2009a. 'The Sensory Experience of Sacred Space: Senso-Ji and Meiji-Jingu, Tokyo' in *MONU: Magazine on Urbanism*. Issue 10: Holy Urbanism, pp. 46–55. Rotterdam: Board Publishers.

Lucas, Ray. 2009b. 'Designing a Notation for the Senses' in *Architectural Theory Review Special Issue: Sensory Urbanism*, Vol. 14, Issue 2, Spring 2009, p. 173.

Lucas, Ray. 2009c. 'Gestural Artefacts: Notations of a Daruma Doll' in Gunn, Wendy (Ed.). *Fieldnotes and Sketchbooks: Challenging the Boundaries between Descriptions and Processes of Describing*, pp.155–174. Bern: Peter Lang Publishers.

Lucas, Ray. 2012. 'The Instrumentality of Gibson's Medium as an Alternative to Space' in *CLCWeb Special Issue: Narrativity and the Perception/Conception of Landscape*. West Lafayette, IN: Purdue University Press. https://doi.org/10.7771/1481-4374.2039. Accessed 31 January 2019.

Lucas, Ray. 2014. 'The Sketchbook as Collection: A Phenomenology of Sketching' in Bartram, A., El-Bizri, N. & Gittens, D. (Eds.). *Recto-Verso: Redefining the Sketchbook*, pp. 191–206. Farnham: Ashgate.

Lucas, Ray. 2016. *Research Methods for Architecture*. London: Laurence King.

Lucas, Ray. 2017a. 'Electricity as Limit in Namdaemun Market, Seoul' in Cross, J., Anusas, M., Schick, L. & Abram, S. (Eds.). in *Our Lives with Electric Things*, Theorising the Contemporary Section, Cultural Anthropology Website. https://culanth.org/fieldsights/1263-our-electric-controls. Accessed 31 January 2019.

Lucas, Ray. 2017b. 'The Discipline of Tracing in Architectural Drawing' in Johannessen, Christian Mosbaek & van Leeuwen, Jacob (Eds.). *The Materiality of Writing: A Trace Making Perspective*, pp. 116–137. London: Routledge.

Lucas, Ray. 2018a. 'Threshold and Temporality in Architecture: Practices of Movement in Japanese Architecture' in Bunn, S. (Ed.). *Anthropology and Beauty: From Aesthetics to Creativity*, pp. 279–290. London: Routledge.

Lucas, Ray. 2018b. 'Script and Score: Revisiting Nelson Goodman at Sanja Matsuri' in Browne, Jemma, Frost, Christian & Lucas, Ray (Eds.). *Architecture, Festival & the City*, pp.81–96. London: Routledge.

Lucas, Ray. 2019a. *Drawing Parallels: Knowledge Production in Axonometric, Isometric and Parallel Projection*. London: Routledge.

Lucas, Ray. 2020. 'Threshold as a Social Surface: The Architecture of South Korean Urban Marketplaces' in Simonetti, C. & Anusas, M. (Eds.). *On surfaces: Contributions from Anthropology, Archaeology, Art and Architecture*. London: Routledge (Forthcoming).

Lucas, Ray & Romice, Ombretta. 2008. 'Representing Sensory Experience in Urban Design' in *Design Principles and Practices: An International Journal*, Vol. 2, Issue 4, pp. 83–94. Common Ground Publishers.

Lukas, Scott. 2012. *The Immersive Worlds Handbook: Designing Theme Parks and Consumer Spaces*. London: Routledge.

Lund, Katrin & Lorimer, Hayden. 2008. 'A Collectible Topography: Walking, Remembering and Recording Mountains' in Ingold, Tim & Lee Vergunst, Jo (Eds.). *Ways of Walking*, pp. 185–200. Aldershot, Hampshire: Ashgate.

Lynch, Kevin. 1960. *The Image of the City*. Cambridge, MA: MIT Press.

MacDougall, David. 2006. *The Corporeal Image: Film, Ethnography, and the Senses*. New York: Princeton University Press.

Marchand, Trevor H. 2009. *The Masons of Djenne*. Bloomington, IN: Indiana University Press.

Mauss, Marcel. 1947. 'Techniques of the Body' in *Economy and Society*, Vol. 2, Issue 1, pp. 70–78.

Mauss, Marcel. 2002 [1954]. *The Gift*. London: Routledge.
Merleau-Ponty, Maurice. 2002 [1962]. *Phenomenology of Perception*. London: Routledge.
Message, Kylie. 2006. *New Museums and the Making of Culture*. Oxford: Berg.
Metz, Christian. 1984. *Psychoanalysis and Cinema: The Imaginary Signifier*. London: Macmillan Press.
Miller, Daniel. 2001. *Home Possessions: Material Culture behind Closed Doors*. Oxford: Berg.
Miller, Daniel. 2010. *Stuff*. Cambridge: Polity Press.
Miyazaki, Hirokazu. 2010. 'Gifts and Exchange' in Hicks, D. & Beaudry, M. C. (Eds.). *The Oxford Handbook of Material Culture Studies*, pp. 246–264. Oxford: Oxford University Press.
Mooshammer, Helge & Mörtenböck, Peter. 2008. *Networked Cultures: Parallel Architectures and the Politics of Space*. Rotterdam: NAi Publishers.
Mooshammer, Helge & Mörtenböck, Peter. 2015. *Informal Market Worlds: The Architecture of Economic Pressure: Atlas*. Rotterdam: NAi/010 Publishers.
Mooshammer, Helge & Mörtenböck, Peter. 2016. *Visual Cultures as Opportunity*. London: Sternberg Press.
Mooshammer, Helge, Mörtenböck, Peter, Cruz, Teddy & Forman, Fonna (Eds.). 2015. *Informal Market Worlds: The Architecture of Economic Pressure: Reader*. Rotterdam: NAi/010 Publishers.
Oliver, Paul. 2003. *Dwellings: The Vernacular House Worldwide*. London: Phaidon.
Orwell, George. 2004 [1946]. *Why I Write*. London: Penguin Great Ideas.
Orwell, George. 2013 [1946]. *Politics and the English Language*. London: Penguin Modern Classics.
Ozawa De-Silva, C. 2014. 'Hatsumōde, the Visitation of Shinto Shrines: Religion and Culture in the Japanese Context' in Idler, E. L. (Ed.). *Religion as a Social Determinant of Public Health*. Oxford: Oxford University Press, chapter 8, pp. 71–76.
Pallasma, Juhani. 1996. *The Eyes of the Skin*. London: Academy Editions.
Pallasmaa, J. 2009. *The Thinking Hand*. Oxford: Wiley.
Pekkanen, Robert J., Tsujinaka, Yutaka & Yamamoto, Hidehiro. 2014. *Neighborhood Associations and Local Governance in Japan*. London: Routledge (Nissan Institute/Routledge Japanese Studies Series).
Perec, Georges. 1997. *Species of Spaces and Other Pieces*. London: Penguin.
Pevsner, Niklaus. 2009. *An Outline of European Architecture*. London: Thames & Hudson.
Pink, Sarah. 2004. *Home Truths: Gender, Domestic Objects and Everyday Life*. Oxford: Berg.
Pink, Sarah. 2007. *Doing Visual Ethnography: Images, Media and Representation in Research*. London: Sage.
Pink, Sarah, Leder Mackley, Kerstin, Moroşanu, Roxana, Mitchell, Val & Bhamra, Tracy. 2017. *Making Homes: Ethnography and Design*. London: Bloomsbury.
Ponciroli, Virginia (Ed.). 2004. *Katsura Imperial Villa*. Milan: Electa Architecture.
Porcu, E. 2012. 'Observations on the Blurring of the Religious and the Secular in a Japanese Urban Setting' in *Journal of Religion in Japan*, Vol. 1, pp. 83–106. Leiden: Brill.
Price, C. 2003. *Re: Cedric Price*. Basel: Birkhauser Verlag.

Rabinow, Paul, Marcus, George E., Faubion, James D. & Rees, Tobias. 2008. *Designs for an Anthropology of the Contemporary*. Duke University Press [kindle edition].
Rasmussen, Steen Eiler. 1962. *Experiencing Architecture*. Cambridge, MA: MIT Press.
Rendell, Jane. 1996. '"Industrious Females" & "Professional Beauties" or Fine Articles for Sale in the Burlington Arcade' in Borden, Iain, Kerr, Joe, Pivaro, Alicia, Rendell, Jane (Eds.). *Strangely Familiar: Narratives of Architecture in the City*, pp. 32–36. London: Routledge.
Robertson, Stephen. 2014. 'Monozukuri and Machizukuri: Crafting Community in Contemporary Japan' paper presentation on *Forging Futures* panel at IUAES 2014 conference, Chiba, May 2014.
Rossi, Aldo. 1982. *The Architecture of the City*. Cambridge, MA: MIT Press.
Rudofsky, Bernard. 1981. *Architecture without Architects*. London: John Wiley & Sons.
Rudofsky, Bernard. 1987. *Architecture without Architects: A Short Introduction to Non-Pedigreed Architecture*. Albuquerque, NM: University of New Mexico Press.
Ruskin, John. 1969 [1856]. *The Elements of Drawing*. New York: Dover Books.
Said, Edward. 2003 [1978]. *Orientalism*. London: Penguin Books.
Sansi, Roger. 2015. *Art, Anthropology and the Gift*. London: Bloomsbury.
Schatzki, T. R., Cetina, K. K. & Von Savigny, E. (Eds.). 2001. *The Practice Turn in Contemporary Theory*. London: Routledge.
Scheer, David Ross. 2014. *The Death of Drawing: Architecture in the Age of Simulation*. London: Routledge.
Schmidtpott, Katja. 2012. 'Indifferent Communities: Neighbourhood Associations, Class and Community in Pre-War Tokyo' in Brumann, Christoph & Schulz, Evelyn (Eds.). *Urban Spaces in Japan: Cultural and Social Perspectives*, pp. 125–146. London: Routledge.
Schwanhäusser, Anja. 2016. *Sensing the City*. Basel: Birkhauser.
Sen Arijit & Silverman, Lisa (Eds.). 2014. *Making Place: Space and Embodiment in the City*. Bloomington: Indiana University Press.
Sennet, R. 2008. *The Craftsman*. London: Penguin Books.
Shephard, Wade. 2015. *Ghost Cities of China: The Story of Cities without People in the World's Most Populated Country*. London: Zed Books.
Simone, Abdoumaliq. 2010. *City Life from Jakarta to Dakar: Movements at the Crossroads*. London: Routledge.
Skyes, K. 2007. 'Subjectivity, Visual Technology and Public Culture: Watching the Ethnographic Film, *Malanggan Labadama* in New Ireland' in *The Sociological Review*, Vol. 55, Issue 1, pp. 42–56.
Smith, Rachel Charlotte, Vangkilde, Kaspar Tang, Kjærsgaard, Mette Gislev, Otto, Ton, Halse, Joachim & Binder, Thomas (Eds.). 2016. *Design Anthropological Futures*. London: Bloomsbury [kindle edition].
Sousanis, Nick. 2015. *Unflattening*. Cambridge, MA: Harvard University Press.
Stanek, Łukasz. 2012. 'Miastoprojekt Goes Abroad: The Transfer of Architectural Labour from Socialist Poland to Iraq (1958–1989)' in *The Journal of Architecture*, Vol. 17, Issue 3, 1 June 2012, pp. 361–386.
Stoller, Paul. 1989. *The Taste of Ethnographic Things: The Senses in Anthropology*. Philadelphia: University of Pennsylvania Press.

Strathern, Marilyn. 1988. *The Gender of the Gift: Problems with Women and Problems with Society in Melanesia*. Berkeley: University of California Press.

Strathern, Marilyn. 2001. 'The Patent and the Malanggan' in *Theory, Culture and Society*, Vol. 18, Issue 4, pp. 1–26.

Sudnow, David. 2001 [1978]. *Ways of the Hand: A Rewritten Account*. Cambridge, MA: MIT Press.

Sutton, David E. 2001. *Remembrance of Repasts: An Anthropology of Food and Memory*. Oxford: Berg.

Tafuri, Manfredo. 1976. *Architecture and Utopia: Design and Capitalist Development*. Cambridge, MA: MIT Press.

Tarkovsky, Andrey. 1986. *Sculpting in Time*. Austin: University of Texas Press.

Taussig, Michael. 2011. *I Swear I Saw This: Drawings In Fieldwork Notebooks, Namely My Own*. Chicago: University of Chicago Press.

Tester, Kieth (Ed.). 1994. *The Flâneur*. London: Routledge.

Thiel, Philip. 1996. *Paths, People, and Purposes: Notations for a Participatory Envirotecture*. University of Washington Press.

Tschumi, Bernard. 1996. *Architecture and Disjunction*. London: Academy Editions.

Turner, Victor. 1987. *The Anthropology of Performance*. New York, NY: PAJ Publications.

Van Gennep, Arnold. 1961. *The Rites of Passage*. Chicago: University of Chicago Press.

Venturi, Robert, Scott Brown, Denise, Izenour, Steve, et al. 1977. *Learning from Las Vegas*. Cambridge, MA: MIT Press.

Warnier, Jean-Pierre. 2006. 'Inside and Outside: Surfaces and Containers' in Tilley, Christopher, Keane, Webb, Küchler, Suzanne, Rowlands, Mike, Spyer, Patricia (Eds.). *Handbook of Material Culture*, pp. 186–195. London: Sage.

Welter, Volker M. 2003. *Biopolis: Patrick Geddes and the City of Life*. Cambridge, MA: MIT Press.

Woods, Lebbeus. 1996. *War and Architecture (Pamphlet Architecture 15)*. New York: Princeton Architectural Press.

Woods, Lebbeus. 1997. *Radical Reconstruction*. New York: Princeton Architectural Press.

Yaneva, Albena. 2009. *Made by the Office for Metropolitan Architecture: An Ethnography of Design*. Rotterdam: 010 Publishers.

Yelavich, Susan & Adams, Barbara (Eds.). 2014. *Design as Future-Making*. London: Bloomsbury.

de Zegher, Catherine (Ed.). 2000. *Drawing Papers 4. The Body of the Line: Eisenstein's Drawings*. New York: The Drawing Center.

# Index

Adapon, Joy 186, 198
Adorno, Theodore 31, 200
agency 4, 22, 45, 48, 83, 99 n.4, 124, 143, 147, 158, 201, 206, 209, 218; of the home 51–7; in *Invisible Cities* (Calvino) 67; and the gift 112; in *Art and Agency* (Gell) 186, 198
alterations/adaptations 2, 6, 50–1, 76, 126, 135, 143, 146, 160
anti-object 133, 237. *See also* Kuma, Kengo
Appadurai, Arjun 20, 103, 112–13
Archigram 122, 124
architectural anthropology 4–7, 17, 22, 29, 65, 189, 217–20, 229
Arnheim, Rudolf 38–40, 42
Asakusa 21, 167–84, 212–13. *See also* Tokyo; Sanja Matsuri; Senso-ji
Ashkenazi, Michael 170, 174, 186–7, 189
Ashkenazi and Jacob 202–3, 208–10
attention 25, 37–8, 64, 70 n.16, 204, 221, 227–31
Augoyard, Jean-Francois 21, 138, 140–7

Bachelard, Gaston 65–7
Banham, Reyner 152
Barthes, Roland 166, 183 n.8
Bateson, Gregory 26
Baudelaire, Charles 35–7, 40
Baudrillard, Jean 19, 72, 74, 80, 84–7, 99 n.6
being, ways of being 2, 18, 35, 43, 50, 64, 68, 78, 106–8, 139, 148, 190
bell 116, 153–4, 172, 174, 176, 180
Benjamin, Walter 35, 200
Bergson, Henri 14

Bestor, Theodore 103, 114–16, 118, 168
Binzasara 178, 184 n.13
Boas, Franz 11
Borden, Iain 146, 182
Borges, Jorge Luis 198, 219, 225
Bourdieu, Pierre 48, 73, 102–3, 107–9, 135 n.5

Cairns, Stephen 126, 136 n.14
Calvino, Italo 65, 67
Cartesian coordinates 106, 127, 176–7
Cheonggyecheon, Cheonggye Stream Restoration 90–3
choreography 20, 202
Classen, Constance 74
co-production 2, 14, 19, 29, 74, 187, 217, 223, 230
cognition 11, 30, 37–8, 40
collection 2, 19
commodity 20, 104, 112–15
Computer Aided Design (CAD) 26, 28
condiments 209, 211
conservation 2, 19, 72, 88, 100 n.15, 220–2
convention (drawing) 17, 25, 27, 109, 194, 218, 224–5
cos-play zoku 40
counterman 202–4
cross-programming 223. *See also* Tschumi, Bernard
cuisine 21, 40, 186–92, 198, 204, 222

Daegu 17
Daniels, Inge 48, 58–62, 135 n.6, 208
Daruma 227, 231 n.12
De Certeau, Michel 103–7, 140
design anthropology 3, 6, 13, 15, 23 n.8, 26, 29, 219
diegetic space 21, 161–7

# INDEX

dirt, matter out of place 19, 46, 53, 87
dismantling 88, 126, 134, 136 n.14
Dongdaemun Design Plaza 96, 135. *See also* Zaha Hadid Architects
Douglas, Mary 19, 22, 53–4, 66, 87, 186, 189–90
draughting 27, 218, 225
drawing 15–18, 67, 69–70 n.16, 109, 122, 141–2, 156 n.9, 194; architectural drawing 13, 25–43; in Sensory Notation 217–19, 220–4. *See also* Graphic anthropology
dressage 139
dwelling 1–2, 5, 17–19, 43, 46–7, 51–2, 56, 148, 163, 187, 218; dwelling perspective 22, 63–8, 69 n.13

economics 3, 6, 20, 26, 48, 52, 55–7, 59, 76, 133, 160, 187–90; economic anthropology 101–4; practices of 107–10; material culture of 113–15, spatiality of 119–20
Edo-Tokyo Open Air Museum 76, 83–7
education, pedagogy 27, 72–3, 186, 228
Eisenstein, Sergei 33–4, 163, 166
electrical power 88, 133, 135
emergence 14, 178, 188, 200
envirotecture. *See* Thiel, Philip
ethnography 1, 3, 5, 10, 12, 15–16, 22 n.1; auto-ethnography 23 n.7, 23 n.9, 28–9, 48, 58, 69–70 n.16, 74, 103, 114, 118, 122, 219–20
exchange. *See* economics; gift
extravagance 110, 112, 136 n.10

festival 17, 21–2, 111, 135 n.7, 137, 150–6, 156 n.12, 158–83, 192, 211–14, 215 n.8, 227. *See also* Sanja Matsuri
fire 61, 66, 68, 134, 152–4, 168, 170, 188, 215 n.1
flow 34, 39, 58; *of materials* 61, 91–3, 124–5, 133, 138, 142, 163, 177, 221, 223
food event 22, 185–215, 222
Fourth Plinth, Trafalgar Square, London 82–3

fourth wall 161, 163
frames, frame analysis 163–4, 221, 223
Frazer, James 8–9, 11, 168
*furoshiki* (wrapping cloth) 62, 135 n.6
futures 13–14

Geddes, Patrick 104–5, 135 n.1, 225
Gell, Alfred 22, 99 n.4, 103, 112, 118–19, 186, 189, 225
gender 9, 46–54, 68 n.1, 106, 108, 138
generosity 101, 110, 112, 155. *See also* extravagance
geometrical space 106, 177, 192, 220
gesture 25, 32, 36, 63, 110, 191, 218
Gibson, James J. 26, 38, 42, 64, 69 n.13, 127, 133, 136 n.15, 176–9, 192. *See also* medium; surface; substance
gift 20, 61–2, 69 n.12, 99 n.4, 101, 103, 108, 109–12, 135 n.5, 135 n.6, 169, 223
gilet 129
Goffman, Erving 158, 160, 163–4, 223–4
Golden Gai, Shinjuku, Tokyo 196
Goody, Jack 185–9
graphic anthropology 29, 122, 158, 218, 224–30
Greenblatt, Stephen 72, 99 n.2, 99 n.6
Gunn, Wendy 23 n.8, 26, 230 n.1
gusteme 21, 188, 222
Guys, Constantin 35–7

habitus 101–9, 120, 126, 134, 148, 220
Hann, Chris & Hart, Keith 101, 103
hanok housing 19–20, 73, 76, 87–90, 97–8, 100 n.16
Hatsumōde 150–6, 156 n.13. *See also* New Year
Hawker Centre 143–4
Helliwell, John & Putnam, Robert 169
Hendry, Joy 19, 62, 69 n.12, 78–80, 83, 135 n.6
Heschong, Lisa 152
High Line, New York 92

# INDEX

Himeji Castle 32–5
home 18–20, 22, 45–69, 71, 80, 97, 120, 148, 157, 168, 182; *Home within Home within Home within Home within Home* (artwork by Do Ho Suh) 70 n.19; intimacy of 76 as ideal 87–9; and New Year festivity 151–2; eating at home 185–6, 189, 208–9; being at 221–2
Housing & Development Board (HDB) Block 143–4
Howes, David 74

Imai, Heide 196
informality 20, 22, 107, 120–2, 128–9, 132–5, 143, 153, 185, 205, 223
Ingold, Tim 1, 18, 28, 148–9, 156 n.3, 177, 231 n.4; on ethnography 15–16; on dwelling 19, 22, 64, 69 n.13; on lines 44 n.6; critique of landscape 135 n.2; on navigation and wayfinding 105, 135 n.3; on co-construction of people and environments 159. *See also* dwelling perspective (in *dwelling*); Knowing from the Inside
ink 31–5, 37–9
inscription 218, 227
inscriptive practice 16–23, 25–9, 38, 40, 44 n.6, 122, 218, 224–7
intertextuality 60
Isozaki, Arata 69 n.10, 69 n.11, 148
izakaya 40, 185, 191, 195–8, 200, 202, 206

Jacob, Jeanne 186–7, 189, 201–2, 204, 208–10, 215 n.4
Jacobs, Jane M. 126, 136 n.14
Jinnai, Hidenobu 170
Joya no kane 153. *See also* new year

Kabuki 21, 158, 161–7; Kabuki-za Theatre, Tokyo 164, 166
kaiseki 22, 185, 191, 198–201, 202, 206, 215 n.4
Kannon Bosatsu 170
Kannushi (Shinto Priest) 171, 183 n.12
Kappabashi, Tokyo 42

katsu 201, 205–6
Katsura Rikyu (Imperial Villa) 69 n.11, 211
Knowing from the Inside (KFI) 17, 28, 65, 69–70 n.16, 122, 231 n.13
knowledge production 13, 26, 122, 219–24
Kodai-ji Temple, Gion, Kyoto 153–4
Koolhaas, Rem 103
Küchler, Suzanne 19, 71, 74–6, 80–2, 99 n.4, 107
Kuma, Kengo 12, 21, 133, 162
kura-house 61
Kurosawa, Akira 60, 227
Kyoto 17, 21, 69 n.11, 137, 139, 150–6, 211

Laban notation 142, 150, 218, 227
LDK home 59–60
Le Breton, David 191
Le Corbusier 63–8, 84, 182
Lefebvre, Henri 138–9, 167
Levi-Strauss, Claude 10–11, 21, 44–8, 52, 63, 69 n.6, 185, 188–90
lifeworld 2–4, 5, 13, 18, 22 n.1, 56–7, 64–5, 72, 101–2, 158, 229
liminality 21, 54, 157–83, 223
Lorimer, Hayden 149–50
Lund, Katrin 149–50

machine for living in 63
Malanggan 19, 71, 74–6, 99 n.4, 107
Malanowski, Bronislaw 11
Marker, Chris 40, 44 n.7
material culture 13, 18–20, 46, 48, 54–5, 57–8, 62, 68 n.2, 71–2, 74, 103, 112–14, 139, 175, 187, 203, 208, 221, 229
medium: in drawing 32, 35; in Gibson, James J. 127, 133, 176–7, 179. *See also* drawing; Gibson, James J.; substance; surface
memory machine 66. *See also* Douglas, Mary
Merleau-Ponty, Maurice 44 n.9
methodological philistinism 3, 5, 9, 62, 222
Metz, Christian 162–3, 183 n.4

# INDEX

*Mikoshi* 168–81, 183–4 n.12, 227
Miller, Daniel 48, 54–7, 68 n.2, 221
mobility 103, 122, 133, 137, 221
modular cart 126, 129, 131–3, 135, 136 n.17. *See also* Namdaemun market
Mooshammer, Helge & Mörtenböck, Peter 120, 132
museum 2, 19, 22, 46, 72–81, 83–9, 92, 96, 98, 217, 222

Namdaemun market, Seoul 102, 113, 121–35
narrative 13, 18, 21, 73, 75, 78, 83, 87, 92, 98, 105, 135, 142, 145–6, 154, 158, 160–3, 165–7, 177, 183 n.1, 183 n.3, 188, 190, 210, 224
new year 21, 115, 137, 139, 150–6, 170
Neighbourhood Association (NHA) 168–70
Nō, Noh 161–2, 183 n.2
Noryangjin market, Seoul 117, 136 n.12, 186
notation: general 25, 27, 28, 38, 142, 150, 158, 165, 219, 225; Laban notation 142, 150, 218, 227, 229, 231 n.12; sensory notation 192–4, 197, 203, 206, 210, 214, 215 n.7, 225

o-mikuji (fortunes) 154–5
Okera Mairi (rope burning) 152
Orientalism. *See* Said, Edward
Orwell, George 30–4, 42–3, 43 n.4, 145
otherness 2, 62, 77, 158

Pallasmaa, Juhani 138, 178, 198
paper 31–3, 35, 37, 44 n.5, 79, 151, 154, 172, 197
Parent, Claude 122
participant-observation 3–4, 11–13, 15, 28, 58, 142
pathological monument. *See* Rossi, Aldo
patina 87
Pekkanen, Tsujinaka & Yamamoto 168–70, 176, 183 n.9
Perec, George 40, 43–4 n.4, 192

performance 1, 21–2, 79–80, 111, 150, 175–83, 190, 201, 203, 223, 230
Pevsner, Niklaus 134
Pink, Sarah 22, 23 n.7, 48–54, 59, 182
porter 102–3, 114, 122, 126, 129–30
potlatch 110–11
Price, Cedric 124, 183–4 n.16
production of self, selfhood 46, 49–51, 55, 112, 181, 218
propelling monument. *See* Rossi, Aldo
prototype 6, 15, 20, 63, 134, 190, 219

Rasmussen, Steen Eiler 138
reciprocity 101, 103, 109–11, 125, 135 n.6, 169
resonance 72, 79, 98, 99 n.2
rhythmanalysis 139
Robertson, Stephen 170
Rossi, Aldo 96, 100 n.12
Rudofsky, Bernard 22 n.3, 127, 133
Ruskin, John 39

Said, Edward 71, 77–8, 99 n.9
Sanja Matsuri 21, 135 n.7, 151, 167–83, 211–14, 215 n.8, 231 n.12
Sansi, Roger 12, 112
Science & Technology Studies (STS) 12
self-identification 52–3
Sen, Arijit & Silverman, Lisa 181–2
Sennett, Richard 178
Seoul 17, 19–20, 87–98, 102, 121–35, 186
Seoul City Hall 90–6
shabu shabu 208–11
shitamachi 168, 170, 210
shrine, Shinto 40, 58, 69 n.11
*shukahachi* (Flute Music) 171
Simone, Abdoumaliq 120
sketch, sketchbook 13, 16, 25, 27–8, 33, 36–41, 99 n.6, 212, 218, 223–4
skill, skilled practice 2, 9, 18, 26–7, 38, 43 n.1, 53, 101–4, 109, 114, 120, 128, 134, 137–8, 178, 200, 208–9, 220, 222, 230
social drama 159–61
social relations 1, 45, 46–8, 49–50, 56–8, 101, 119–20, 134, 190

social structures 47–8, 52, 56, 108, 119, 161
space syntax 4, 138, 225
spatial practices 104–6, 122, 129, 134, 139, 144–5, 158
spectatorship 37, 86, 158, 162, 227
spillage 125, 129
Stoller, Paul 190
Strathern, Marilyn 99 n.4, 112
studio 1, 16, 18, 22, 26–7, 35, 99 n.6, 217, 223
study (drawing) 37, 42
substance 127, 133–4, 176–9. *See also* Gibson, James J.; medium; surface
Sudnow, David 178
Sumo 33–4, 227–9
surface 23 n.10, 25, 32, 37, 107, 122, 126–9, 132–4, 136 n.16, 148, 176–7, 179, 218–19. *See also* Gibson, James J.; Medium; Substance
Sutton, David 191

*tachinomi* 196
tarpaulin 123–6, 175, 212
tatami 59–60, 148, 199
techniques of the body 20, 148
temple, Buddhist 137, 150–5, 170–1, 183 n.11, 211–14
tempura 186, 201–4
theme park 62, 77–80, 100 n.10
Thiel, Philip 225
threshold 21, 39, 54, 65, 68, 102, 120, 151, 156, 158, 159, 161, 164, 167, 218, 223

Tokyo 17, 20–1, 40, 87, 88, 102–3, 141–2, 158, 170, 183, 192, 196, 210, 227
Tschumi, Bernard 223, 231 n.6
Tsukiji market, Tokyo 102–3, 114–18, 136 n.11
Turner, Victor 21, 159–62
twine, thread 65–8, 69 n.15
typology 1, 4, 46, 61, 71, 80–1, 90, 98, 102–4, 120, 132, 134, 143, 196, 198, 235

Van Gennep, Arnold 159
vendor 20, 103, 107, 118, 122, 124–9, 132–3, 171, 197, 212, 223
Venturi, Scott-Brown & Rauch 79, 129
visual anthropology 3, 23 n.6, 29, 158

walking 3, 20–1, 36, 104, 106, 138–56, 176, 218, 221
Warburg, Aby 74
wonder 35, 72–3, 98, 99 n.2. *See also* resonance
*Writing Culture* (Clifford and Marcus) 18, 28–30

Yamanote 168
Yasaka Shrine, Gion, Kyoto 152–3
yatai 185, 196, 211–14
yokochō 196–7
Yoo Kerl & iArc Architects. *See* Seoul City Hall

Zaha Hadid Architects (ZHA) 96, 135, 222

www.ingramcontent.com/pod-product-compliance
Ingram Content Group UK Ltd.
Pitfield, Milton Keynes, MK11 3LW, UK
UKHW022318131225
466018UK00009B/200